Experiencing America's Past

A Travel Guide to

Museum Villages

Experiencing America's Past

A Travel Guide to

Museum Villages

GERALD & PATRICIA GUTEK

A Wiley Press Book
JOHN WILEY & SONS, INC.
New York • Chichester • Brisbane • Toronto • Singapore

Publisher: Stephen Kippur
Editor: Elizabeth G. Perry
Managing Editor: Katherine Schowalter
Design: Laura Ferguson
Production Services: G&H/SOHO, Ltd.

Library of Congress Cataloging-in-Publication Data

Gutek, Gerald Lee.
Experiencing America's past.
1. Historic sites—United States—Guide-books. 2. Historical museums—United States—Guide-books. 3. Villages—United States—Guide-books. 4. Historic buildings—United States—Guide-books. 5. United States—History, Local.
I. Gutek, Patricia, 1941-   II. Title. III. Title: Museum villages.
E159.G87   1986   917.3'04927   85-29565
ISBN 0-471-82892-0

Printed in the United States of America

86 87 10 9 8 7 6 5 4 3 2 1

To our daughters:
Jennifer, the reluctant historian,
and Laura, always the enthusiast,
who shared a healthy skepticism about their parents' book.

PHOTO AND ILLUSTRATION CREDITS

CONTENTS

INTRODUCTION

Over the past fifteen years, we have visited a wide variety of America's museum villages. Our first village was Historic New Harmony, Indiana, where we spent part of a summer doing research in the archives of the Workingmen's Institute for a book on the history of American education. New Harmony, the scene of two utopian communities, excited our curiosity about America's restored heritage.

Our early visits were to Midwestern locations that we could travel to on weekends from our home in LaGrange, Illinois, near Chicago. After these short family excursions, we embarked on longer trips to museum villages in New England, the South, and other regions of the country. This book is the result of many rewarding trips to America's past.

VISITING A MUSEUM VILLAGE

Visiting a museum village is a way of rediscovering our roots as Americans. Trips to these restored cross sections of American life can satisfy many purposes, ranging from pure recreation to escape to education. Unlike a visit to a typical museum, where the exhibits are protected in glass cases, the exploration of a historic village enables you to be a time-traveler, nearly an active participant in the past. It offers the opportunity to step out of the hurried pace of modern life and to recapture life in an earlier time. It can be a totally enriching experience.

This introduction provides a general perspective or orientation to make your exploration of America's past a heightened and enriching experience. To begin, let's identify the various types of museum villages that you will discover in your travels.

TYPES OF MUSEUM VILLAGES

Museum villages are generally carefully selected and arranged collections of original buildings grouped to illustrate the way of life— architecture, economics, industry, furniture, society, and culture—of a community representative of a particular period. Among the various types of museum villages are the *restored* village, once an actual

1

community, with original buildings on their original sites; the *recreated* village, composed of either original buildings or well-researched, newly constructed facsimiles brought together on an arbitrary site; and the *reconstructed* village, rebuilt on its original site but consisting primarily of new structures.

The Restored Village

In most instances, the buildings in a restored village were actually lived in by the community members. Their restoration recreates the buildings, furnishings, and environment of a particular period. Examples of restored villages are Colonial Williamsburg in Virginia; Deerfield Village in Massachusetts; Historic New Harmony in Indiana; Old Salem in Winston-Salem, North Carolina; and the various Shaker communities.

Many restored villages were once the locations of religious communal societies such as the Shakers, the Rappites at Old Economy in Pennsylvania, the Separatists at Zoar in Ohio, and the Inspirationists at Amana in Iowa. These groups sought to create perfect communities, often in isolated regions, where they could practice their religion without interference. The communities of religious societies such as the Shakers and Rappites endured for a much longer time than those of secular groups such as the Owenites at New Harmony. A shared set of beliefs generally sustained the religious communitarians, but the nonreligious groups often disintegrated because of internal conflicts.

At times, extensive rebuilding has been done in restored villages. The plan is generally to restore the buildings to their original sites as they were at a particular time in history. These restorations follow the architectural design and style of the original buildings. Furniture and other artifacts usually date from the period portrayed in the village but are not necessarily original to that site.

The Recreated Village

In a recreated community, historic buildings such as homes, shops, stores, and offices are transported to a particular location, usually from the nearby vicinity. These buildings are then restored to the period that the village is meant to portray, and authentic artifacts are assembled for display. Examples of recreated villages are Old World Wisconsin; Greenfield Village, Michigan; and Old Sturbridge, Massachusetts. Some of these villages were developed because antique collectors' collections outgrew their space. In studying historic preservation, we often see this pattern: one or two people with a passion for collecting and the means and good taste with which to do it, leaving a valuable legacy for society. The Wells brothers at Old Sturbridge, the Rockefellers at Williamsburg, the Du Ponts at Winterthur, Henry Ford at Greenfield Village, and Electra Havemeyer Webb at Shelburne Museum all carried out massive tasks of restoration and preservation that are to America's benefit.

A second type of recreated village neither has original buildings nor is on an original site. The buildings are facsimiles built in the style of the time depicted. Such a village also often houses an extensive collection of authentic artifacts in the buildings in which they would have been used. Examples of this type of recreated village are Stonefield in Wisconsin and Wheaton Village in New Jersey.

The Reconstructed Village

In some instances, where an actual village has been completely destroyed, total reconstruction has been done. Using archaeological research, the foundations of the original buildings are located. Based upon historical documents such as drawings, blueprints, or diaries, facsimile structures are built. This has often been done in the case of forts and military installations. Schoenbrunn in Ohio is an example of a completely restored eighteenth-century Moravian frontier village and Indian mission. Another example is New Salem in Illinois, where Abraham Lincoln once lived.

A Total Environment

Regardless of its type, the museum village has the advantage of depicting a complete historical environment in relationship to its natural setting. It portrays religious, cultural, social, and economic life by showing us where people prayed, worked, and lived. Entering their homes, their shops, and their churches transports us not only to another time but also tells us who we were and who we might become.

A VISITOR'S OVERVIEW OF THE HISTORIC VILLAGE

To appreciate a historic village, you should be a traveler in space and time rather than a harried tourist. Allow yourself to become a part of the museum village experience by taking the time to place it in context.

Many museum villages have visitors' centers that provide brochures, maps, and guides. Some time spent at the visitors' center before you begin your journey through the village streets and shops will give you an overall perspective. Rather than seeing isolated buildings, you can gain a total mental landscape. If the visitors' center has a film or slide presentation, take the time to view it. Many of the larger historic villages have such visual presentations. Smaller villages that operate with limited staffs and budgets may be unable to provide a visitors' orientation, but they should not be overlooked; they still have much to offer. In these instances, travelers should do their own preliminary orientation. In either case, the descriptions in this book provide background information for your journey into the American heritage.

In addition to the orientation at the visitors' center, some museum villages provide guided tours, on which a trained guide will narrate the history, tell you about the people, and describe the art and artifacts of the community. If such a tour is available, it will further enhance your visit.

After getting a perspective of the museum village, begin your personal exploration. See the village in terms of the functions that its buildings performed in the total life of the people who lived there.

Each traveler has his or her own interests, and a historic village can satisfy all of them. Some people may be interested in the style of architecture, which may range from colonial to Federal to crude log cabin or to sophisticated plantation manor. Others may be interested in the decorative arts and artifacts—the utensils, wall hangings, china-ware, quilts, and furniture. Still others may want to concentrate on the gardens. It is possible to see how families lived by studying the design of their homes, or to see how they shopped by visiting their stores, or to see how they were educated by visiting the town school.

USING THE BOOK

The museum villages described in this book are organized into the following geographic regions: New England, the Middle Atlantic, the South and Southeast, and the Midwest. The regional arrangement facilitates planning trips to a number of villages located in the same geographic area. Within a region, the museum villages are then grouped by state.

Each entry for a museum village begins with a listing of facts, identifying and categorizing the village, giving its location, address, phone number, operating months and times, and pointing out restaurants, shops, facilities, and special features. We have indicated admission fees, but it should be noted that these are subject to change. In our descriptions, we have used the following abbreviations: NR, which signifies that the site is included in the National Register of Historic Places; NHL, which identifies the site or structure as a National Historic Landmark; and HABS, which identifies the structure as being included in the Historic American Building Survey.

To facilitate your travel planning, we have included a "Where to Stay" section that lists accommodations located in the vicinity of each museum village. These accommodations—resorts, inns, bed and break-fast lodgings, motels and hotels, and campgrounds—are arranged by town. Dollar signs after each lodging entry indicate the following price ranges for a double room: $, under $40; $$, from $40 to $70; $$$, from $70 to $95; $$$$, $95 and up. Because campgrounds do not have a wide range of costs and are usually economical, no indication of price has been included.

To provide an orientation to the site and its significance, the text describes the history of the site and the people who lived there. (Because several of the villages discussed in this book were established by the Shakers, we have provided a brief history of the sect itself in the Appendix.) The history is followed by the "Tour" section, which includes a detailed description of the buildings, their uses, and furnishings.

For added interest and convenience, we've included brief descriptions of side trips to other points of interest in the vicinity of most of the villages.

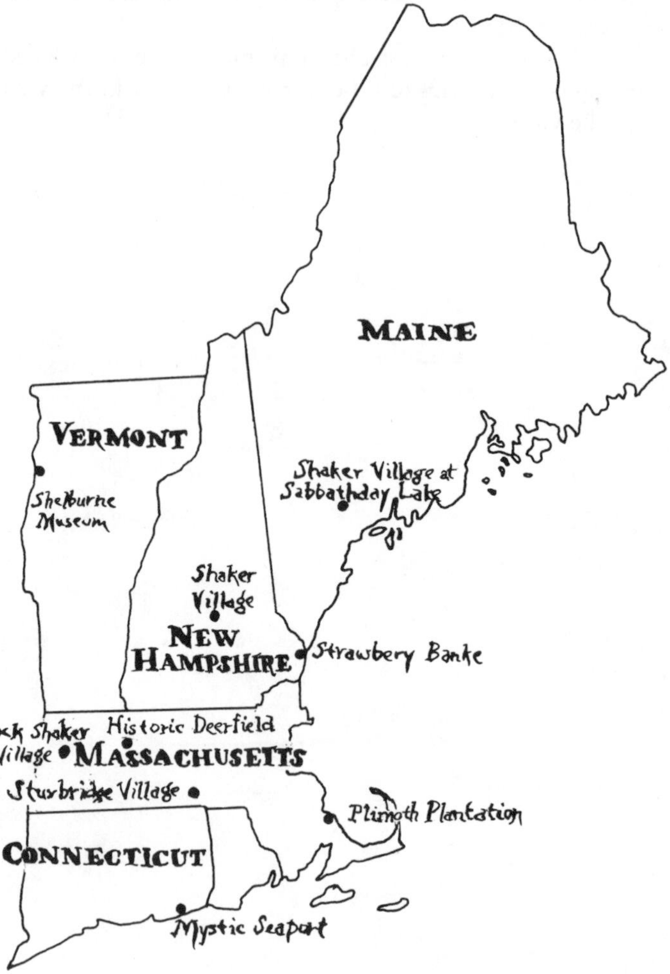

MAINE

VERMONT

Shelburne Museum

Shaker Village at Sabbathday Lake

Shaker Village

NEW HAMPSHIRE

Strawbery Banke

Hancock Shaker Village

Historic Deerfield

MASSACHUSETTS

Old Sturbridge Village

Plimoth Plantation

CONNECTICUT

Mystic Seaport

New England

CONNECTICUT
　　Mystic Seaport, Mystic

MAINE
　　Shaker Village at
　　　　Sabbathday Lake, Poland Spring

MASSACHUSETTS
　　Historic Deerfield, Deerfield
　　Hancock Shaker Village, Pittsfield
　　Plimoth Plantation, Plymouth
　　Old Sturbridge Village, Sturbridge

NEW HAMPSHIRE
　　Strawbery Banke, Portsmouth
　　Shaker Village, Canterbury

VERMONT
　　Shelburne Museum, Shelburne

CONNECTICUT

Recreation of a nineteenth-century maritime village

Address: Mystic, CT 06355
Telephone: (203)572-0711
Location: On Route 27, 1 mile south of I-95 Exit 90
Open: Daily, 9:00 A.M. to 5:00 P.M., May to October; 9:00 A.M. to 4:00 P.M., November to April; closed Christmas Day
Admission: Adults, $8.50; children 5 to 15, $4.50. Two-day pass: Adults, $10.50; children, $5.25. Group rates available.
Restaurants: The Galley, a cafeteria; The Seamen's Inne
Shops: Museum Store, nautical gifts; Mystic Maritime Gallery, contemporary art
Facilities: 4 ships and 300 boats, maritime museum, library, picnic area, accessible to handicapped

WHERE TO STAY
Bed and Breakfast, Mystic: 1833 House, 33 Greenmanville Avenue, 06355, (203)572-0633, $–$$; Camolli's Bed & Breakfast House, 36 Bruggeman Place, 06355, (203)536-8723, $$
Motels/Hotels, Mystic: Day's Inn, Route 27, P.O. Box 88, 06355, (203)572-0574, $$; Howard Johnson's, on Route 27 at I-95 Exit 90,

P.O. Box 159, 06355, (203)536-2654, $$; Inn at Mystic, Route 1, 2 miles south of I-95 Exit 90, 06355, (203)536-9604, $$–$$$$; Old Mystic Motor Lodge, Route 27 at I-95 Exit 90, 06355, (203)536-9666, $$; Ramada Inn, on Route 27 north of I-95 Exit 90, P.O. Box 427, 06355, (203)536-4281, $$; Seaport Motor Inn, at junction of I-95 and Route 27, Coogan Boulevard, 06355, (203)536-2621, $$

Bed and Breakfast, Old Mystic: Red Brook Inn, P.O. Box 237, Route 184, 06372, (203)572-0349, $$–$$$

Camping, Old Mystic: Seaport Campgrounds, Route 184, P.O. Box 104, 06372, (203)536-4044

Bed and Breakfast, Groton Long Point: Shore Inn, 54 East Shore Road, 06340, (203)536-1180, $

Camping, East Lyme: Rocky Neck State Park, Route 156, P.O. Box 676, 06357, (203)739-5471; Camp Niantic by the Atlantic, Route 156, P.O. Drawer FF, 06357, (203)739-9321; The Island, Islanda Court, P.O. Box 2, 06333, (203)739-8316; Ponderosa Park & Campgrounds, Chesterfield Road, Route 161, 06333, (203)739-2629

HISTORY

Mystic Seaport is a maritime museum that recreates a New England coastal village of the mid-nineteenth century. The town of Mystic is actually composed of sections of two other towns, Groton and Stonington, which lie on either side of the Mystic River, and has been jointly governed by them since 1705.

Shipbuilding began on the Mystic River as early as the seventeenth century. A five-mile stretch along the river several miles inland from the Atlantic Ocean provided Mystic with excellent shipbuilding sites. After the War of 1812, the revival of sealing and whaling and the increase in southern trade stimulated rapid growth at Mystic, which was becoming the home of shipbuilders and whaling captains.

George Greenman and Company was one of the most famous Mystic shipbuilders, and its shipyards are now the site of Mystic Seaport Museum. The Greenman Company built many of America's renowned packets and clipper ships, and its shipyards launched nearly 100 vessels between 1838 and 1878. One of them, the *David Crockett*, regularly traveled the difficult Cape Horn route to San Francisco. The *Crockett* was one of the fastest clippers, and its average performance on more than twenty-five runs around Cape Horn was never equaled. Another active Mystic shipbuilder was Charles Mallory, who had been an apprentice sailmaker. In the 1830s, Mallory produced a fleet of nine whalers that was used in the lucrative whale oil business. Exhibits describing the story of Mystic's shipbuilding industry are housed in the Seaport's **Mallory House** (see page 12).

During the Civil War, the demand for ships increased, and Mystic's shipyards received a good deal of business. The *Galena*, the navy's first seagoing ironclad, was built at the Maxson and Fish shipyards. By the end of the war, Mystic shipyards had built fifty-six steamers for the navy, many of which measured 230 feet or more in length. Mystic shipyards launched 30,000 tons of shipping in the nineteenth century.

Toward the end of the nineteenth century, shipbuilding at Mystic declined because of decreased demand for wooden ships. Also, the Mystic River was not deep enough for construction of modern, steel-hulled ships. Shipbuilding was revived briefly during World War I. Since then, however, only small numbers of yachts and fishing craft have been produced at Mystic.

In 1929, the Marine Historical Association, Inc., was founded by Mystic residents Dr. Charles K. Stillman, Edward E. Bradley, and Carl C. Cutler. The purpose of the association was to establish a museum of the U.S. maritime past. This nonprofit, educational maritime museum, now known as Mystic Seaport Museum, Inc., includes 60 historic buildings, 4 major vessels, more than 300 boats, a research library, and a large collection of maritime artifacts.

TOUR

Mystic Seaport, the nation's largest maritime museum, occupies seventeen acres along the Mystic River. The site is the former shipyards of George Greenman and Company, a prominent Mystic shipbuilder. There are so many ships, boats, museum buildings, and village sites that you should plan to spend the whole day, if possible.

The feature that truly sets Mystic Seaport apart from other historic villages is the opportunity to board four major vessels from another era. Reading is no substitute for stepping on board a clipper ship or whaler. It's only then that you begin to understand the experiences of their crews. Board the *Joseph Conrad*, built in Copenhagen in 1882. It served as a training ship for the Danish merchant service until 1934 and was also used by the U.S. Maritime Commission during World War II. Before it was berthed at Mystic, Alan Villiers, the Australian sea captain who brought Plymouth's *Mayflower II* to America, sailed the *Conrad* on a 58,000-mile, two-year voyage around the world. Visitors may also board the *L. A. Dunton*, a Gloucester fishing schooner built in 1921.

Seeing Mystic Seaport from the water is a special treat. The *Sabino*, a 1908 steamboat built in East Boothbay, Maine, makes half-hour passenger runs on the Mystic River from mid-May to mid-October; there is a small fee. Longer cruises to Fishers Island Sound are available in the evenings. The *Sabino* originally served the islands of Casco Bay, Maine, and is believed to be the last operating coal-fired passenger steamer in the United States.

All the vessels in Mystic's collection are maintained by the **Henry B.**

duPont Preservation Shipyard. This unique facility has the equipment and craftsmen needed to restore and preserve wooden vessels. Visitors may observe the restoration work from the gallery that overlooks the main ship, carpenters' ships, an eighty-five-foot spar lathe, and a rigging loft. There is also a 375-ton-capacity lift dock, which is used to lift ships out of the water for repair.

Many of the more than 300 small craft in the museum's collection are displayed in the **Small Craft Exhibit** and the **North Boat Shed,** and some are afloat at the docks. Replicas of historically significant small craft are built by the staff for use on the Mystic River.

The village area is a recreation of a nineteenth-century shipbuilding seacoast village primarily composed of original New England buildings moved to the site. However, some buildings that belonged to the Greenman family, who owned a mill after shipbuilding declined, were on the property and have been restored.

The **Thomas Greenman House** is a two-and-a-half-story Greek Revival home built in the mid-1800s. The **Edmundson House**, also in the Greek Revival style, was built in 1860 for the George Greenman and Company's shipyard foreman. Weaving is demonstrated in the Edmundson House.

One of the textile mill buildings, the three-story, 1865 **Stillman Building**, is now used to exhibit ship models, marine paintings, and scrimshaw. An exhibit called **New England and the Sea**, which traces the development of the region's maritime communities from the seventeenth through the nineteenth centuries, is also in the Stillman Building.

The 1890 **Wendell Building**, a former machine shop, houses an exhibit of ship figureheads and wood carvings. The **Mallory Building** tells the story of the Mallory family's shipping business during the nineteenth and twentieth centuries, as well as that of the shipbuilding industry in Mystic.

Many demonstrations by skilled craftspeople take place in the village. Ironwork is forged at the 1885 **Shipsmith**, while at the **Cooperage**, barrels for shipping goods are made. Wood-carvers work at the **Shipcarver's Shop**, and sails are made at the 1836 **Sail Loft**, where Charles Mallory was once a sailmaker. Instruments are repaired at the **Nautical Instruments Building**, and nineteenth-century printing methods are employed at the **Mystic Press**.

The **Ship Chandlery** carries the vast array of supplies needed for a voyage. The fishing industry is represented by the 1840 **Salmon Shack**, containing fishing gear; the 1874 **Oyster House**, where oysters are sorted; the **Oystering**, which has oyster boats and fishing gear; and the **Whaleboat Exhibit**, which features a fully equipped whaleboat.

Maritime properties moved to Mystic include the 1845 **New York Yacht Club Building** from Hoboken, New Jersey, and the 1874 **New**

Shoreham Life-Saving Station from Block Island. The longest building at Mystic is the 1824 **Plymouth Cordage Company's Ropewalk**, a gray-shingled building that was part of a rope-making facility.

The village also contains buildings found in most New England towns, including an 1833 **bank** with a shipping office upstairs, an 1889 **chapel**, an 1870 **drugstore** with a doctor's office, an 1880s one-room **schoolhouse**, an 1890s **dry goods store**, and a **tavern**.

Children of all ages will love the **Children's Museum**, which features a replica of a ship's cabin that served as the living quarters for a captain's family. Children are welcome to explore the cabin, lie on the bunks, and play with the reproduction nineteenth-century toys and clothing.

Mystic also has a **planetarium** that offers daily programs explaining how navigators used the stars to determine their position at sea. A small admission fee is charged.

There are many special events held annually at Mystic. They include a lobster weekend in May, a sea music festival in June, an Independence Day celebration and an antique and classic boat rendezvous in July, a photo day in September, and chowder days in October. Sailing classes and a day camp for children are also available.

SIDE TRIPS

The **Mystic Marinelife Aquarium** displays over 6,000 specimens of undersea life. Especially appealing to children are the hourly demonstrations with whales, dolphins, and sea lions. In Mystic, on Coogan Boulevard, I-95 Exit 90. (203) 536-9631. Open daily from 9:00 A.M. to 5:00 P.M. Adults, $5.75; children 5 to 17, $2.75.

Had enough of ships and maritime life? If not, try the **See Submarines by Boat** cruise that passes the **U.S. Submarine Base** and the **Coast Guard Academy**. The cruise leaves from 193 Thames Street, in nearby Groton. (203)445-8111. From Memorial Day to Labor Day, it runs daily, 10:00 A.M. to 3:00 P.M. Adults, $4.75; children, $2.50. You can also visit the Submarine Base, the largest in the free world. Its **museum** traces the history of submarines from their invention to the Tridents of today. Located on Route 12, Groton. (203)449-4779. Open daily from 10:00 A.M. to 3:00 P.M., late June to Labor Day.

Southeastern Connecticut towns were settled as early as the seventeenth century and abound with historic houses and sites. Groton has a historic district, including the remains of **Fort Griswold**, which was the site of a major Revolutionary War battle. In 1781, British troops commanded by Benedict Arnold massacred the colonial defenders of the fort. Located at Fort Griswold State Park, Monument Street and Park Avenue. (203)445-1729. Open daily, 9:00 A.M. to 5:00 P.M., mid-April to mid-October; 9:00 A.M. to 3:00 P.M., mid-October to mid-April. Free.

New London's historic district has buildings dating from the late eighteenth to the twentieth centuries, including the **Lawrence Hospital Building** (1790), **New London Customhouse** (1833), **New London Railroad Station** (1886), and the restored **Nathan Hale Schoolhouse** (1774), which is open Monday to Friday, 10:00 A.M. to 3:00 P.M., Memorial Day to Labor Day. Free. (203)447-3106.

The **Joshua Hempstead House**, at 11 Hempstead Street, has also been restored. Built in 1678, it is one of the oldest dwellings in Connecticut. (203)247-8896. Open Tuesday to Sunday, 1:00 to 5:00 P.M., mid-May to mid-October. Adults, $1.00; children, 25 cents. **Monte Cristo Cottage** (1888) was the childhood home of playwright Eugene O'Neill. 325 Pequot Avenue. (203)443-0051. Open Monday to Friday, 1:00 to 4:00 P.M. Adults, $2.00; children, 50 cents.

Old Lyme, Stonington, and Norwich also offer opportunities for leisurely strolls through their charming historic districts.

Shaker Village at Sabbathday Lake

Restoration of an eighteenth- and
nineteenth-century Shaker community;
NR, NHL, HABS

Address: Poland Spring, ME 04274
Telephone: (207)926-4597
Location: On Route 26, 8 miles north of Gray; 12 miles south of Auburn
Open: Monday to Saturday, 10:00 A.M. to 4:30 P.M., Memorial Day to Columbus Day
Admission: Guided tour of museum: Adults, $2.50; children 6 to 12, $1.25. Walking tour of village: Adults, $3.75; children, $2.00. Group rates available.
Shops: Bookstore, Shaker books; Gift Shop, herbs and crafts
Facilities: 7 restored buildings, 1,900 acres

WHERE TO STAY
Motels/Hotels, Poland Spring: The Inn at Poland Spring, Route 26, 04274, (207)998-4351, $$–$$$$ (includes meals). A 143-room hotel open from the end of May to the end of October; enjoy the medicinal effects of the famous Poland Spring water.
Camping, Poland: Range Pond Campground, 04273. On Plains Road, 2½ miles east of Poland Road. (207)998-2624

Motels/Hotels, Auburn: Holiday Inn, Washington Avenue, 04210, (207)783-1454, $$; Pineland Motel, 711 Washington Avenue, 04210, (207)783-2044, $$; The Best Western Manor Inn, P. O. Box 414, 04210. On Route 202, 4 miles south of Maine Turnpike Exit 12. (207)783-1454, $$

Resorts, Bridgton: Tarry-A-While Resort, Ridge Road, 04009, (207)647-2522, $$$$ (modified American plan). On Highland Lake with good view of Presidential Range.

Inns, Bridgton: Pleasant Mountain Inn, Mountain Road, 04009, (207) 647-2431, $$$ (modified American plan). On Moose Pond at the foot of Pleasant Mountain.

Camping, Naples: Sebago Lake State Park, 04055. On Route 302. (207)693-6613. This 1,300-acre park 2 miles south of Naples has a lake 12 miles long and 8 miles deep. Swimming beaches, fishing for landlocked salmon, and boat rentals available.

Camping, North Windham: Sebago Basin Camping Area, P.O. Box 178R, 04062. On Route 302, 7 miles west of Route 115 from Maine Turnpike Exit 11. (207)892-4839.

HISTORY

On April 19, 1794, the Sabbathday Lake community, or New Glouces-ter United Society of Believers in Christ's Second Coming, was founded under Trustees Nathan Merrill and Barnabus Briggs. (See the Appendix for a brief history of the Shakers.) It was one of three Shaker societies in Maine (Alfred and Gorham were the other two).

Initially, Sabbathday Lake converts met at Gohan Wilson's farm-house; but before long, the work of building the community was started. The first order of business was a meetinghouse, the place of worship. Moses Johnson, a Shaker brother and architect, designed, framed, and built the meetinghouse at Sabbathday Lake. Gradually, other buildings were added, forming three parallel rows on both sides of what is now Route 26.

A three-and-a-half-story central dwelling house, built in 1795, faced the meetinghouse. When it was no longer large enough for its family, the central dwelling house was moved sixty-five feet northeast and replaced with a five-story brick dwelling house, completed in 1884.

To achieve its goal of self-sufficiency, the New Gloucester commu-nity became involved in many businesses, including tannery and cooper shops; herb and garden seeds; lumber; and flour, carding, and spinning mills. These were in addition to the crafts, such as furniture, basketmaking, and textiles, for which the Shakers are so well known.

Despite prosperity, membership in Shaker communities declined. The Gorham community ended in 1887; in 1931, the Alfred commu-nity merged with Sabbathday Lake, which remains an active Shaker community with approximately eight members. The Shaker Museum, founded by Sister Ethel Peacock in 1931, exhibits artifacts made and used at the community over the past three centuries.

TOUR

Like all truly historic places, the Shaker community at Sabbathday Lake, Poland Spring, is unique. Part of its uniqueness lies in the fact that despite being 200 years old, the community is still active, an extremely rare occurrence.

There were three brothers and five sisters living at Sabbathday Lake when we visited. Admittedly, the community is quite small; but when a woman Shaker, known as a *sister*, waits on you in the craft shop, you get a feeling for what it was really like in past times. It's a wholly different experience from dealing with a museum guide whose job requires dressing in traditional Shaker garb.

As with all the Shaker villages we have been to, the impressive architecture, pastoral settings, and well-done preservation and restoration are worth any detour necessary to make the visit. The added ingredient of a living community at Sabbathday Lake makes it something very special.

The tour, which takes a couple of hours, is not strenuous. There are seventeen original buildings remaining on the site, and seven of them are visited on the walking tour. All the buildings are eighteenth- and nineteenth-century frame except the **Dwelling House**, which is brick. Originally, the Shakers owned 2,700 acres; now, they have 1,900.

The tour begins in the **Boy's Shop**, which now serves as the **Reception Center**. It is a white, two-story building built in 1850; and although it was partially destroyed by fire in 1965, the facade is original. The building was used to house young Shaker boys until they reached their midteens, along with the brothers who took care of them.

The first floor houses a **bookstore** with a good collection of Shaker books and some reproduction Shaker items. All the rooms on the second floor are furnished with original Shaker furniture, most of it from Sabbathday Lake.

On our visit, some authentic Shaker-made antiques were for sale, displayed on the grass outside the Reception Center. The work was beautiful and tempting—but expensive.

The 1794 **Meetinghouse**, which now serves as the **Shaker Museum**, was the first building on this site. It was one of ten Shaker meeting-houses built by Moses Johnson, all with gambrel roofs. Chimney bricks were made by brethren near the Sabbathday Pond, and the nails were handmade by Joseph Briggs. In 1839, an ell was added to the north side.

Religious services still take place in the first-floor meeting room; on Sundays, they are open to the public. A divided stairway leads to the second floor, where Shaker costumes are on display. The four rooms on the second floor originally housed the two elders and two eldresses who headed the community. Among the notable items contained in the rooms are a weasel, the Shaker invention used to measure a skein of yarn; a framed patent for chair tilters (one of the few Shaker inventions ever patented); and a sewing desk made by Joshua Bussell.

The three rooms on the third floor were used as guest rooms for visiting ministers. One of the rooms displays a rare Shaker quilt, which is quilted but not pieced. All the rooms have built-in cupboards.

Because the lack of insulation made the meetinghouse extremely cold to live in, the elders moved into the **Ministry's Shop**, which was built in 1839 and has insulated walls. This building was used by the two elders and two eldresses as both home and workplace. As the spiritual leaders, they governed the community. In addition to their administrative duties, they were required to do physical labor or craftwork, so the building contains a sewing room and a tailor's room, as well as offices.

When the Alfred, Maine, Shaker community ended, Sabbathday Lake received much of its furniture and artifacts. One room of the Ministry's Shop contains pictures and drawings of the Alfred community, done in folk art style by Elder Joshua Bussell. These drawings are noteworthy because the Shakers banned all decoration; they were meant to be utilitarian records of the Alfred and Sabbathday Lake property sites rather than decorative.

The **Sisters' Shop**, originally used as a laundry, houses a mail-order herb business on its second floor. From barrels of herbs, sisters fill small metal cans. Herb can labels are printed in the community **printshop**. This is only one of the businesses operating here; being self-supporting is a Shaker principle.

In your tour of the Sisters' Shop, you will see the original washing machine, invented by the Shakers, and a large press that chemically treated material. Permanent-press material is also a Shaker invention.

The **Girls' Shop** was built in 1796. It burned and was rebuilt in 1901. It is a Victorian-style house, very much out of sync with traditional Shaker architecture, but it demonstrates the adaptability of the Shakers. Some of the Shaker-made furniture has Victorian features, and unlike other Shaker dwellings, this house has rugs, wallpaper, and curtains.

The only brick building on the site, the six-story, forty-eight room **Dwelling House**, was built in 1883–84 to replace a three-story frame building that was moved next door. This is the home of the brother and sister residents, who eat, sleep, work, and worship here. Therefore, only a few rooms on the main floor are open to tourists. The building contains a Shaker **library** founded by Elder Otis Sawyer over 100 years ago. The **Winter Chapel** has stenciling around the ceiling, which is probably a recent development. The **gift shop** sells herbs, herbal teas, and craft items.

Historic Deerfield

Restoration of an eighteenth-century village; NR, NHL, HABS

Address: P.O. Box 321, Deerfield, MA 01342
Telephone: (413)774-5581
Location: 6 miles north on Routes 5 and 10 from I-91, Exit 24 or 25
Open: Monday to Saturday, 9:30 A.M. to 6:00 P.M., and Sunday, 11:00 A.M. to 6:00 P.M., July 1 to October 31; Monday to Saturday, 9:30 A.M. to 4:30 P.M., Sunday, 11:00 A.M. to 4:30 P.M., November 1 to June 30; closed Thanksgiving, Christmas Eve, and Christmas Day
Admission: Individual buildings: Adults, $1.00 to $3.00; children 6 to 14, 50 cents to $3.00. Combination tickets: 3 houses, $4.50; 12 houses, $15.00.
Restaurants: Deerfield Inn: Coffee Shop, Beehive Parlor, Dining Room
Shops: J. G. Pratt Museum Shop, books, cards, needlepoint kits, reproductions
Facilities: Information center, picnic area, partially accessible to handicapped

WHERE TO STAY
Inn, Deerfield: Deerfield Inn, P.O. Box 305, The Street, 01342, (413)774-5587, $$$. Built in 1884, the Deerfield Inn has been

extensively restored and enlarged. All 23 rooms are decorated in colonial style. Reservations are essential. The inn is highly recommended for its charm, convenience, and the cuisine in the formal but comfortable dining room.

Bed and Breakfast, Shelburne Center: Parson Hubbard House, Old Village Road, 01370, (413)625-9730, $

Motels/Hotels, Greenfield: Candlelight, 208 Mohawk Trail, 01301, (413)772-0101, $$; Howard Johnson's, 125 Mohawk Trail, 01301, (413)774-2211, $$–$$$

Camping, Erving: Erving State Forest, Route 2A, 01364, (617)544-3939; Pine Ridge Family Campground, Mountain Road, 01344

Camping, Northfield: Baron Cove Nature Area, Rural Route 1, Box 377 BC, 01360, (413)863-9300

Camping, Shelburne Falls: Springbrook Family Camping Area, RFD 1, Box 52, 01370, (413)625-6618

HISTORY

Historic Deerfield is important for its restored houses of late colonial and early Federal architectural styles, the furniture collections they hold, and the Deerfield Academy.

Deerfield's history goes back more than 300 years to 1667, when 8,000 acres in the Connecticut River Valley were purchased from the Pocumtuck Indians for four pence an acre. The first settler, Samuel Hinsdell, arrived in the spring of 1669. By 1673, twenty families occupied the town, which for a brief time was called Pocumtuck. Residents laid out its village street and apportioned its house lots essentially as they are now.

An Indian attack in September 1675 left so many Deerfield men dead that the demoralized survivors decided to abandon the town. By 1682, however, people had returned, and the town was rebuilt. Because of its vulnerable geographic location, Deerfield was attacked by Indians several times. In February 1784, a company of Indians and Frenchmen led by Governor de Vandreuil of Canada attacked Deerfield. Of the town's 291 inhabitants, 48 were killed, and 111 were taken prisoner and forced to march to Canada in winter. Many did not survive the ordeal.

Most of the town was burned during the attack, although the Frary House and Sheldon House remained standing. The fifty Deerfield men and women and seventy-five children who survived started to rebuild again. In 1735, a peace treaty was signed with the Indians.

Deerfield became a prosperous center for wheat and cattle. Many fine houses were built and furnished with handsome furniture made by Connecticut Valley craftsmen. In 1782, Rev. William Bentley of Salem wrote of Deerfield in his diary: "The street is one measured mile, running north and south, about 60 houses in the street in better style than in any towns I saw" [*The Diary of William Bentley, D.D.*, vol. 1 (Salem, Mass., 1905; reprinted Gloucester, Mass., 1962, p. 92)]. Twenty-nine of the houses viewed by Bentley are still standing, and there are thirteen others that date from the first quarter of the nineteenth century.

After the Revolution, Deerfield became less agricultural; and with the establishment of Deerfield Academy in 1797, it became a center for learning. A sense of history among Deerfield residents was evident early on. The Memorial Hall Museum was opened by the Pocumtuck Valley Memorial Association in 1880. Preservation was begun in the 1890s, when Charlotte Alice Baker restored the Frary House as a historic house museum.

Many Deerfield homes were in a finely preserved condition when Henry and Helen Flynt enrolled their son in Deerfield Academy in the early 1940s. They purchased the Allen House and began restoring it. Subsequently, they bought and renovated the Deerfield Inn and six more houses. They furnished the houses with pieces from their outstanding collection of early American decorative arts. In 1952, the Flynts organized the Heritage Foundation, which was renamed Historic Deerfield, Inc., in 1971.

TOUR

Visitors are well advised to allow sufficient time if they wish to visit all of Deerfield's homes. Official statements recommend at least three days. We spent a day and a half at Deerfield but were unable to see it all. Viewing is by guided tour only. At each house, there is a well-trained, knowledgeable docent who describes the house, especially its furnishings, in a thorough and detailed manner. Each tour lasts from forty-five minutes to an hour, and only six persons may tour at a time. This carefully arranged touring permits the visitor to see the furnishings at close range and to ask questions.

Deerfield is ideal for the person who already has some background in the furnishings of the period, but it does not seem to be well suited to young children, who would have difficulty with the slow pace. Nevertheless, we did see groups of schoolchildren touring.

Deerfield is one of those rare restorations, like Shaker Village at Pleasant Hill, Kentucky (see page 127), where you can eat, sleep, and sightsee without leaving the site. You can be totally immersed in the past.

The houses lining Deerfield's mile-long street, known earlier as Old Deerfield Street and now simply called The Street, reflect the prosperity of their owners. They are large, elegant, and well furnished with locally made or imported furniture. There are no log cabins, mud floors, or crude furnishings in this pioneer town.

The **Wright House**, a large, three-story, Federal-style brick house, was built in 1824 by Asa Stebbins for his son and his bride. A frame ell was added later. Federal characteristics evident in the sunny dining room are the mantel and the sideboard. In the parlor hangs a rare portrait of George Washington painted by Jane Stuart, Gilbert Stuart's daughter.

The **Ebenezer Hinsdale Williams House** is a departure from the other Deerfield house museums because it is still being restored by Historic Deerfield; it can be viewed as a restoration in progress until 1989, when it should be completed. Tour leaders emphasize the problems that restorers face and the alternatives from which they must choose. Because this large house has been remodeled several times, it will be a challenge to restore it to its early nineteenth-century appearance.

The **Helen Grier Flynt Fabric Hall** (1872) is a Victorian barn that holds an overwhelming collection of textiles and exquisite handmade clothing from the seventeenth to nineteenth centuries. Included are hand-embroidered French and English costumes displayed on mannequins; a large number of early bed rugs; handmade and embroidered quilts; hand-stenciled Indian cotton; rare eighteenth-century fabrics from England and India; jacquard coverlets; rugs; needlepoint and flame-stitch upholstered furniture; and a marvelous collection of our favorites, samplers.

The **Parker and Russell Silver Shop** is a small, two-story, gambrel-roofed frame house that was built in Deerfield in 1814. It was moved to Greenfield in 1872 and returned to its original site in 1960. Historic Deerfield added a fireproof cinder-block wing, camouflaged with old boards, to hold the village's extensive silver collection. Glass cabinets display English and American silver pieces by Paul Revere, Jeremiah Dummer, and Isaac Parker and John Russell, the two Deerfield silversmiths after whom the house was named. A silversmith's shop, including a forge and many eighteenth-century tools, is displayed, and demonstrations are given.

The **Allen House** was the home of Henry and Helen Flynt, the founders of Historic Deerfield, Inc. It was the first house they purchased and restored. The house is shown by appointment only, and tours must be arranged at **The Hall Tavern Information Center**.

Simon Beaman, a garrison soldier, and Hannah Beaman, the first schoolteacher in Deerfield, began building their house around 1700. During the Indian massacre of 1704, the Beaman House burned down, and the Beamans were captured. Though they were forced to march to Canada, they survived and returned in 1705 to start building their house again.

The **Asa Stebbins House**, built in 1799, was the first brick house in Deerfield. This Federal-style house had a gambrel-roofed ell with dormer windows in back that was changed in 1879 to a pitched-roofed ell with a full second story. Asa Stebbins was the son of a prosperous tanner and operated a very successful gristmill with his brother, Joseph. This lavishly furnished house reflects the wealth of its owner. In the south parlor hangs a Gilbert Stuart portrait of Robert Stoddard in its original frame. The French wallpaper in the south bedroom and hall, depicting Captain Cook's voyage, was originally in the Ruel Williams' mansion in Augusta, Maine. Designed and made in France in 1804, the paper was brought to Williams by James Bowdoin, U.S. ambassador to France. When the Williams house was demolished, the paper was moved to the Stebbins House.

The Hall Tavern, which is used as Historic Deerfield's Information Center, was moved to Deerfield from Charlemont, Massachusetts, where it had been a stagecoach stop. This frame building in the elongated saltbox style was built in 1760; a wing containing a ballroom was added in 1807. The barroom features a fine cage bar. A pewter collection is displayed here, along with the pewterer's shop, complete with a forge and the actual tools used by Samuel Pierce, a skilled pewterer from nearby Greenfield. Upstairs, the large, low-ceilinged ballroom is striking because of the extensive wall stenciling, which was done by an anonymous artist and has been restored.

Frary House is one of the few Deerfield structures that survived the Indian massacre of 1704. Its occupants weren't as lucky; Samuel Frary was murdered, and his wife was killed during the march to Canada. In 1763, Major Salah Barnard bought the house and turned it into an inn. Barnard's Tavern was a popular Whig gathering place during the Revolutionary War. In 1775, Benedict Arnold stayed there when he came to Deerfield to purchase 15,000 pounds of beef for the army.

The Frary House passed through many hands and was in a neglected state when Charlotte Alice Baker, a Frary descendant, purchased it in 1890. Miss Baker carefully restored the house and eventually willed it to the **Pocumtuck Valley Memorial Association** as the first of Deerfield's house museums. A couple of "touch it" rooms in the Frary House, where children—and adults, too—can touch everything in the room and even lie on the bed, make this the best place in Deerfield to take children.

You will find a **borning room** next to the kitchen. This room, equipped with a bed, enabled a new mother to prepare meals with the least inconvenience. The Federal-style ballroom, which was added by Major Barnard, is bright and airy, with a vaulted ceiling, arched alcoves, benches along the walls, a musicians' gallery, and fine old chandeliers. The first meeting of the trustees of Deerfield Academy was held there in 1797.

Ebenezer Wells built the central section of the **Wells-Thorn House** in 1717. It consisted of two rooms: a keeping room and several steps below, following the slope of the land, a kitchen. In 1751, Wells added the two-story, frame front section that now forms the major part of the house. The earlier section has exposed beam ceilings and is furnished with simple seventeenth- and eighteenth-century furniture. The newer part of the house is elegant and decorated with oriental rugs, chandeliers, and draperies.

The **Dwight-Barnard House**, a two-story, timber frame that has weathered to a tobacco brown hue, was built in 1743, and a rear wing was added in 1802. George Sheldon, who was the founder of the Pocumtuck Valley Memorial Association and author of *History of Deerfield*, was born here. The furnishings include many eighteenth-century pieces made in Deerfield.

Ashley House, located at the northern end of The Street, was built around 1730. It is a two-story house with unpainted clapboards, narrow windows, and a double-door entrance. It has a gambrel roof in front and saltbox sweep behind. Jonathan Ashley, a preacher who had graduated from Yale, purchased the house in 1733 for £251. Having strong Tory sympathies, he was often involved in political controversy during the Revolution and religious controversy with Preacher Jonathan Edwards, a fellow Yaleman. The British coat of arms is displayed above the fireplace and on the fireback. Many of Ashley's belongings and pieces of furniture are displayed throughout the house; among them is a portrait of King George III.

SIDE TRIPS

Deerfield is a very small and atmospheric town. In addition to its mile-long street of eighteenth-century houses, it is the home of several famous prep schools, including **Deerfield Academy**, which was founded in 1797.

Memorial Hall Museum, built in 1798, was the academy's first building. Since 1880, the Pocumtuck Valley Association has maintained the museum, which contains colonial and Indian artifacts. (413)773-5206. Open Monday to Friday, 10:00 A.M. to 4:30 P.M.; Saturday and Sunday, 12:30 to 4:30 P.M.; May to October. Adults, $2.00; students, $1.50; children 6 to 12, 75 cents.

For the student of American decorative arts, Historic Deerfield offers seminars on topics such as needlepoint, crewel embroidery, colonial blacksmithing, ceramics, wall stenciling, quilting, silver and pewter, and New England furniture. Seminars are conducted by experts and are quite reasonable. For more information, write or telephone the Historic Deerfield Museum (see page 19 for address and phone number).

MASSACHUSETTS

Hancock Shaker Village

Restoration of a Shaker community to the 1830s; NHL, NR, HABS

Address: P.O. Box 898, Pittsfield, MA 01202
Telephone: (413)443-0188
Location: 5 miles west of Pittsfield at the junction of Routes 41 and 20 in the Berkshire Hills
Open: Daily, 9:30 A.M. to 5:00 P.M., Memorial Day to October 31
Admission: Adults, $6.00; children 6 to 12, $2.00; senior citizens and students, $5.00; family, $15.00. Group rates available.
Restaurants: Lunchroom in the Visitors' Center
Shops: Bookstore, books, needlework kits, herbs, baked goods
Facilities: Visitors' Center, 20 restored buildings, library and archives, picnic area

WHERE TO STAY

Inns, Stockbridge: The Red Lion Inn, Main Street, 01262, (413)298-5545, $$–$$$. This classic white frame inn is featured in the Norman Rockwell painting of Stockbridge's main street. It was rebuilt in 1896 after a fire. There are 108 rooms decorated in the colonial style and a rambling front porch. Williamsville Inn, Route 41, West Stockbridge, 01266, (413)274-6580, $$$. An eighteenth-century inn featuring French country cuisine. The Inn at Stockbridge, Route 7, P.O. Box 2033, 01262, (413)298-3337, $$$–$$$$

Motels/Hotels, Pittsfield: Berkshire Hilton Inn, Berkshire Common at West Street, 01201, (413)499-2000, $$$–$$$$; Heart of the Berkshires Motel, 970 West Housatonic Street, 01201, (413)443-1255, $; Liberty Court Motel, Albanz Road, 01201, (413)443-9431, $

Camping, Pittsfield: Pittsfield State Forest, Cascade Street, 01201, (413)442-8992; Bonnie Brae Cabins and Campsites, 108 Broadway, 01201, (413)442-3754

Resorts, Lenox: Foxhollow Resort, 251 Kemble Street, 01240, (413)637-2000, $$$–$$$$

Inns, Lenox: The Gateway Inn, 71 Walk Street, (413) 637-2532,

$$-$$$$; Wheatleigh, P.O. Box 824, West Hawthorn Road, 01240, (413)637-0610, $$$$; Apple Tree, P.O. Box 699, 224 West Street, 01240, (413)637-1477, $$$

Camping, Lee: October Mountain State Forest, Woodland Road, 02138, (413)243-1778; Maple Glade Campground, 02138, (413)243-1528

HISTORY

Hancock Shaker Village began in August 1783 when Mother Ann Lee, founder of the Shakers, conducted a meeting at the home of Daniel Goodrick, Sr., in Hancock. (See the Appendix for a brief history of the Shakers.) As a result of Mother Ann's visit, several families in the area accepted the Shaker creed and joined their lands and possessions to form a new Shaker settlement. In 1790, Calvin Harlow became the first elder of Hancock, with the approval of Elder Joseph Meacham, the first American-born leader of the church. In 1791, Sarah Harrison was appointed eldress of the Hancock community sisters.

In 1796, the members of the Hancock community drew up their first written covenant, pledging to "devote themselves and services, with all they possess, to the Service of God and the support of the Gospel forever, solemnly promising never to bring debt nor damage, claims nor demand, against the Society, nor against any member thereof, for any property or service which they have devoted to the uses and purposes of the institution" [John Harlow Ott, *Hancock Shaker Village, A Guidebook and History* (Hancock, Mass.: Shaker Community, Inc., 1976, p. 25)].

The early decades of the nineteenth century brought an increase to the ranks and prosperity of the Hancock Shakers. In 1803, the community's 142 members were engaged in farming, blacksmithing, milling, and manufacturing items for sale. Shaker garden seeds, medicinal herbs, and flat brooms were well-known items produced there.

During the Shaker's period of spiritual renewal in the early 1840s, Hancock Village was renamed the City of Peace, and a mountain near the settlement was called Mount Sinai and used for religious services. Hancock residents received spirit communications in the form of songs or drawings (see the Appendix for a description of Shaker spirit drawings and songs). After the period of spiritualism ended, the drawings were placed in drawers and forgotten. It has been said that they were discovered by Edward Deming Andrews, a Shaker scholar and collector who lived near Hancock, when he noticed a sister lighting a fire with a rolled-up spirit drawing. Andrews's rescue of Shaker drawings was a valuable addition to American folk art, and this extensive collection is one of the outstanding features of the Hancock restoration.

The population at Hancock reached a peak of 247 members organized into six families in 1829. In 1846, membership was 217; and by

1853, it had dropped to 193. Membership gradually declined until only 3 sisters remained in 1959, and the Central Ministry at Canterbury, New Hampshire (see page 47), closed the community. In 1960, the remaining 900 acres and seventeen buildings were sold to Shaker Community, Inc., a group of local citizens who wanted to develop the site for an outdoor museum interpreting the Shaker way of life. Restoration of the buildings started soon after.

TOUR

Hancock Shaker Village is situated on a 1,000-acre site in the Berkshire Mountain area of western Massachusetts, only a few miles from the New York State border. Twenty of the approximately sixty buildings that once made up the community have been restored to the 1830 period. These buildings belonged to the Church family, one of the six families living at Hancock in its heyday.

The **Visitors' Center**, where tickets are sold and tour information is available, is housed in a modern wooden building. Visitors are advised to allow at least two hours for touring the village; we spent an enjoyable five and a half hours, including a lunch break. The **lunchroom**, located in the Visitors' Center, serves homemade soups, a large list of sandwiches, and homemade desserts from 11:00 A.M. to 3:00 P.M. The center also houses the **bookstore**, which sells books on crafts, some needlework kits, herbs, and baked goods.

If you take a guided tour, you will meet your guide in the three-and-one-half-story brick **Dwelling House**, built in 1830. It was home for the 100 members of the Church family, who slept, cooked, ate, and worshiped here. On the lowest floor, you'll find the kitchen, a very large room with a brick oven capable of baking fifty loaves of bread at a time. At meals, men sat on the east side of the dining room and women on the west at long tables. They ate their hearty meals in silence. The small dining room was for elders and eldresses, who always ate apart from the others.

Some of the retiring rooms on the upper floors in the dwelling house are furnished to portray rooms in other buildings that have since been demolished. Consequently, there is a deacon's office, a deaconess's sewing room, a physician's office, an infirmary (which contains cradles for sick adults), and a pharmacy. All the furniture in the Hancock restoration is Shaker, and much of it was made in Hancock.

One of the highlights of Hancock Shaker Village is the imposing **Round Dairy Barn**. The three-story stone barn, built in 1826, was twice destroyed by fire and faithfully reconstructed, the last time in 1968. Inside, the scope of the barn is majestic. The soaring ceiling, with its cupola, and the huge open space gives it the feeling of a cathedral, not a barn. However, the Shakers built it this way for functional reasons: one man could easily feed fifty-two head of cattle working the circular area. The hay was stored in a central area. All three levels are ramped, which enabled wagons pulled by teams of horses to reach the highest level for unloading hay. Still considered an architectural treasure, the round barn alone justifies a visit to Hancock.

The **Meetinghouse,** designed and built by Moses Johnson in 1793, was originally located in Shirley, Massachusetts, but was moved to Hancock in 1962. It replaced the original Hancock meetinghouse, also built by Johnson, which had been dismantled by the Shakers in 1938 because it had fallen into disuse. Like Johnson's other meetinghouses, it is a two-story, white frame building with a gambrel roof and two front entrances, one for men and one for women. (See the Appendix for a description of Shaker services.) The **Ministry's Shop,** constructed around 1874, was where the two elders and two eldresses, who constituted the ministry, carried out their administrative duties. Like the other members of the community, the ministry was required to do manual labor, so the building had both administration offices and craft workshops. This building was restored after a fire in 1968 destroyed the rear wing.

Many Shaker crafts are demonstrated at Hancock. Visitors can watch the making of oval boxes, brooms, and clocks at the **Brethren's Shop** and weaving and spinning in the **Sisters' Dairy and Weave Shop.** There is a blacksmith's shop and a cabinetmaker in the **Tan House,** which also has equipment for making apple cider. A printing office, which still produces announcements needed at Hancock on the antique presses, is in the **Hired Men's Shop and Printing Office.**

The **Machine Shop and Laundry** has an ironing room with a conical stove that warmed twenty-five irons at a time. There is an herb and seed exhibit upstairs.

The Shakers established a school in 1791; and by 1817, it had become a public school. The **Village Schoolhouse** is a reconstruction on the original foundation. The original schoolhouse still exists, but it was moved to nearby Route 41 in the late 1920s.

The **Trustees' House** was the site of the offices of the trustees, who were charged with regulating trade and administering the lands, monies, and property of the family, as well as with conducting business with all visitors to Hancock. The Trustees' Office, built in 1813, was remodeled in 1895, and the austere Shaker building was converted into a High-Victorian structure with a tower, bay windows, bracketed porches, and awnings and was decorated inside with wallpaper. Victorian furniture, lace curtains, and machine-turned woodwork reflect the changing tastes of the Shakers.

The brick **Poultry House** features a display of spirit drawings. One of the most interesting was received from Mother Ann Lee in the 1840s and shows the locations of famous persons in heaven. Mother Ann and

Christopher Columbus have prominent places in the front row. The well-known Shaker tree of life, a drawing by Hancock resident Sister Hannah Cohoon, also hangs in the exhibit.

The **Horse Barn** is now an **Education Center**, with benches set up for programs. Interpretation of artifacts and restoration are done here. On our visit to Hancock, we heard a demonstration of historic songs, which were regarded as gifts from heaven. The young woman who gave the performance learned the songs from surviving Shakers or from accounts written by "world's people" who had visited Shaker communities.

The Hancock Community Industries Program occupies the 1910–1939 **Barn Complex**. The program reproduces and sells Shaker furniture and trains apprentices and students in woodworking.

There are a number of special events at Hancock. *An Evening with the Shakers* is a candlelit tour led by costumed interpreters and featuring readings from Shaker letters and diaries and performances of Shaker music. These *Evenings* are held Friday and Saturday at 7:30 P.M. during July. *World's People's Dinners*, Shaker-style meals, are also held one week in late July, Monday to Saturday at 6:00 P.M. and Sunday at 1:00 P.M. An antique show is held in October, and there is an antiquarian book fair in November.

SIDE TRIPS

Hancock Shaker Village is located near Pittsfield in the Berkshire Hills vacation area, which is rich in natural beauty, cultural activities, and historic attractions. Pittsfield, known as a winter ski area, was home to Herman Melville from 1850 to 1863. He completed *Moby Dick* at **Arrowhead**, his home, 780 Holmes Road, (413)442-1793. Arrowhead is open for guided tours daily, 10:00 A.M. to 4:30 P.M., from June 1 to October 31. Adults, $2.00; children, $1.00.

The charming Main Street of nearby Stockbridge, a popular summer resort town, was captured in a Norman Rockwell painting. The **Norman Rockwell Museum** in the **Old Corner House** on Main Street (the childhood home of author Rachel Field) has the only permanent collection of Norman Rockwell paintings in the country. Open daily except Tuesdays, 10:00 A.M. to 5:00 P.M.; closed the last two weeks in January; (413)298-3822. Adults, $3.00; children, $1.00. Also on Main Street is the **Berkshire Playhouse**, site of the annual summer Berkshire Theater Festival, which features American drama; (413)298-5576.

Chesterwood, the summer residence and studio of Daniel Chester French, is near Stockbridge. French was the sculptor of the Lincoln Memorial and the Minuteman statue in Concord. The buildings and gardens are open daily, 10:00 A.M. to 5:00 P.M., May to October; P.O. Box 248, Stockbridge, (413)298-3579. Adults, $3.50; children, $1.00.

The town of Lenox is famous for its annual **Berkshire Music Festival**, with concerts running from early June to late August, Wednesdays through Sundays; (413)639-1940. The festival is held at **Tanglewood**, Nathaniel Hawthorne's 210-acre estate. Most of Tanglewood's formal gardens are open daily and can be visited free except during the festival. The estate contains a replica of Hawthorne's **Little Red House**.

A third important summer cultural event is the **Jacob's Pillow Dance Festival**, held at the **Ted Shawn Theater**, 9 miles east of Lee, P.O. Box 287, Lee, 01238, (413)243-0745. The festival features celebrated dancers and classic ballet.

Reconstruction of the 1627 Pilgrim settlement

Address: P.O. Box 1620, Plymouth, MA 02360
Telephone: (617)746-1622
Location: 3 miles south of Plymouth on Route 3A and Exit 4 off Route 3
Open: Daily, 9:00 A.M. to 5:00 P.M., April to November. *Mayflower II*, operated by Plimoth Plantation: daily, 9:00 A.M. to 5:00 P.M., April to June and September to November; stays open until 6:30 P.M., July to August.
Admission: Adults, $6.00; children 5 to 13, $3.50. *Mayflower II*: adults, $3.00; children, $2.00. Combination ticket for Plimoth Plantation and *Mayflower II*: adults, $8.00; children, $5.00. Group rates available.
Restaurants: Reception Center, cafeteria
Shops: Reception Center, gift shop, bookstore
Facilities: Reception Center, theater, picnic area, partially accessible to handicapped

WHERE TO STAY
The Visitors' Information Center, located at the waterfront on Park Avenue, will provide information on accommodations, restaurants, and attractions. (617)746-4779.

Inns, Plymouth: Colonial House Inn, 207 Sandwich Street, (617)746-2087, $$

Motels/Hotels, Plymouth: Cold Spring, 188 Court Street, 02360, (617)746-2222, $$; Pilgrim Sands, Warren Avenue, Route 34, (617)747-0900, $$$; Governor Bradford Motor Inn, Water Street, 02360, (617)746-6200, $$; The Governor Carver Motor Inn, Summer Street at Town Square, 02360, (617)746-7100, $$; The Sleepy Pilgrim, 182 Court Street, 02360, (617)746-1962, $$

Camping, Plymouth: Ellis Haven, Federal Furnace Road, 02360, (617)746-0803; Sandy Pond Campground, 2 Paula Road, 02360, (617)224-3707; Indianhead Resort of Plymouth, State Road, RFD 8, (617)888-3688

HISTORY

Although Jamestown, Virginia, was the site of the first English settlement in the New World, Plymouth, Massachusetts, is the legendary home of America's Founding Fathers. The original settlers of Plymouth have been called a company of saints and strangers.

The saints were Separatists, Protestants who opposed the formal and popish rituals of the Anglican Church and seceded from it. The strangers were people recruited by a capitalist, Thomas Weston, who sought economic prosperity in the New World. Altogether, 101 passengers and 20 crew set sail on the *Mayflower* from Southampton, England, on September 6, 1620.

After nine weeks of cold, stormy seas and little food, the *Mayflower* sighted Cape Cod on November 9. On November 11, at Provincetown Harbor, the Mayflower Compact was drawn up. The forty-one men who signed it agreed to be self-governing and to abide by whatever laws would be made. John Carver was named governor.

After several expeditions, Plymouth was chosen as the site for the colony, and the *Mayflower* anchored in Plymouth Harbor on December 16, 1620. Plymouth prospered despite the fact that half the original party died during their first year there. Other ships from England brought new arrivals. By 1630, Plymouth's population was about 300; and by 1650, almost 1,000.

After the Revolution, Plymouth grew into a thriving fishing and trading post. Throughout the nineteenth century, it shared in New England's commercial and industrial development. Its historical significance made it an attractive destination for tourists.

In 1945, Henry Hornblower II founded Plimoth Plantation, an educational, not-for-profit organization dedicated to building a Pilgrim memorial village. In 1957, a site on a hill above the Eel River physically resembling that of the original Plymouth Colony was selected for a replica of the 1627 village. The Fort Meeting House was reconstructed there, although replicas of First House and 1627 House were built near Plymouth Rock.

TOUR

Tickets for Plimoth Plantation are sold at the **Reception Center**, which also has restrooms, a **gift shop**, a **cafeteria**, and a **picnic area**. The first stop on your tour will be the **Orientation Center**, which shows a fifteen-minute slide presentation about Plimoth. There are also two exhibits, one on rural life in the seventeenth century and the other on the Wampanoag Indian Program.

Plimoth Plantation is comprised of a five-acre site with a 1627 **Pilgrim Village** and the **Wampanoag Summer Settlement**. None of the village's sixteen buildings is original, but authentic methods were employed in their construction. Even the site is not original, although it closely resembles the original, which is not far away. The houses are small, dark, cramped, and smoke-filled, with rough, uncomfortable-looking rope beds and chairs. The furnishings and artifacts are period pieces or careful reproductions. The reconstruction, based on extensive archaeological and documentary research, successfully conveys the hard and unglamorous life of the Pilgrims.

Resident guides dressed in period costumes are usually hard at work conducting musket drills, shearing sheep, milling logs in a sawpit, weaving wattle fences, cooking, or baking. They use authentic methods and tools. Each has assumed the identity of an original resident of Plymouth and plays only that role. In Elizabethan accents, they introduce themselves and talk about themselves, their problems, or whatever task they are engaged in. Children, especially, enjoy talking with such Pilgrims as Myles Standish and John and Priscilla Alden.

Plimoth Plantation has an amazingly realistic feel. While you are there, you have a keen sense of what life was like 350 years ago. Fires are lit and cooking is done indoors even in the heat of August, so the smells are particularly strong. Chicken, pigs, and sheep roam freely through the streets.

The plantation is a fortified town enclosed by a palisade, or wooden fence. The town is small, barely covering an acre of ground. A main street runs through the middle and is intersected at the center by a cross street. At the cross street is a small, square structure, a miniature fort, which has four small ordnances, or cannons, mounted on swivels, making it possible to shoot down every street. The purpose was to repel any rebellion within the town.

Houses, each with a small garden in the rear, line both sides of the main street. Most are generally one-room structures with a half loft above for sleeping. Exteriors are unpainted clapboard. Clapboards were handmade by splitting a log lengthwise, then shaping the pieces with a two-handled blade called a *drawknife*. Roofs are thatched with rushes, and the chimneys have a wooden framework filled with wattlework (rods and twigs woven together) and daubed with clay. Tiny windows are covered with oilpaper and cloth to keep out the cold. The floors are of packed earth.

Thatched roofs often caught fire, so in 1627, they were outlawed. Wooden roofs replaced them. Eventually, many of the small, cramped houses were replaced with larger homes built around central brick chimneys and with kitchens, parlors, and bedrooms upstairs. Floors were of wide pine boards, windows had diamond-paned-glass casements, and both inside and outside walls were of cedar.

The **Fort** is the dominant structure at Plimoth. In 1627, Isaack de Rasieres, an agent for the Dutch West India Company, described it as "a large square house, with a flat roof, made of thick sawn planks, stayed with oak beams, upon the top of which they have six cannons, which shoot iron balls of four and five pounds, and command the surrounding country. The lower part they use for their church" [Cyril Leek Marshall, *The Mayflower Destiny* (Harrisburg, Pa.: Stackpole Books, 1975, p. 58)].

The fort and palisade reflect the Puritan concern for security. They feared Indian attacks and even carried muskets to Sunday services. However, their first encounter with an Indian was with Samoset, who walked into the village alone and greeted the Pilgrims with "Welcome, Englishmen." Astonished and pleased, the Pilgrims responded warmly to Samoset, who had learned some words from English traders. Soon after, Governor Carver and Chief Massasoit signed a peace treaty that lasted for fifty years.

The Indians taught the Pilgrims how to plant corn, fish, hunt, and preserve food, skills that helped them survive in the early years. A few Indians lived with the Pilgrims, including Squanto, who had been to England and became the Pilgrims' interpreter. Indians were guests at the celebration of the Pilgrims' first harvest at Plymouth. They brought five deer to this first Thanksgiving feast in October 1621.

The **Wampanoag Summer Settlement** recreates a typical 1627 encampment of the Indian families who came to the New England coastal area to fish, hunt, and grow crops during the summer. The settlement is directed and staffed by Wampanoags, who, using first-person narrative, tell the story of their people who lived in this area centuries before the Pilgrims' arrival. There are demonstrations of basket weaving, food preserving, cooking, and tepee building.

A full-scale replica of the *Mayflower* was built in England and sailed to Plymouth in 1957. The **Mayflower II**, which is operated by Plimoth Plantation, now occupies a permanent berth at State Pier on Water Street.

SIDE TRIPS

A must when visiting Plymouth is **Plymouth Rock**, located on the harbor at Water Street and protected by a Greek templelike colonnade. It is considered the place where the Pilgrims from England landed. Just north of Plymouth Rock are **First House** and **1627 House**, replicas of early Pilgrim dwellings.

Plymouth is a treasure chest of historic houses, ranging from the very early **Richard Sparrow House** (1640) to the **Antiquarian House** (1809). The houses are furnished with fine seventeenth- to nineteenth-century antiques. At some houses, visitors can watch demonstrations of pottery making, weaving, spinning, and candle making. There are also displays of collections of china, dolls, toys, and costumes. A small admission fee is charged for each house. (617) 746-9697; (617) 747-1240.

Another interesting site is **Pilgrim Hall**, 75 Court Street, the oldest public museum in the country. It was built in 1824 by the Pilgrim Society to house its collection of Pilgrim possessions, including items brought to the New World and others produced in Plymouth. There are displays of firearms, portraits, furniture, and housewares. The library and manuscript collections contain both books owned by the Pilgrims and those written about them. The Bibles of John Alden and Governor Bradford are in the collection. The Pilgrim Hall is open daily, 9:30 A.M. to 4:30 P.M., (617) 746-1620. Admission: adults, $2.50; children 6 to 15, 50 cents.

Coles Hill, south of Plymouth Rock, is the burial site of the *Mayflower* voyagers who died during their first year at Plymouth. Their graves were not marked because the Pilgrims feared an Indian attack if the Indians knew that half of the Pilgrims were dead.

Ocean Spray Cranberries, Inc., operates the **Cranberry World Museum** on Water Street and offers tours of the cranberry bogs. The museum is open daily, 10:00 A.M. to 5:00 P.M., April to November. Admission is free. (617) 747-1000.

Old Sturbridge Village

Recreation of an early nineteenth-century village

Address: Sturbridge, MA 01566
Telephone: (617)347-3362
Location: On Route 20, 1 mile west of junction of I-86 Exit 3 and Massachusetts Turnpike I-90 Exit 9
Open: Daily, 9:00 A.M. to 5:00 P.M., April to October; Tuesday to Sunday, 10:00 A.M. to 4:00 P.M., November to March; closed on Mondays from December through March and on Christmas and New Year's Day
Admission: Adults, $8.50; children 6 to 15, $4.00; people in wheelchairs, free
Restaurants: Bullard Tavern: Taproom, New England Buffet, cafeteria
Shops: Grant's Store, film, postcards, reproductions; Museum Gift Store and New England Bookstore, reproductions, books, crafts, toys
Facilities: Information Center, picnic areas, craft demonstrations, wagon rides, special events, motel, library

WHERE TO STAY
Resorts, Sturbridge: Sheraton-Sturbridge Resort, Routes 20 and 131, 01566, (617)347-7393, $$$
Inns, Sturbridge: The Publick House, Main Street, P.O. Box 1876, 01566, (617)347-3313, $$. Originally a tavern, this 1771 colonial inn is famous for its Yankee cooking. Colonel Ebenezer Crafts Inn, Fiske Hill Road, 01566, (617)347-3313, $$$. Managed by the Publick House.
Motels/Hotels, Sturbridge: Old Sturbridge Village Motor Lodge, Route 20, P.O. Box 481, 01566, (617)347-3327, $$. Adjacent to the village; there are 49 units in 7 buildings resembling colonial cottages. Carriage House Motor Lodge, Route 20, 01566, (617)347-9311, $$; Sturbridge Coach Motor Lodge, Route 20, 01566,

(617)347-7327, $; Quality Inn Colonial, Route 20, P.O. Box 399, 01566, (617)347-3306, $$

Camping, Sturbridge: Wells State Park, Route 49, Mountain Road, 01566, (617)347-9257

Camping, Charlton: Applewood Campground, Kings Road, P.O. Box 330, 01507, (617)248-7017; Wood Lot Campground, Stafford Street, 01507, (617)248-5141

Camping, Brimfield: Quinebaug Cove Campground, Route 20, 01010, (413)245-3232; Long-Vue Campground, Route 20, 01010, (413)245-3504

HISTORY

Old Sturbridge never existed at its present location or in its present form as a village. Neither was it related to a particular group or individual. Old Sturbridge Village is an outdoor museum that recreates a typical small New England community of the 1830s. It is particularly well done, with careful attention to historical detail. Most of the buildings are original, not facsimiles, from New England.

Old Sturbridge was founded by Albert B. and J. Cheney Wells, two brothers from Southbridge, Massachusetts, who collected New England antiques during the early 1920s. They accumulated a wide variety of tables, chairs, beds, china, brassware, tools, and pottery. After amassing a sizable collection that quickly outgrew their houses and barns, the Wells brothers decided to share their collection by placing it in a museum. And because they wanted it to be displayed in appropriate settings, they decided to recreate a small New England rural village.

The Wells brothers purchased a 200-acre tract of land in Sturbridge that had the geographic characteristics of a New England village, including fields, arable land, woodland, a stream and millpond, hills, and ravines. There were two buildings on the property, the Wright House and the Gate House.

Among the first projects that the brothers tackled was moving a barn and two houses onto the green. Next came a gristmill, blacksmith shop, country store, school, meetinghouse, and tavern. There are now more than forty buildings furnished with the Wellses' collection.

The Wellses succeeded in recreating a typical rural New England town of the early nineteenth century. Unlike the coastal cities, Old Sturbridge is representative of interior New England. It is located in south central Massachusetts and has an agricultural as well as an industrial base, using its own source of waterpower. Daily activities at Sturbridge relate to the agricultural, social, political, religious, commercial, and industrial activities of a typical New England community.

Old Sturbridge is also outstanding for its demonstrations of handicrafts that were common in early nineteenth-century New England. Visitors can see weaving, cabinetmaking, tinsmithing, broom making, pottery, candle dipping, and cooking.

Old Sturbridge Village opened officially to the public in 1946, although it had been chartered by the state of Massachusetts as early as 1936 as an independent, nonprofit, educational institution. The village is now administered by an independent board of trustees representing all sections of New England.

TOUR

Old Sturbridge Village is set along the Quinebaug River and is complete with **covered bridge**. The **village green** is particularly picturesque, with historic buildings carefully arranged among trees, shrubs, and flowers. Only horse-drawn vehicles are allowed on the dirt roads. The village is well suited to family recreation because of its spaciousness, wide variety of exhibits, craft demonstrations, and, of course, animals, always a favorite of children.

Old Sturbridge Village has four major areas: **Seasonal Exhibits, Center Village, Countryside,** and **Mill Neighborhood.** Tours begin at the **Visitors' Center,** which has orientation exhibits, a film, and information about special activities. If you want to see everything in the village, plan to spend the whole day.

At **Center Village,** the green is surrounded by the **Meetinghouse,** a **parsonage,** a **law office,** a **tavern,** a **bank,** a **store,** and several **homes.** The **Meetinghouse,** which faces the green, is a classic white New England church with a tall spire. It was built in 1832 and served Fiskdale, Massachusetts, for over a century. Occasionally, it is used for weddings and parties.

The **Fenno House,** which also faces the green, is the oldest dwelling at Sturbridge; it was built in 1704 near Canton, Massachusetts. Each home in the village has its own story, and guides take the roles of residents. Fenno House is inhabited by an elderly widow and her unmarried daughter. They support themselves by weaving blankets and coverlets.

The **Fitch House,** the second-oldest structure in the village, began as a one-room cabin built in 1735 in Windham, Connecticut. Additions were made, and finally, in 1880, the roof was raised to its present half-gambrel appearance. The kitchen has wide-paneled, painted wainscoting and a paneled fireplace wall. The Fitch House is occupied by a country printer, whose office is nearby.

The small **Village Bank,** in country Greek Revival style, was built in Thompson, Connecticut, in 1825. No community would be complete without a general store, and **Miner Grant's Store** served Stafford, Connecticut, from 1802 until it was moved to the village in 1939. The benches on the covered porch still provide visitors with relief for tired feet after an examination of the store's well-stocked shelves. Film, postcards, and reproduction items are also sold at the store.

The fully equipped 1830 **Print Shop** is housed in a small gray building nearby. The shop belonged to Isaiah Thomas of Worcester, Massachusetts, author of A *History of Printing in America* (1810). Broadsides are produced on a Peter Smith handpress by a guide, who sets the type by hand. Folding and sewing of pamphlets and preparation of books for binding in leather and cloth are done in the **Bookstore**, which is also stocked with early nineteenth-century books, papers, ink, slates, and almanacs.

The **Towne Family Home** stands at the east end of the green, facing the meetinghouse. A two-story, white, Federal building, it was the home of Salem Towne, a prosperous farmer, Revolutionary War major general, member of the Constitutional Convention of 1780, and Massachusetts state legislator. This elegant home, built in Charlton, Massachusetts, in 1769, has finely detailed woodwork, including wainscoting, window and door moldings, overmantels, and cornices. The sitting room is furnished with a set of mid-eighteenth-century cherry Chippendale chairs from Connecticut and an early nineteenth-century Massachusetts secretary. The dining room, where one of several Towne portraits hangs, is furnished with New England Empire chairs.

The second-floor ballroom extends across the front of the house. Towne held Masonic meetings here, and the walls have cedars of Lebanon, a Masonic symbol, painted on them. The "all-seeing eye of God," another Masonic symbol, looks down from the ceiling. The ballroom also served as sleeping quarters for the Towne children.

The **Bullard Tavern** is still filling two of its original functions: providing food and drink to tired travelers. The **Taproom** on the main floor serves beer, wine, and cocktails. The **New England Buffet** specializes in chicken pie, baked ham, baked Indian pudding, and deep-dish apple pie. On the lower level is a **cafeteria**. Food service is from 10:00 A.M. to 3:30 P.M..

A red and white saltbox built in Podunk, Massachusetts, about 1748 is known as the **Parsonage**, home of a Congregational minister and his family. This is a "touch it" house, where visitors are allowed to sit in the reproduction chairs and touch the furnishings. A subscription cooking class is held in the parsonage kitchen during the winter months.

You can also visit a small **law office**, which once belonged to John McClellan of Westock, Connecticut; a **shoe store**, with a shoemaker hard at work; and a one-room **district school**, built in Candia, New Hampshire, about 1800.

Craft demonstrations are an important feature of Old Sturbridge Village. Demonstrators have been carefully trained in traditional methods and use the same tools as their 1830 counterparts. In many cases, original tools are on exhibit, but the craftspeople use reproductions. Children, especially, appreciate the willingness of the demonstrators to explain their work and answer questions.

Women's work was carefully separated from men's work in New England rural villages. Women will be found throughout the village giving cooking demonstrations, spinning and weaving, making candles, and milking cows. Men can be seen plowing fields, shearing sheep, blacksmithing, and running the mills.

Wooden barrels are still being made at the 1840 **Cooper Shop**, and pottery is still being fired in the Goshen, Connecticut, **Potter's Shop**. Every mid-nineteenth-century village had a blacksmith, and the **Moses Wilder Blacksmith Shop** still uses the original double forge, built for father and son. This shop was built in Boulton, Massachusetts, around 1810.

The **Mill Neighborhood,** with its weathered buildings and big waterwheels, is the industrial area of the town. Water supplied the power to New England mills, and three kinds of waterpower can be seen at work here. The reconstructed **Gristmill** uses the breast wheel, a seventeenth-century invention, to move the heavy millstones that grind rye, corn, and other grains into flour. The **Carding Mill** came from South Waterford, Maine, where it was built in 1840. The water-powered machines separate, comb, and smooth the wool, replacing tedious hand carding. The carding machines are powered by a tub wheel, a small, vertically mounted wheel, dating from about 1820, encased in a wooden tub. The **Sawmill** is a reconstruction of an 1838 New Hampshire mill. A water-powered turbine operates the mechanism, in which a reciprocating saw cuts logs into boards and planks.

The **Pliny Freeman Farm**, which originated in Sturbridge in 1801, will delight children because of its animals. Like most farmers in the mid-nineteenth-century, Freeman kept oxen and horses as work animals and cattle, sheep, pigs, and chickens for food. Rye, corn, oats, barley, potatoes, pumpkins, and squash were all grown here. Crops not needed to feed the family were traded for needed goods.

The Pliny Freeman Farm is a working farm where agricultural methods of the 1830s are used. Crops grown are 1830s varieties, not modern hybrids, and animals have been back-bred to produce specimens of the same size and appearance as in the mid-nineteenth-century. This is typical of the careful research done at Sturbridge.

The **J. Cheney Wells Gallery** is a traditional museum displaying New England clocks and a folk art collection. A three-tiered **herb garden** grows household, culinary, and medicinal plants. The **Museum Gift Store** sells good reproductions, many produced in the village, along with books relating to the period.

Special events at Old Sturbridge include town meetings, militia days, and Good Housekeeping, in which 1830s methods of spring cleaning are demonstrated. Frequent *Crafts at Close Range* programs allow visitors to spend a day learning a traditional craft such as theorem painting or basketmaking. On the Fourth of July and Thanksgiving Day, 1830s celebrations are reenacted.

Strawbery Banke

Restoration of a seventeenth-century seaport town; NR

Address: P.O. Box 300, Portsmouth, NH 03801
Telephone: (603)436-8010
Location: On the Portsmouth waterfront, bounded by Court and Marcy Streets. Take I-95 Exit 7 to downtown and follow Strawbery signs.
Open: Daily, 10:00 A.M. to 5:00 P.M., May 1 to October 31
Admission: Adults, $5.50; senior citizens, $4.50; children 6 to 16, $3.00; families, $15.00; group rates available
Restaurants: Aaron Conant Coffee Shop
Shops: Dunaway Store, crafts, books; The Shapelz-Cotton House, nautical gifts; Kingsbury House, crafts, books
Facilities: 35 buildings, picnic area

WHERE TO STAY

Inns, Portsmouth: Martin Hill Inn, 404 Islington Street, 03801, (603)436-2287, $$; The Inn at Christian Shore, 335 Maplewood Avenue, P.O. Box 1474, 03801, (603)431-6770, $; The Inn at Strawbery Banke, 314 Court Street, 03801, (603)436-7242, $$
Motels/Hotels, Portsmouth: Howard Johnson's, Routes 1, 4, and 16,

1 Traffic Circle, 03801, (603)436-7600, $$–$$$; Portsmouth Inn, 383 Woodbury Avenue, 03801, (603)431-2500, $–$$$
Inns, York Harbor, Maine: Dockside Guest Quarters, Harris Island Road, P.O. Box 205, York, 03909, (207)363-2868, $–$$. A large white frame house on Harris Island, the Dockside offers panoramic views of the ocean and York Harbor. York Harbor Inn, P.O. Box 573, York Street, 03911, (207)363-5119, $$
Motels/Hotels, York Harbor, Maine: Stage Neck Inn, 03911, (207)363-3850, $$$$
Camping, York Harbor, Maine: Camp Eaton, P.O. Box W, 03911, (207)363-3424; Burnette's Trailer and Tent Area, 45 Railroad Street, York Beach, 03910, (207)363-4756
Camping, Greenland: Liberty Hill Camping Area, Route 101, 03840, (603)431-6359
Camping, North Hampton: North Hampton MHP, 203 Lafayette Road, 03862, (603)964-8103

HISTORY

The spring of 1623 marked the arrival of the first English colonists to a site near the banks of the Piscataqua River. It had been the home of the Pennacook Indians, a tribe whose numbers were decimated by pestilence. The colony grew slowly and was named Strawbery Banke by the residents after the lush crop of wild strawberries that covered the riverbanks. A fort was erected at Odiorne's Point, and in 1653, the fifty families of Strawbery Banke petitioned the Massachusetts General Court for the right to establish a recognized township to be named Portsmouth.

Colonists originally engaged in farming, fishing, and timbering, but shipping gradually became more important. By the end of the 1600s, land was divided into house lots; and artists, merchants, and mariners began building residences and commercial structures. As commerce flourished, the elegant mansions, large taverns, and prosperous shops reflected Portsmouth's accumulating wealth.

Portsmouth has remained a shipping center for 350 years. John Paul Jones's famous ship *Ranger* and the USS *Constitution* were built here. It was the capital of New Hampshire in the early years after independence until 1800, when the more centrally located Concord was designated the capital.

As Portsmouth became secondary to other Eastern seaports and prosperity waned, descendants of the original artisans and mariners began to move away. Their homes were converted to multifamily rental dwellings. The waterfront Strawbery Banke area deteriorated throughout the late nineteenth and early twentieth centuries, but in the 1950s, a local group of preservationists decided to restore the area. In September 1964, Strawbery Banke Incorporated, a private, nonprofit educational institution, purchased ten acres of land and thirty-five buildings, all but five of which are on their original foundations. The buildings reflect architectural changes in the neighborhood over a period of 350 years. Five homes have been fully restored and furnished to reflect the period between 1770 and 1860, and restoration of the others is still going on.

TOUR

Whereas most museum villages are found in rural areas, Strawbery Banke is right in the city of Portsmouth, combining the features of a historic district and a museum village. Admission is by a single ticket, which gives the visitor entry to the restored homes, craft shops, and stores. A visit to Strawbery Banke provides exhibits on the architecture, furnishing, and crafts of the nation's early maritime period.

The **Captain John Sherburne House**, built in 1695, is the oldest structure at Strawbery Banke. It has leaded quarrel casement windows and twin front gables. Inside, there are exhibits on the early architecture and settlement of Portsmouth.

The **Peter Lowd House** dates from 1790. Lowd was a cooper, and his house contains exhibits of nineteenth-century tools used by seacoast builders of houses and dories.

The **Captain John Wheelwright House** (1780) was built in the Georgian style prevalent in New Hampshire from 1725 to 1780. The exterior is painted according to a formula used in the late eighteenth century; it combines linseed oil, turpentine, and iron oxide to produce a deep rust tone. The interior of this furnished house is noted for its excellent wood paneling.

The **James Marden House** (1700) was occupied by three generations of the Marden family, who operated the mast yard.

A working blacksmith occupies the **Dinsmore Blacksmith Shop,** located on the site where a small smithy once stood. However, this building, which dates from 1800, came from the Dinsmore Farm in Dundee, New Hampshire. Items made by the blacksmith are for sale.

The **Yeaton-Walsh House** (1795) contains an exhibit of early photographs of Portsmouth.

The **Joshua Jones House** was built in 1790 and purchased by Joshua Jones, a farmer and trader, in 1796. It is the site of an ongoing archaeological dig.

In one of the **Leonard Cotton Tenant Houses**, built in 1835, a skilled potter demonstrates his craft, explaining his work and answering questions. His fine traditional works are for sale.

The **Winn-Yeaton Houses** were built simultaneously around 1795 by traders Timothy Winn and Thales Yeaton. These dwellings are examples of the compact design necessitated by the space limitations of the urban area. They contain a thorough exhibit on house construction covering the methods used in four major building styles, three of which are represented at Strawbery Banke: medieval (Sherburne), 1600 to 1700; Georgian (Wheelwright), 1710 to 1800; Federal (Winn and Pierce), 1790 to 1830; and Greek Revival, 1820 to 1860. Exhibits cover windows, plaster, doors, hardware, and decoration, including wallpaper and painting appropriate to each period. The Yeaton house also has an exhibit on the spinning and weaving of wool and flax, including the tools used in these processes.

A clock shop currently occupies the **Peacock House**. This small 1821 building is the only one-and-a-half-story house in Strawbery Banke. The craftsmen make a variety of clocks for sale.

The **Ruben Shapley** and **William Cotton Houses** were originally a store and a warehouse, respectively. Today, the two houses contain a gift shop run by the Guild of Strawbery Banke, Inc. Many of the items on sale have either a strawberry motif or a nautical theme.

The **Stephen Chase House** dates from 1762. The Chases, who were in the import-export business, lived there from 1799 to the late 1800s. It then became the Chase Home for Orphans until 1916. The house has been restored to its early nineteenth-century appearance. It does not contain Chase family furniture, but the restorers used inventories left by the Chases to furnish it with pieces that are typical of the period. Upstairs, the **Children of the Past Exhibit** features toys, clothing, and child-sized furniture.

The **Thomas Bailey Aldrich House** (1797) was the home of one of Portsmouth's literary figures. The Aldrich family bought the five-bedroom house in the 1830s, and Thomas Bailey Aldrich's *The Story of a Bad Boy*, a barely fictionalized recollection of his adventures in Portsmouth, immortalized it. The house contains nineteenth-century American furniture that actually belonged to the Aldriches.

The **boat shop**, in a 100-year-old converted stable, holds the contents of the Hiram Lowell Boat Shop, founded in Amesbury, Massachusetts, in 1793. Today, boatbuilders handcraft dories, skiffs, and other boats for sale. Strawbery Banke opened this shop in 1972 to help preserve the dying tradition of building small wooden boats. Copper clench nails, produced at Strawbery Banke on one of the two remaining copper-clench nail machines in the country, are used in the construction. This shop is unique to museum villages and to the region in which this restoration is located.

Space limitations dictated the design of the **Captain Keyran Walsh House** (1796). Because the house was squeezed on a lot shaped like a pie wedge, it has no square corners. Notable for the unusual painted graining and marbling of its interior woodwork, the Walsh House is furnished with Chippendale and Federal furniture.

The **Governor Ichabod Goodwin Mansion** was moved from its original site on Islington Street. Goodwin was governor of New

Hampshire during the Civil War. His Federal-style house, with its balustraded hipped roof, has some Greek Revival touches. It was built in 1811 but is furnished as it would have been when the Goodwins lived here from 1832 to 1882. Among the furnishings are many family pieces.

In addition to viewing these buildings, visitors can see the ongoing restorations of several exteriors. Several significant buildings are awaiting funds for restoration; among them are **Daniel Webster's Home**, New Hampshire's **first State House**, and the **William Pitt Tavern**, which was once visited by George Washington, John Hancock, and the Marquis de Lafayette.

Strawbery Banke maintains a summer calendar of events that ranges from militia encampments to scrimshaw demonstrations to antique shows. There are also programs on herbs, lead soldiers, woodcarving, heirloom appraisal, and a Christmas fair.

SIDE TRIPS

York, Maine, is one of three villages along the York River that together make up **York Historic District**. This area, settled in the 1600s, was a shipbuilding center in the eighteenth century and became a resort area in the late 1800s. Among its many seventeenth- to nineteenth-century buildings are the **Old Gaol Museum** (1720), which was built as a king's prison and is said to be the oldest English public building in the United States. Open Monday to Saturday, 10:30 A.M. to 5:00 P.M.; Sunday, 1:30 to 5:00 P.M.; mid-June to Labor Day. (207)363-3872. Admission: adults, $1.50; children, 50 cents. The **John Hancock Warehouse**, Lindsay Road at York River, was a property used as a wharf, store, and storehouse; John Hancock inherited it at the age of twenty-seven. Open Monday to Saturday, 10:30 A.M. to 5:00 P.M.; Sunday, 1:30 to 5:00 P.M.; July to Labor Day. (207)363-4974. Admission: adults and children, 50 cents.

Fishing and boating are major recreational activities in the area. Viking Cruises offers trips from Portsmouth to the **Isles of Shoals**, nine picturesque islands 10 miles off the coast, which were discovered by Captain John Smith in 1614. Viking also offers dinner cruises and whale-watching cruises. P.O. Box 311, Portsmouth 03801, (603)431-4620.

On coastal Route 1 from Portsmouth to Kennebunk, Maine, there are approximately 15 antique stores. One of them, **Jorgensen's**, had settles, tables, and cupboards of exceptional quality and quantity. On Route 1, Ogunquit, Maine 03907, (207)646-9444.

Shaker Village

Restoration of an eighteenth- and nineteenth-century Shaker community; NR

Address: Canterbury, NH 03224
Telephone: (603)783-9977
Location: 15 miles north of Concord on Route 106
Open: Tuesday to Saturday, 10:00 A.M. to 5:00 P.M., mid-May to mid-October; closed Sundays and Mondays, except holiday Mondays; Friday evening candlelight tour and dinner by reservations only
Admission: Adults, $4.50; children 6 to 12, $1.75; group rates available
Restaurants: Creamery, traditional Shaker meals in the dining room, light meals in the Good Room
Shops: Gift Shop in the carriage house, reproduction furniture, herbs, books, crafts
Facilities: 22 buildings, picnic area

WHERE TO STAY
Motels/Hotels, Concord: Capital Motor Inn, Gulf Street, 03301, (603)224-4011, $$; Hotel New Hampshire Highway, Fort Eddy Road, 03301, (603)225-6687, $$; Ramada Inn, 172 Main Street, 03301, (603)224-9534, $$; Brick Tower Motor Inn, 414 South Main Street, 03301, (603)224-9565, $$
Camping, Concord: Cascade Park Campground, RFD 10, Box 193, 03301, (603)224-3212
Inns, Henniker: Colby Hill Inn, West Main Street, P.O. Box 778, 03242, (603)428-3281, $$
Inns, Sunapee: Dexter's Inn, Stagecoach Road, 03782, (603)763-5571, $$$–$$$$ (modified American plan); The Inn at Sunapee, Burkehaven Road, 03782, (603)763-4444, $$
Motels/Hotels, Sunapee: Burkehaven, Burkehaven Drive, 03782, (603)763-2788, $$; Mount Sunapee Motel, Route 103, Mount Sunapee, 03772, (603)763-5592, $

Camping, Contoocook: Cold Brook Camping, RFD 1, 03229, (603)746-3706

Camping, Chichester: Hillcrest Campground, Routes 4, 9, and 202, 03263, (603)798-5124

Camping, Franklin: Thousand Acres Family Camping, Route 3, 03235, (603)934-4440

HISTORY

Canterbury Village, chartered in 1792, was the seventh Shaker community founded in America (see the Appendix for a brief history of the Shakers). Today, it is one of only two active Shaker communities left in the United States (Sabbathday Lake, Maine, described on page 15 is the other).

The Canterbury community began with meetings held at Benjamin Whitcher's home in the 1780s. Eventually, he donated his 100-acre farm as the communal site. Canterbury's meetinghouse was built in 1792 by the Shaker architect Moses Johnson. By 1850, the village consisted of 100 buildings on 6,000 acres.

The 250 residents were divided into the three families: Church, Second, and North. They produced wooden boxes and washing tubs, maple sugar, seeds, and herbs; had fine orchards; tended large herds of cattle; and ran a printshop that served the entire Shaker movement. One of Canterbury's most successful products was the Dorothy cloak, designed by Eldress Dorothy Durgin and worn by Frances Cleveland, President Grover Cleveland's wife, at the 1893 inaugural ball. The cape became the rage among Victorian women.

Like all Shaker communities, Canterbury began a steady decline about the time of the Civil War. In 1972, the three remaining sisters turned over their twenty-two buildings and 600 acres to Shaker Village, Inc., a nonprofit organization in which they share control.

TOUR

Canterbury is situated on a hilltop surrounded by 600 acres of pastoral land. Its twenty-two buildings, most of them New England–style white frame, form a serene cluster. Two Shaker sisters, Eldress Bertha Lindsay and Eldress Gertrude Soule, who still reside there, are very much involved in museum activities. They personally welcome visitors.

Six of the buildings at Canterbury are open to visitors on guided tours. The **Moses Johnson Meetinghouse**, the village's first building, was completed on September 22, 1792. Like many other Johnson meetinghouses, it is a Federal-style white frame with a gambrel roof. Initially, all interior woodwork was painted a dark blue, as prescribed by the Millennial Laws, and the woodwork in the upstairs rooms still retains its almost-200-year-old paint. Woodwork in the meeting room was repainted light blue in 1875. It houses exhibits of Shaker-made furniture, baskets, medicines, and stoves.

The **Ministry's Shop** was built in 1848. Traditionally, the elders and eldresses lived on the upper floors of the meetinghouse; but as time passed, they occupied a separate building in which they worked, slept, and carried out their administrative duties. Today, the building's sleeping rooms, workrooms, and offices are furnished with Shaker furniture, much of it made at Canterbury. One room was used by Elder Henry Blinn to dry herbs and prepare them for sale. Blinn was also a beekeeper, dentist, and carpenter; he made the bookcase desk displayed in his office.

The **Sisters' Shop**, a white frame, two-story building, dates from 1810. Shakers made their own clothing, and much of the sewing was handled in the Sisters' Shop. Many sisters were involved in cutting and sewing the extremely popular broadcloth Dorothy cloaks. The room in which the cloaks were made features built-in cupboards and a tailoring bench, a combination tailor's table and chest of drawers designed especially for this work.

Doing laundry was another task assigned to the sisters. In the 1813 **Laundry** at Canterbury, clothes, cleaned in a mechanical washing machine, a Shaker invention, were brought upstairs in a dumbwaiter and hung on wooden racks. A steam-operated boiler was used for heating the building and drying the clothes.

School was first taught at Canterbury in 1801 by Hannah Bronsen; she used a room in the **Blacksmith's Shop**. A one-room **Schoolhouse** was built in 1823. The traditional Shaker curriculum was expanded to include agriculture, history, geography, botany, physiology, music, drawing, and elocution.

In 1862, the schoolhouse became a two-story building. Because it was too far from the Church family, it was moved, and a new first floor was added *under* the original building. It was considered easier to add four walls than to raise the roof. Therefore, the second floor of the schoolhouse is forty years older than the first. Moving or adding to buildings was a common practice among the Shakers, along with recycling buildings for other uses. Structures no longer being used were usually torn down.

In the newly restored **Carriage House**, craftspeople demonstrate basketmaking, tinsmithing, woodworking, and sewing. These products are among the items sold in the **gift shop**, which is located in the carriage house. An herbalist has cultivated sixty-two varieties of medicinal and culinary herbs, and some of these are sold in the shop.

Lunch is available from 11:30 A.M. to 3:00 P.M. in the **Creamery**. Shaker meals are served in the dining room, and the **Good Room** has sandwiches, desserts, and beverages.

SIDE TRIPS

Canterbury is about twelve miles from **Concord**, the state capital. The **State Capitol Building**, a neoclassical structure of Concord granite and Vermont marble, is the nation's oldest state capitol in which a legislature still meets in its original chambers.

Concord's historic district is predominantly residential, with brick and frame houses dating from the 1730s to mid-twentieth century. A pleasant way to spend an afternoon is to walk through this district, which is bounded by North State Street, Horse Shoe Pond, the B & M railroad tracks, and Church Street.

The **Pierce Manse** at 14 Penacook Street was the home of President Franklin Pierce from 1838 to 1849. Open Monday to Friday, 11:00 A.M. to 3:00 P.M., June to Labor Day. (603)224-9620. Admission: adults, $1.50; children, 50 cents. Pierce is buried in **Old North Cemetery**, off North State Street.

Don't miss the **League of New Hampshire Craftsmen** at 36 North Main Street. This is one of several locations throughout the state where jewelry, pottery, needlework, and wooden objects by the finest New Hampshire craftspeople are sold in state-run stores. Open Monday to Saturday, 10:00 A.M. to 5:00 P.M., (603)228-8171.

The town of **Franklin**, north of Canterbury, is the site of **Daniel Webster's Birthplace**. The restored two-room frame farmhouse, where Webster was born in 1780, is located on Route 127. Open daily, 9:00 A.M. to 5:00 P.M., late June to Labor Day. Admission: adults, 50 cents; children, free.

North of Canterbury is the **lakes region**, which encompasses Lake Winnipesaukee, New Hampshire's largest, and three other lakes. This recreational area has good fishing, hiking, water-skiing, beaches, and boating. **Laconia**, located in the lakes area, is also the headquarters of the **White Mountain National Forest**, though most of this national forest lies farther north. Its 730,000 acres offer some of the most beautiful, unspoiled scenery in the East.

Outdoor museum; eighteenth- and nineteenth-century New England buildings

Address: Shelburne, VT 05482
Telephone: (802)985-3344, -3346
Location: 7 miles south of the I-89 Burlington interchange on Route 7
Open: Daily, 9:00 A.M. to 5:00 P.M., mid-May to mid-October; Sundays only, 11:00 A.M. to 4:00 P.M., mid-October to mid-May
Admission: Adults, $9.00; children 6 to 17, $3.50; group rates available
Restaurants: Tuckaway Barn, a cafeteria
Shops: Museum Store, gifts and reproductions; Diamond Barn, bookstore
Facilities: Museum, library, picnic area, accessible to handicapped

WHERE TO STAY

Motels/Hotels, Shelburne: Shelburne Inn, Route 7, on the Village Green, P.O. Box 2, 05482, (802)985-3305, $$; T-Bird, Shelburne Road, 05482, (802)985-3663, $–$$; Yankee Doodle, RFD 2, Box 2990, Shelburne Road, 05482, (802)985-8004, $$; Econo Lodge, Route 7, Shelburne Road, 05482, (802)985-3334, $$

Camping, Shelburne: Shelburne Camping Area, Route 7, RFD 1, Box 300, 05482, (802)985-2540

Inns, Burlington: The Yellow House, P.O. Box 118, 05401, (802)864-4002, $

Motels/Hotels, South Burlington: Best Western Redwood, 1016 Shelburne Road, 05401, (802)862-6421, $$; Brown, 165 Shelburne Road, 05401, (802)862-5708, $; Holiday Inn, 1068 Williston Road, 05401, (802)863-6363, $$; Ramada Inn, P.O. Box 2306, 1117 Williston Road, 05401, (802)658-0250, $$; Radisson Hotel, Burlington Square, 05401, (802)658-6500, $$$

Camping, South Burlington: Burlington Beach Camp Ground, Institute Road, 05401, (802)862-0942

HISTORY

Shelburne Museum is not a recreated village, but a collection of collections. It can be considered an outdoor museum, too, because one of the collections is of eighteenth- and nineteenth-century New England buildings. The folk art at Shelburne is widely regarded as the best collection of Americana in New England.

Electra Havemeyer Webb is the person responsible for Shelburne Museum. Born in 1889, she was the daughter of Henry Havemeyer, president of the American Sugar Refining Company. Mr. Havemeyer and his wife, Louisine, were avid collectors of European Impressionist and old master paintings. Under the guidance of their friend, the artist Mary Cassatt, they assembled a fine collection that now hangs in New York's Metropolitan Museum of Art.

The Havemeyers were dismayed when they learned that their daughter was collecting folk art and Americana, terms that had not even been coined in 1907, when Electra bought her first cigar-store Indian. She collected quilts, weather vanes, merchants' trade signs, ships' figureheads, dolls, carousel animals, carved eagles, decoys, pewter, toys, hatboxes, carriages, sleighs, covered bridges, and, believe it or not, the steamboat *Ticonderoga.* Electra's early interest in folk art is supposed to have stimulated others, leading to important collections by Abby Aldrich Rockefeller, Henry Ford, and Henry du Pont.

In 1910, Electra Havemeyer married J. Watson Webb, whose family owned a large estate in Shelburne on Lake Champlain. The Webbs had five children, but Mrs. Webb still found time to add to her extensive folk art collection.

After decades of voluminous collecting, Electra wanted to display her acquisitions. Her husband, a great-grandson of Commodore Vanderbilt, was interested in local architecture, so the Webbs began acquiring buildings in Shelburne for the purpose of displaying the collections.

The Shelburne Museum was founded in 1947 and opened to the public in 1952. Most of the objects on display, as well as the twenty-five historic structures, date from the early to late nineteenth century. Nearly forty buildings are distributed informally in a forty-five-acre park of fruit trees, ornamental shrubs, roses, and formal gardens. Paved paths are a boon to handicapped visitors.

Although all the buildings of a typical New England town can be found at Shelburne, they are not arranged in a village setting. Apparently, Mrs. Webb saw recreated villages as less than honest. She was more interested in preserving the past than in recreating it. Both Mr. and Mrs. Webb died in 1960. The museum is now a public, nonprofit educational organization.

TOUR

Shelburne, a small town chartered in 1763, borders Lake Champlain and is nestled between the Adirondack Mountains to the west and the Green Mountains to the east. Shelburne has a distinctive flavor, different from that of any of the other sites covered in this guide. Although it contains vast and important collections of folk art and other Americana, it has a certain lack of focus and a touch of eccentricity as well. Its collections are massive rather than representative. Still, its displays of samplers and quilts, in particular, are outstanding.

All of Shelburne Museum's collections are unique, including the collection of buildings. In addition to typical New England homes, barns, churches, and shops, there is a railroad station complete with train, a lighthouse, a covered bridge, a sawmill, a steamboat, and specially designed buildings housing a miniature circus parade and the Webbs' Park Avenue apartment.

The **Information Center** is located in the **Shelburne Railroad Depot**, a Victorian structure built in 1890 by Dr. W. Seward Webb, president of the Rutland Railroad. The restored station displays all manner of railroadiana. Outside the station sit a 1915 **Baldwin steam locomotive** and the **Grand Isle**, a sumptuous private car built around 1890 as a gift from Dr. Webb to Governor Edward C. Smith of Vermont.

The SS *Ticonderoga*, a steamboat listed in the National Register and a National Historic Landmark, is the most unusual item found at Shelburne. This 1906 steel-hulled, 220-foot-long, side-paddle-wheel vessel served as an excursion boat on Lake Champlain from 1906 to 1953. The *Ticonderoga* is the only extant ship of its kind. A film about the arduous overland journey to get it to Shelburne is shown aboard. Prints, paintings, broadsides, and photographs related to the steam transportation era are displayed inside the ship.

For many years, the *Ticonderoga* sailed past the **Colchester Reef Lighthouse** on Lake Champlain, and now they are located next to each other at the museum. The small, white frame lighthouse was built in 1871 to warn ships about treacherous Colchester Reef near Grand Isle. It was decommissioned in 1933 and sold by the Coast Guard in 1952 and brought piece by piece to Shelburne. It now houses a display of maritime and whaling paintings and prints, ships' figureheads, scrimshaw, early maps and charts, and Currier and Ives prints.

The **Circus Building** displays a hand-carved miniature circus parade, complete with sixty bandwagons, cage wagons, animals, riders, clowns, and musicians created by contemporary artist Roy Arnold. It stretches 518 feet in the new, horseshoe-shaped building custom-made for it. The Circus Building also displays forty hand-carved, full-sized carousel figures and a collection of circus posters.

The first building moved to Shelburne in 1947 was the **Vergennes Schoolhouse**, a one-room brick structure resembling a meetinghouse. It was built in 1830 at Vergennes, Vermont, by General Samuel Strong, who rented the school to the town for an annual fee of one kernel of

Indian maize. Today, it houses an exhibit of early maps and calligraphic drawings.

The 1783 **Stagecoach Inn** comes from Charlotte, Vermont, where it was on the stage route between Canada and southern New England. Hezakiah Barnes's spacious inn, complete with ten fireplaces, now exhibits folk art, including carved eagles, cigar-store Indians, trade signs, and weather vanes.

Decoys, another part of the Webb folk art collection, fill the **Dorset House**, a Greek Revival structure built in 1840 in East Dorset, Vermont.

Textile arts are displayed in the **Hat and Fragrance Unit**. Quilts, coverlets, hooked and bed rugs, samplers, homespun cloth, and lace from the eighteenth century to the present are exhibited in tremendous quantities. The quilt collection is said to be one of the largest in the world. Rooms filled with dollhouses and miniature furniture also abound.

Electra Havemeyer Webb began collecting dolls when she was a child. Her 1,500 dolls are displayed in the **Variety Unit**, a red brick two-story house built in 1835. Originally known as the Weed House, it is the only building at Shelburne still on its original site.

The **Toy Shop** also commemorates a child's world with handmade wooden toys, banks, trains, and music boxes, just to name a few of the playthings on display.

Over 200 carriages, sleighs, farm wagons, Conestoga wagons, stage-coaches, and trade wagons occupy the **Horseshoe Barn and Annex**. This newly constructed building is based on a horseshoe-shaped barn near Georgia, Vermont. Many of the vehicles were from the Shelburne estate of Electra Webb's father-in-law, Dr. William Seward Webb, where they had been maintained and stored in a coach house until 1946. At that time, they were offered to Electra just as she was founding her museum. Horse-drawn farm machinery and other farm implements are in the **Red Shed**.

Although not arranged as a village, Shelburne has assembled and restored many original New England buildings. There is the well-stocked 1804 **general store** from Shelburne; the **Charlotte Meeting House**, a brick 1840 church from Charlotte, Vermont; the **Castleton State Jail**, a solid brick and slate 1890 structure from Castleton, Vermont; a **sawmill**; a **smokehouse**; an 1800 hand-hewn log cabin called **Sawyer's Cabin** from East Charlotte, Vermont; and the 1840 **Little Stone Cottage** from South Burlington, Vermont.

Period houses that have been restored and furnished with American furniture are the **Prentice House**, the oldest house at Shelburne, a saltbox built in 1733 by the Dickenson family of Hadley, Massachusetts; the **Dutton House**, a red saltbox built in 1782 at Cavendish, Vermont; and the charming 1790 Cape Cod cottage from Columbus,

New York, known as **Stencil House** because of its beautifully stenciled walls done by an itinerant artist, possibly Moses Eaton.

The **Shaker Shed** is from the Shaker village in Canterbury, New Hampshire (see page 47). Built in 1834 for horses and carriages, this large, two-and-a-half-story building houses a display of tools and household implements built around the extensive Frank H. Wildung collection of woodworking tools.

The children of J. Watson and Electra Webb built an unusual memorial to their parents at Shelburne: a Greek Revival building that contains six of the seventeen rooms from their **Park Avenue apartment**. Faithfully reconstructed in every detail, the rooms are decorated with the couple's fine furnishings and filled with art inherited by Mrs. Webb from her parents, Henry and Louisine Havemeyer. Paintings by Monet, Degas, Cassatt, Goya, and Rembrandt hang throughout the apartment.

Three centuries of American artwork, including primitive folk art and early portraits, are displayed in the **Webb Gallery**.

The **Tuckaway Barn**, an 1835 structure from Shelburne, houses the cafeteria. The **Museum Store** stocks gifts and reproductions, and a bookstore can be found in the **Diamond Barn**.

SIDE TRIPS

The Shelburne Museum is only a few miles away from beautiful **Lake Champlain**, a popular recreation area. Ferries cross the lake to New York from Charlotte and Burlington. For information, call (802)864-9804. You can take a paddle-wheeler cruise on the *Spirit of Ethan Allen*, which also has dinner and dancing. For information, call (802)862-8300.

Nearby **Burlington** hosts a **Mozart Festival** during late July and early August. P.O. Box 512, Burlington, 05402, (802)862-7352. The **University of Vermont** in Burlington presents a **Shakespeare Festival** during July and August, at 109 South Prospect Street, (802)651-2094. And the **Lake Champlain Discovery Festival** in June combines jazz, sailboat races, and ballooning. For information, call (802)863-3489 or contact the Lake Champlain Regional Chamber of Commerce, 209 Battery Street, P.O. Box 453, Burlington, 05402.

The University of Vermont is the fifth-oldest university in New England, and the **University Green** is a historic district.

Shelburne Farms, the summer estate of Dr. William Seward Webb and his wife, Lila Vanderbilt, was established in 1885 on 4,000 acres along the shore of Lake Champlain. Tours of the 110-room **Shelburne House**, **barn**, and **coach barn**, and the 1,658 remaining acres, landscaped by Frederick Law Olmsted, are available in summer. Located on Harbor Road, 1 mile west of Shelburne, (802)985-3222.

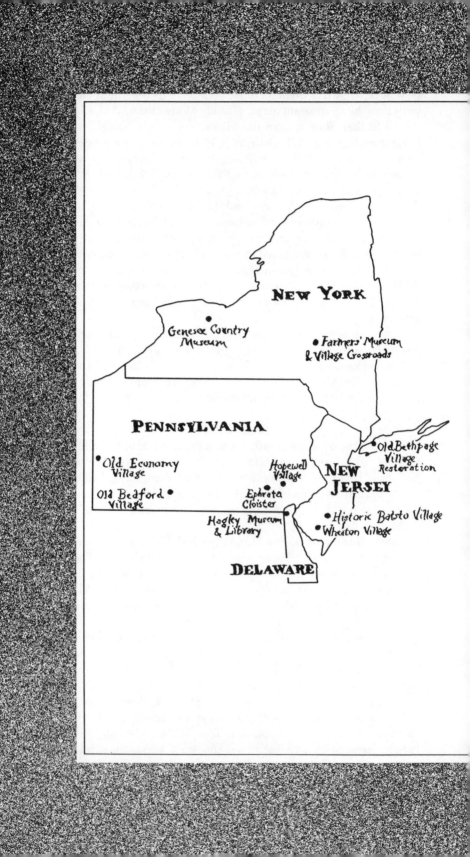

Middle Atlantic

DELAWARE
Hagley Museum and Library, Wilmington

NEW JERSEY
Wheaton Village, Millville
Historic Batsto Village, Hammonton

NEW YORK
Farmers' Museum & Village Crossroads,
Cooperstown
Old Bethpage Village Restoration, Long Island
Genesee Country Museum, Mumford

PENNSYLVANIA
Old Economy Village, Ambridge
Ephrata Cloister, Ephrata
Hopewell Village, Elverson
Old Bedford Village, Bedford

Hagley Museum and Library

**Restoration of a nineteenth-century black
powder mill; NHL, NR**

Address: Route 141, P.O. Box 3630, Wilmington, DE 19807
Telephone: (302)658-2400
Location: I-95 Exit 7 to Route 100 north to Route 141 north, or I-95
Exit 8 to Route 141 south
Open: Daily, 9:30 A.M. to 4:30 P.M., April to December; Monday to
Friday, 1:00 to 4:30 P.M., Saturday and Sunday, 9:30 A.M. to 4:30
P.M., January 2 to March 31; closed holidays
Admission: Adults, $5.00; senior citizens and students, $4.00; chil-
dren 6 to 14, $2.00; families, $14.00; group rates available
Shops: Museum store, books, craft items
Facilities: Picnic area, library

WHERE TO STAY
Motels/Hotels, Wilmington: Hotel DuPont, Rodney Square, 11th
and Market Streets, 19899, (302)656-8121, $$$$; The Radisson
Wilmington, 700 King Street, 19801, (302)655-0400, $$$;
Wilmington Hilton, I-95 and Naaman's Road, Claymont, 19703,
(302)792-2701, $$$; Best Western El Capitan, 1807 Concord Pike,
19803, (302)656-9436, $$; Holiday Inn, 4000 Concord Pike,

19803, (302)478-2222, $$; Sheraton Motor Hotel, 4727 Concord Pike, 19803, (302)478-6000, $$$

Camping, New Castle: Delaware Auto Court Motel and Park, 235 South Dupont Highway, 19720, (302)328-3114

Motels/Hotels, Kennett Square, Pennsylvania: Longwood Inn, 815 East Baltimore Pike, 19348, (215)444-3515, $$

Inns, Mendenhall, Pennsylvania: Mendenhall Inn, Kennett Pike, 19357, (215)388-1181, $$

Inns, Chadds Ford, Pennsylvania: Chadds Ford Inn, Routes 1 and 100, 19317, (215)388-7361, $$

Camping, Unionville, Pennsylvania: KOA West Chester, P.O. Box 502, 19375, (215)486-0447

HISTORY

During the eighteenth and early nineteenth centuries, economic development was closely tied to water power. Small-scale industries, such as the Du Pont black powder mill, were located on the banks of rivers. Hagley Museum and Library tells two stories: the history of nineteenth-century industrialization and the history of the du Pont family of Delaware, founder of E. I. du Pont de Nemours & Company, today one of the largest industrial concerns in the world.

Eleuthère Irénée du Pont, his brother Victor, and their father, Pierre Samuel du Pont de Nemours, emigrated to America from France in 1800. E. I. du Pont, who had worked in black powder manufacturing in France, decided to establish a black powder mill in America. Upon arriving in Delaware, he purchased property along the Brandywine River.

The sixty-mile-long Brandywine River was the site of flour, cotton, paper, saw, snuff, and black powder mills. Originating in the Welsh Mountains of Pennsylvania, the Brandywine has a daily volume of 60,000 tons of water and drops 125 feet in its last five miles. Moreover, it was surrounded by fertile land and close to well-traveled trade routes. Du Pont chose a site along the Brandywine not only because of good water power but also because ingredients needed to make black powder (sulfur from Italy and saltpeter from Bengal) could be shipped to nearby Wilmington. Another ingredient, charcoal, was produced from willow trees that grew on or near du Pont's property.

In 1802, E. I. du Pont began construction of powder mills, a home, and a garden. The home, now known as Eleutherian Mills, was built on the hillside overlooking the mills so that du Pont could direct operations from his home. Business was conducted from the house until 1837, when the first office of the Du Pont Company was built near the northwest corner of the family dwelling. It served as the company office until 1891. Thus, both the du Pont family and its business were based at Eleutherian Mills for almost a century.

Although du Pont had the advantage of being able to see and direct his mills' operations from home, there was a serious disadvantage. When the inevitable accidental explosion occurred in the mills, the home usually sustained damage. A particularly severe blast in 1890 drove Louisa du Pont, wife of E.I.'s son Henry, and their daughter, Evelina, from their home permanently.

In France, E. I. du Pont had learned a method of refining that produced black powder superior to any made in America. His business was so successful that in 1810, he purchased additional land along the Brandywine that included the Hagley Mill. The Hagley property allowed du Pont to build an additional powder yard and increase his business significantly. Du Pont black powder was used in mining, canal construction, and war.

Du Pont's first powder mills were powered by water. However, other energy sources were adopted as they became available. In the 1840s, waterwheels started to be replaced with more efficient water turbines; and by the 1880s, turbines had replaced all the company's waterwheels. Because turbines also relied on the sometimes inadequate water power, steam engines were purchased beginning in 1855, and a central steam plant was constructed in 1884. By the late 1880s, electrical power provided current for lighting the mills. In 1900, the New Century Power House was built to provide electrical power; it remained in operation until 1921.

The Du Pont Company became the largest powder manufacturer in America under the leadership of E. I. du Pont's son Henry and was incorporated in the early 1900s. Expansion led to the production of other chemical products. The company supplied forty percent of all the explosives used by the Allied forces in World War I.

In 1921, powder manufacturing was discontinued along the Brandywine. The company decided to sell the land to the du Pont family. Henry Algernon du Pont, a grandson of the original owner, purchased the home for his daughter, Mrs. Louise Evelina du Pont Crowinshield. They renovated the building and in 1952, the 150th anniversary of the Du Pont Company, gave the home, powder works, and museum to the Eleutherian Mills–Hagley Foundation, a nonprofit educational corporation.

TOUR

The **Hagley Museum** is a site of great natural beauty. There are 200 wooded acres in addition to the Brandywine River. The Brandywine is a wildlife preserve and home to Canada geese. Most buildings on the site, and indeed countless buildings in the Brandywine River valley, are made of locally quarried stone. These attractive buildings seem a natural part of the peaceful landscape.

Tours start at the **Hagley Museum Building**, a three-story Delaware stone building constructed in 1814 as a cotton-spinning mill. It was purchased by the Du Pont Company in 1884 and converted to the production of metal powder kegs. Tickets may be purchased on the first floor of the museum or at the kiosk outside. Knowledgeable guides conduct bus tours that take two hours.

Exhibits on the first floor of the museum relate to the harnessing of Brandywine water power for industrial use. Dioramas of mill operations, along with tools and items relating to du Pont family and company history are exhibited. Exhibits on the second floor continue the story of America's industrial development and are not limited to the local area, focusing on the changing methods of producing iron, steel, textiles, paper, cotton, and wool.

The restoration has two areas: the **Hagley area** focuses on the powder years with the **Black Powder Exhibit Building,** powder mills, a waterwheel, turbine, hydroelectric plant, and stone quarry; the **Eleutherian Mills area** has the E. I. du Pont residence, the first Du Pont Company office building, a barn, cooper shop, and garden.

The Black Powder Exhibit Building, a restored machine shop, was built in 1858 and used for repairing power yard machinery. Exhibits explain E. I. du Pont's superior process of black powder manufacture. If visitors stop here first, they can follow the steps in manufacturing black powder as they visit other restored buildings.

Twenty-one **powder mills** still stand at Hagley, but only some have been restored. They are constructed of three heavy stone walls with the fourth wall and roof of lighter material. They were designed to channel the force of an explosion toward the river rather than toward nearby powder-filled structures.

Black powder was originally mixed in stamping mills; by 1822, these were replaced by roll mills, where huge cast-iron wheels ground the ingredients. Demonstrations of turbine-powered roll mills are given throughout the day at the **Eagle Roll Mills**, which was constructed in 1839 and rebuilt in 1886. The powder was then pressed hydraulically in the **press house** and reduced to grains at the **graining mills**. The next step was to tumble the powder in glazing barrels at the **glaze mill** to round the grains. Then powder was either dried in the **dry house**, which was heated by the **steam engine house**, or spread on dry tables outdoors in the sun. Demonstrations are conducted at the engine house and the dry table area. Powder was then packaged in wrappers, metal canisters, and wooden kegs at the **pack house** and shipped by Conestoga wagon or ship and, later, railroad.

Opposite the Black Powder Exhibit Building is a **stone quarry** where demonstrations of drilling, cutting, and transporting stone are conducted.

Noteworthy but not open to the public are the **Gibbons-Stewart House**, the only remaining example of the many workers' row houses that once crowded the hillsides on both sides of the Brandywine, and the **Brandywine Manufacturers' Sunday School**, a one-story stone building dating from 1817. Many children worked in the mills, and their day off was Sunday. The only education offered to them was this Sunday School, which at its height was attended by 200 children.

The Eleutherian Mills area is dominated by the 1802 two-and-a-half-story residence, which was renovated by E. I. du Pont's great-granddaughter, Louise Crowinshield, in 1923. Mrs. Crowinshield decorated the house with traditional American furniture, but only one or two pieces were originally owned by the du Pont family. The house, although attractively furnished, has not been restored to its original condition.

The small **Old Stone Office** has been restored to its appearance in 1850, when Henry du Pont, E.I.'s son, was president of the company. There are several Bob Cratchett–type desks and stools for the book-keepers and a large vault where money and company papers would be safe from an explosion. During the company's 120 years on the Brandywine, over 100 people lost their lives in explosions.

The du Pont family also engaged in farming, raising corn, oats, rye, and fodder crops to feed workhorses, mules, and oxen. The **Stone Barn** was built in 1802 and enlarged and reconstructed in 1844, with stone buttresses added to resist the force of explosions. The most impressive of the vehicles on display is the man-dwarfing Conestoga wagon. Several teams of oxen or horses were needed to haul its load of explosives to market.

E. I. du Pont's gardens and orchards were planted in 1802 and designed in the French manner, with vegetables and flowers side by side. The lovely restored garden is composed of four quadrants, each bordered by dwarf fruit trees. It also contains a reconstructed pump, a summerhouse, and an arbor.

The **Eleutherian Mills Historical Library** is housed in a modern stone building nearby. A research library which contains 125,000 volumes and six million manuscripts, it includes the archives of the Du Pont Company and du Pont family papers, in addition to materials on nineteenth-century industry in Delaware, Pennsylvania, New Jersey, and Maryland.

SIDE TRIPS

The Brandywine Valley is an area of natural beauty, historical significance, and cultural attractions. Because of its proximity to Philadelphia and Wilmington, it is a busy area, with fairly heavily traveled roads. Consequently, reservations are a must at hotels, motels, popular restaurants, and some of the sights.

The Hagley Museum is not the only property associated with the du Pont family that is open to visitors. **Winterthur Museum and Gardens** is a museum of American decorative arts in a house built in 1839 for

James Antoine and Evelina Gabrielle du Pont Bidermann, E. I. du Pont's daughter and son-in-law. In 1927, it was inherited by Henry Francis du Pont, a grandnephew of the Bidermanns and a collector. He greatly enlarged the house to a sprawling nine-story building with 196 rooms and display areas.

The collection of Americana housed in Winterthur is considered one of the finest and largest in the world. Not content simply to collect furnishings, Henry Francis also collected entire rooms, complete with such architectural elements as fireplaces, walls, floors, and ceilings, so that the furnishings would be displayed in appropriate settings. Therefore, the house is really a collection of rooms that have been moved and installed in their entirety, representing the history of American furnishings and interior architecture. There are even some building facades arranged around a courtyard.

Henry Francis du Pont was also a gardener and a landscape artist. There are 60 acres of display gardens in addition to 900 acres of woods and farmland.

Winterthur is located on Route 52, 6 miles northwest of Wilmington, Exit 7 off I-95 in Wilmington. Open Tuesday to Saturday, 10:00 A.M. to 4:00 P.M.; Sundays, noon to 4:00 P.M.; closed Mondays (except holiday Mondays) and holidays. General admission: adults, $7.00; senior citizens and children 12 and over, $5.50; children under 12, free.

Reserved tours with very well-trained guides are available January 2 through April 2 and June 6 through November 10. Admission: adults, $10.00; children 12 to 16, $5.00. Children under 12 are not permitted on these tours. Reservations must be paid for in advance. For information, call (302)654-1548.

The **Delaware Art Museum** houses an extensive collection of American art from traditional to contemporary, including works of Howard Pyle, the father of American illustration. Located at 2301 Kentmere Parkway, Wilmington. Open Monday to Saturday, 10:00 A.M. to 5:00 P.M.; Sunday, 1:00 to 5:00 P.M. For information, call (302)571-9590.

Nemours, the chateau of Alfred I. du Pont, great-grandson of E. I. du Pont, contains fine examples of European antique furniture, oriental rugs, tapestries, and paintings dating to the fifteenth century. Fine French-style gardens surround the chateau. On Rockland Road, off Route 141, Wilmington. Tours available Tuesday to Sunday, May to November. Admission: $6.00 (visitors must be over 16 years old). For information, call (302)651-6912.

Longwood Gardens is a 1,000-acre property; some 350 acres are gardens open to the public. Some of the property was originally owned by William Penn, who sold it to a Quaker family named Peirce in 1700. The Peirces created one of America's first tree parks. Pierre S. du Pont, a great-grandson of E. I. du Pont, was deeply interested in horticulture and landscape design. He purchased the property in 1906 and began designing gardens and building conservatories. There are twenty indoor gardens in glass conservatories; they are magnificent in their color, quantity, and design. Outdoors, carefully laid-out gardens feature the seasonal foliage. In addition, tours of the **Peirce–du Pont House** are available.

Longwood Gardens is on Route 1 in Kennett Square, Pennsylvania. The outdoor gardens are open every day from 9:00 A.M. to 6:00 P.M., April to October, and from 9:00 A.M. to 5:00 P.M., November to March; the conservatories are open from 10:00 A.M. to 5:00 P.M. year-round. Admission: adults, $5.00; children 6 to 14, $1.00; children under 6, free. Restaurant and picnic areas. For information, call (215)388-6741.

Kennett Square calls itself the Mushroom Capital of the World; it is known for mushroom cultivation and is home to a mushroom museum. **Phillips Mushroom Place**, on Route 1, explains the history and lore of mushrooms through exhibits. Phillips is also an informal restaurant that serves soups, salads, and mushroom snacks. Open daily, 9:00 A.M. to 6:00 P.M., (215)388-6082.

The **Brandywine River Museum** on Route 1 in nearby Chadds Ford, Pennsylvania, exhibits paintings by three generations of the Wyeth family—N. C. Wyeth, Andrew, and Jamie—in a converted century-old gristmill. Open daily, 9:30 A.M. to 4:30 P.M. Admission: adults, $2.50; senior citizens and children 6 to 12, $1.25. For information, call (215)388-7601.

The **Brandywine Battlefield Park**, Route 202 in Chadds Ford, commemorates the Battle of Brandywine (September 11, 1777), a defeat for George Washington that led to the capture of Philadelphia by the British. Open daily except holidays, 9:00 A.M. to 8:00 P.M. Visitors' Center open Tuesday to Saturday, 9:00 A.M. to 5:00 P.M.; Sunday, noon to 5:00 P.M.; closed Mondays. Admission: adults, $1.00; senior citizens, 75 cents; children 6 to 17, 50 cents. For information, call (215)459-3342.

The reconstructed headquarters of General George Washington in the **Benjamin Ring House**, and the restored headquarters of Washington's aide, General Marquis de Lafayette, in the **Gideon Gilpin Farmhouse**, can be toured June through September, from 9:00 A.M. to 5:00 P.M., Tuesday to Saturday, and noon to 5:00 P.M. on Sunday.

See Ephrata Cloister, page 94, and Hopewell Village, page 102.

Wheaton Village

Restoration of an 1888 glass-manufacturing town

Address: Millville, NJ 08332

Telephone: (609)825-6800

Location: At 10th and G Streets, near Routes 47, 49, and 55; 42 miles southeast of Philadelphia

Open: Daily, 10:00 A.M. to 5:00 P.M., April 1 to December 30; closed Mondays and Tuesdays, January 2 to March 31 and Christmas, New Year's Day, Easter, and Thanksgiving; reduced exhibits and food service, January to March

Admission: April 1 to December 30: adults, $4.00; senior citizens, $3.00; children 6 to 17, $2.00; families, $8.00. January 2 to March 31: adults, $2.50; senior citizens, $1.75; children, $1.50; families, $5.50. Group rates available.

Restaurants: Craftsmen's Cafe, a cafeteria; T. C. Wharton Pharmacy, ice-cream parlor

Shops: Located throughout the village, selling tinware, paperweights, pitchers, pottery, wood carvings

Facilities: Glass museum, playground, library, accessible to handicapped

WHERE TO STAY

Motels/Hotels, Millville: Millville Motor Inn, South Delsea Drive, 08332, (609)327-3300, $$

Motels/Hotels, Vineland: Best Western Executive Inn, Route 55 and
West Landis Avenue, 08360, (609)696-1010, $$; Circle Plaza, 62
South Delsea Drive, 08360, (609)691-6685, $
Motels/Hotels, Bridgeton: Highway 77, 1040 North Pearl Street,
08302, (609)455-2500, $
Camping, Elmer: Parvin State Park, RFD 1, 08318, (609)682-7039
Camping, Woodbine: Belleplain State Forest, P.O. Box 450, 08270,
(609)861-2404

HISTORY

Southern New Jersey has been a center of the glassmaking business for
over 100 years. Silica sand, one of the ingredients needed to make
glass, is plentiful in this part of the state. As Carl Sandburg put it,

> Down in southern New Jersey, they make glass. By day and by
> night, the fires burn on in Millville and bid the sand let in the light
> . . . . Big, black fumes, shooting out smoke and sparks, bottles,
> bottles, bottles, of every tint and hue, from a brilliant crimson to the
> dull green that marks the death of sand and birth of glass.
>   Carl Sandburg, "In Reckless Ecstasy"
>   (Galesburg, IL: Asgard Press, 1904)

The T. C. Wheaton Glass Company was founded by a doctor who
moved to Millville in 1883. In addition to his medical practice, Dr.
Wheaton operated several pharmacies and became interested in medi-
cine bottles. In 1888, he purchased the Shull-Goodwin Glass Company
of Millville, a manufacturer of pharmaceutical bottles. The T. C.
Wheaton Glass Company is still family-owned and employs over
10,000 people at various locations. Its Millville plant is across the street
from Wheaton Village.

The village, which is a recreation of a southern New Jersey glassmak-
ing town in 1888, has a Victorian flavor, with many of the facsimile
buildings built in Victorian style. The Wheaton Museum of American
Glass covers the development of glassmaking from the glassworks at
Wistarburgh, New Jersey, in 1739 to contemporary glass production.
The village's other outstanding feature is the working replica of the
1888 Wheaton glass factory, in which glassmakers still use traditional
methods.

The village was incorporated in 1968 and is administered by the
Wheaton Historical Association.

TOUR

There are about fourteen buildings at Wheaton Village. Although it is
attractively laid out on a wooded, eighty-eight-acre site, the village has

only a few historic structures, and many of the facsimile buildings are used as shops. A pleasant stop for a family on a Sunday afternoon, it's an absolute must for glass collectors, especially those interested in bottles and paperweights.

The **Museum of American Glass** is housed in a replica Victorian-era building based on a turn-of-the-century Cape May resort hotel. The lobby is decorated with Victorian furnishings.

Exhibits in the museum trace the development of glassmaking techniques in the United States from free-blowing, part-size molding and mold-blowing, pressing, and cutting to automated manufacture. More than 6,000 glass objects are displayed, including flasks, figured bottles, early art glass, glass housewares, lighting devices, insulators, paperweights, pattern glass, cut glass, Art Nouveau glass, studio art glass, and contemporary manufacturing goods such as fiber optics and lasers.

The collector can find examples of most American-made glass, including Stiegel, Sandwich, New England, Hobbs, Corning, Pittsburgh, T. C. Wheaton, Durand, Tiffany, Steuben, carnival, and depression glass.

The **Arthur Gorham Paperweight Room** displays a wide assortment of paperweights, including antique Sandwich, pinchbeck, antique Baccarat, Durand, and Steuben. The **Arthur Gorham Paperweight Shop**, located in a village shop, sells paperweights made by contemporary artists and village artisans.

A library with over 1,000 volumes is also available for the student of glass manufacturing.

The **factory**, which uses 1888 glassmaking methods, is in an authentic reconstruction of the 1888 Wheaton factory in Millville, which burned down in 1889. It is a barnlike frame structure, fireproofed with steel and concrete blocks. The huge cylindrical brick furnace that dominates the interior is fired by natural gas, but the original furnaces were fueled by wood or coal. The temperature inside the furnace averages 2100 degrees Fahrenheit.

Although glassmaking is being done continuously in the factory, narrated demonstrations are held three times daily, at 11:00, 1:30, and 3:30. Shaping molten glass into a finished product takes infinite patience and skill, and it's fascinating to watch a shapeless blob develop into a recognizable object. A unique feature at Wheaton is that adult visitors can make their own paperweight under the guidance of a glassmaking expert. The cost is $35.00, and an appointment is necessary.

Other factory exhibits include wooden and iron molds, mechanical presses, grinding and polishing equipment, and hand tools.

The **Crafts and Trades Row Building** houses working potters, woodcarvers, and lamp makers. The craftspeople provide very thorough answers to visitors' questions.

A working tinsmith occupies a separate, small **tin shop**, which was moved to Wheaton Village. Other historic structures moved to Wheaton include an 1876 **schoolhouse** from nearby Centre Grove, a **printshop** containing turn-of-the-century printing equipment, and an 1897 **railroad station** from Palermo, New Jersey. There is a half-scale replica of the 1863 **C. P. Huntington Railroad Train**, which visitors can ride for the three-quarter-mile trip around the village.

The remainder of the buildings are facsimiles of Victorian-style shops that sell products made in the village, including paperweights, pitchers, pottery, wood carvings, and tinware. The T. C. Wheaton Pharmacy displays pharmaceutical bottles; it doubles as an ice-cream parlor during the summer. A **barn** has an agricultural display, and the **Craftsmen's Cafe** is a cafeteria-style restaurant.

The village hosts several annual events, including an antique bottle show, a wood-carvers' show, an antique auto show, an antique fire apparatus muster, and a large general antique show.

NEW JERSEY

Historic Batsto Village

Restoration of an eighteenth- and nineteenth-century iron-making village; NR; State Historic Site

Address: Wharton State Forest, RFD 4, Batsto, Hammonton, NJ 08037

Telephone: (609)561-3262

Location: On Route 542, 7 miles east of Route 30 or 12 miles west of Route 9; 15 miles northwest of Atlantic City

Open: Daily, 10:00 A.M. to 6:00 P.M., Memorial Day to Labor Day; 11:00 A.M. to 5:00 P.M., after Labor Day to before Memorial Day; closed Thanksgiving, Christmas, and New Year's Day

Admission: Adults, $1.50; children 6 to 11, 75 cents

Shops: Gift shop in Visitors' Center, books, souvenirs

Facilities: Visitors' Center, stagecoach rides, picnic area, post office, partially accessible to handicapped

WHERE TO STAY

Motels/Hotels, Hammonton: Hammonton Motor Inn, South White Horse Pike, 08037, (609)561-5700, $; Wharton State Forest (cabins), RFD 4, Batsto, 08037, (609)561-0024, $

Camping, Hammonton: Wharton State Forest, RFD 4, 08037, (609)561-0024; Paradise Lakes Campground, Route 206, Box 46, 08037, (609)561-7095; Indian Branch Park, Route 322, RFD 6, Box 457, 08037, (609)561-4719

HISTORY

Batsto Furnace was built in 1766 by Charles Read of Burlington, New Jersey, a distinguished lawyer, Supreme Court justice, assemblyman, and ironmaster. The furnace was located on Batsto River above its junction with the Atsion River. The name Batsto is derived from the Swedish *batsta* (pronounced baat-stoo), which refers to a bathhouse or bathing place. Local New Jersey Indians, the Lenni-Lenape, borrowed the word and used it to designate one of their bathing places on the river.

William Franklin, Benjamin's son and colonial governor of New Jersey, signed into law an act by the New Jersey provincial legislature giving Read permission to build a dam over "Batstow Creek" so that bar iron could be made from the ore found in the bogs. Read then acquired timber rights to 60,000 acres of land surrounding Batsto (1,000 acres of timber were needed to provide enough charcoal to fuel the furnace for one year).

The furnace produced iron pots, kettles, Dutch ovens, fish kettles, skillets, gristmill rounds, weights, stoves, pestles and mortars, and forge hammers. In 1770, Batsto Furnace was sold to John Cox of Philadelphia.

When the American colonies began their struggle for independence from England, Colonel Cox, who was a patriot and an assistant quartermaster general, changed production at Batsto from peacetime to wartime necessities, which included cannon and ball, iron fastenings and fittings for caissons, wagons, and ships, and pans for evaporating salt water for salt needed by the army. Batsto was so important to the Continental forces that its employees were exempt from military duty except in case of invasion. Shipping military products was not always easy. Many people in nearby New Jersey towns were not sympathetic to the revolutionary cause, and Tory spies reported military shipments from Batsto.

Batsto Furnace was not the only site in the neighborhood that engaged in anti-British activities. A nearby town called The Forks was a center for privateersmen and their boats, which captured British vessels along the Jersey coast and Delaware Bay. Goods and vessels were sold at auction unless they contained military supplies, which were then shipped to Washington's army. Another town in the vicinity, Chestnut Neck, served as the supply depot for the privateersmen.

Batsto Furnace, The Forks, and Chestnut Neck constituted an important military target for the British. The Provincial Congress directed John Cox and The Forks' Richard Wescoat and Elijah Clark to erect earthwork defenses at Chestnut Neck. Sir Henry Clinton, commander-in-chief of the British forces in America, sent a naval force to attack Chestnut Neck. The British burned the entire village to the ground. Before reaching The Forks or Batsto Furnace, the British massacred about forty people at Tuckertown but were later halted by Pulaski's foreign legion.

In 1781, the Batsto Forge was built along Nescochague Creek. Four iron firebacks produced at the forge were sold to George Washington, and two can still be seen at Mount Vernon.

After the Revolutionary War ended, William Richards acquired the Batsto Furnace. He rebuilt the facilities, made additions and improvements, built a hilltop mansion, and ran the furnace during its period of greatest prosperity. The furnace made ball and shot for the War of 1812.

Prosperity waned, however, when the discovery of coal in Pennsylvania in the mid-1830s made iron making in that state more economical. In 1846, a glassworks was added at Batsto in an attempt to improve the site's profitability. However, in 1848, the furnace closed down, and the workers left to find other jobs. In 1874, a fire swept the village and the furnace, destroying nearly half the workers' houses.

Ownership was assumed by Joseph Wharton, a Philadelphia speculator, who remodeled the mansion in 1876 and used it for his country home. His total holdings in the area amounted to 96,000 unspoiled acres. In the early 1950s, the Air Force announced plans to build a giant jet-airport supply depot on a 17,000-acre site near Batsto. Governor Alfred Driscoll of New Jersey, a conservationist, opposed the plan, and the state eventually acquired the 96,000-acre Wharton tract. Restoration at Batsto Village began in 1958. The remaining acreage became a state forest and recreational area.

TOUR

A quarter of a million people visit Batsto Village annually. In addition to the industrial site, there is a village with houses, stores, and a post office.

Start your tour at the **Visitors' Center**. Then view the 150-year-old modified Durham boat, which was excavated from the bottom of Batsto Lake. Durham boats, the type used by George Washington to cross the

Delaware, are long, narrow, shallow-draft barges that were adapted for transporting raw bog ore to the furnace.

The **Bog Ore Exhibit** displays the raw material from which iron was extracted by the furnace. Bog ore is found in the stream and swamp bottoms of southern New Jersey, where drainage is poor. It forms as a thick and heavy mud, scale, and pebbles or larger rocklike concretions. After being dug out of beds, it was loaded on boats to float downstream to the furnace.

The most imposing building on the site is the **Ironmaster's House**. This thirty-six-room great house or big house was the residence of the manager of the ironworks. It is thought that some of the foundation walls from the first manager's house (1766) may be incorporated in the present structure. The oldest part of the house is the rear; the front portion was built by the Richards family in the 1820s. Joseph Wharton added the five-story tower and extensively remodeled the interior in the 1870s. It is elegantly decorated with carpeting, drapes, oil paintings, richly upholstered furniture, and all the other trappings of a successful businessman's household. Tours of the big house are conducted regularly.

Nearby is the stone **Ice and Milk House**, where dairy products were stored. Ice cut from Batsto Lake during the winter cooled the house.

The **Company Store** served the needs of the employees. Purchases would be recorded on the employees' accounts and then balanced against their wages. The eastern portion of the building predates the Revolutionary War; the western section was added in 1847. The company store was also the site of the Batsto Post Office, which operated from 1852 until 1911. The post office was reopened in 1966 and operates daily except Monday.

The **Gristmill** was built in 1828 by Thomas S. Richards. Originally, it was operated by a waterwheel, which was replaced by a turbine later in the nineteenth century. The restored mill is still used to mill corn.

Agricultural buildings include a large stone **horse barn** built in 1830, an early **mule barn**, a **range barn** used for storing feed for cattle and built by Joseph Wharton, a **corncrib** built of iron pipe probably cast at Batsto, a **pig slaughterhouse** containing a huge cauldron most likely made at Batsto, a **stable**, and a frame **threshing barn** built during the latter half of the nineteenth century.

The **Sawmill** was built in 1884 by Joseph Wharton. It has been completely restored and produces lumber and shingles used in the village restoration. Motive power for the massive log carriage and circular saw blade comes from the Batsto River, which is diverted into the original iron turbine under the mill.

Unfortunately, Batsto's iron furnace, with its thirty-foot stone stack that was fired day and night, is gone, as is the glassworks, which operated from 1846 to 1867. However, seventeen **workers' houses** remain. These two-story houses are sheathed in clapboards of Jersey cedar, which blackens with age and weather. One house has been simply furnished as a typical worker's home, with country-style chairs and tables in the downstairs rooms. The others are used by working craftsmen who demonstrate traditional crafts such as weaving, chair caning, candle making, wood carving, and pottery making.

There was a church on the Batsto property as early as 1712. The present **church** dates to 1808, and services are still being held in the **Batsto–Pleasant Mills Church** for its congregation.

Nature House is devoted to exhibits relating to fauna and flora of the Jersey pine barrens, with emphasis on the Batsto region.

SIDE TRIPS

Historic Batsto Village is in **Wharton State Forest**. This 108,000-acre forest has swimming, fishing, hunting, canoeing, picnicking, and camping. There are miles of pine and oak trees, many streams and ponds, cedar swamps, and cranberry bogs, along with several hiking trails. **Atsion Lake**, within the forest, has 9 cabins on its sandy beach. Wharton State Forest, RFD 4, Batsto, Hammonton, 08037, (609)561-3262 or (609)561-0024.

Atlantic City, the popular beach and gambling resort, is about fifteen miles from Batsto. The casino hotels tend to be quite expensive, but the **City Visitors' Bureau**, Convention Hall, 08401, (609)348-7044 and the **Atlantic City Convention and Visitors' Bureau**, 16 Central Pier, 08401, (609)345-3305 can provide a list of accommodations and special events.

Farmers' Museum & Village Crossroads

Recreation of a 1783–1840 farming village

Address: P.O. Box 800, Cooperstown, NY 13326
Telephone: (607)547-2593
Location: On Lake Road, Route 80, 1 mile north of Cooperstown
Open: Daily, 9:00 A.M. to 6:00 P.M., May to October; Tuesday to Sunday, 10:00 A.M. to 4:00 P.M., April, November, and December; closed January to March
Admission: Farmers' Museum & Village Crossroads: adults, $4.00; children 7 to 15, $1.50. Combination ticket with Fenimore House: adults, $6.25; children, $2.25. Combination ticket with Fenimore House and Baseball Museum: adults, $9.00; children, $3.00. Group rates available.
Restaurants: Snack bar
Shops: Gift shop, books, prints, cards
Facilities: American folk art museum (Fenimore House), library, picnic area

WHERE TO STAY
Resorts, Cooperstown: Otesaga Hotel, P.O. Box 311, 13326, (607)547-9931, $$$$ (modified American plan). An elegant Georgian inn on Otsego Lake.

Inns, Cooperstown: Cooper Inn, Main and Chestnut Streets, 13326, (607)547-2567, $$$. A Federal-style inn operated by the Otesaga Hotel. Tunnicliff Inn, 34–36 Pioneer Street, 13326, (607)547-9611.

Motels/Hotels, Cooperstown: Deer Run Motel, RFD 2, Box 722, 13326, (607)546-8600, $$; Hickory Grove Motor Inn, RFD 2, Box 896, 13326, (607)547-9874, $–$$; Lake 'n Pines Motel, RFD 2, Box 784, 13326, (607)547-2790, $–$$; Terrace Motor Inn, RFD 2, Box 1938, 13326, (607)547-9979, $$

Camping, Cooperstown: Beaver Valley, P.O. Box 704, 13326, (607)293-7324; Cooperstown Shadow Brook Campground, RFD 2, Box 646, 13326, (607)264-8431; Ringwood Farms Campground, RFD 2, Box 721, 13326, (607)547-2896

HISTORY

The village of Cooperstown, on the southern shore of Otsego Lake, was founded by William Cooper in 1786. In 1790, he and his wife, Elizabeth Fenimore, decided to move their family from Burlington, New Jersey, to Cooperstown. Fourteen-month-old James was the youngest of the Coopers' seven children. Later in life, he added his mother's name, and the world knew him as the famous novelist, James Fenimore Cooper.

In his well-known *Leather-Stocking Tales,* such as *The Last of the Mohicans,* Cooper wrote about the American wilderness and civilization on the frontier. Our visit to Cooperstown conjured up images of the long rifle, Natty Bumppo, Chingagook, and other characters of Cooper's tales of frontiersmen, Indians, and fur trappers during the French and Indian wars.

Although Cooperstown was prosperous, it was bypassed by the canal, the railroad, and later, the interstate highways. It remained primarily agricultural. In 1943, Stephen C. Clark, a local philanthropist, proposed the creation of a museum of agricultural and rural life at Cooperstown. Clark wished to preserve craft and agricultural tools, as well as the skills and techniques needed to use them. The museum was designed to depict the life of the average farmer from 1776 to 1860, the decades from the Revolutionary War to the Civil War. Buildings were acquired and moved to Cooperstown to form a typical crossroads village. The buildings, all from upstate New York, were carefully restored and decorated.

The site of the museum is the former estate of Edward Severin Clark, Stephen Clark's brother. His home, Fenimore House, on the shore of Lake Otsego, one mile north of Cooperstown, became the Folk Art Museum; his barn now houses the Farmers' Museum.

The Farmers' Museum & Village Crossroads is a private, nonprofit educational organization administered by the New York State Historical Association, whose headquarters are located in Fenimore House.

TOUR

The scenic twenty-eight-mile drive from the interstate highway to Cooperstown takes one through lush valleys and past sparkling lakes. Cooperstown itself is a jewel, a picturesque village of large homes on tree-lined streets on the shore of Lake Otsego.

The first of the compound's two main areas, the **Village Crossroads,** is a collection of about a dozen original nineteenth-century structures that recreates a typical upstate New York preindustrial village.

The **Country Store,** dating from 1828, was moved from Toddsville. It is stocked with spices, patent medicines, coffee, tea, candy, shoes, cloth, dishes, and tin pans—items that farmers and their families were unable to produce themselves. The store also served as the post office.

The 1827 **Blacksmith Shop,** moved from New Berlin, is loaded with tools and has a working forge. Blacksmithing demonstrations are given regularly, and tools made here are for sale.

A newspaper and broadsides are still being produced on the Washington flatbed press in the **Printing Office** (1829), which served as the newspaper office of George Shafer of Middlefield.

Used by physicians in Westford for over a century, the **Doctor's Office** dates from 1825 and is fully furnished and equipped with medical instruments. The **Druggist Shop** (1832), originally a Hartwich doctor's office, contains herbal medicines and perfumes.

Samuel Nelson, a country lawyer who later became a U.S. Supreme Court justice, practiced in Cooperstown's small, white frame, two-room **Lawyer's Office** (1830). The small, white **New England Church** was built in Durham in 1791 and later moved to Cornwallville.

The **Lippitt Homestead** was a pioneer home built in Hinman Hollow by Joseph Lippitt in 1797. Food is cooked in the kitchen's fireplace and beehive oven; butter and cheese are made in the bakery. Located behind the house is the **Brooks Barn** (1795), from South New Berlin. It is built of logs sheathed in hemlock and is home to geese, chickens, and cows.

The 1811 **Schoolhouse** from Filers' Corners was considered a model of school design because it was warmer and lighter than others of that time. It has a small library and a cloakroom.

The **Bump Tavern,** built in Ashland in 1795 by Jehiel Tuttle, is a typical turnpike tavern, complete with barroom, ladies' parlor, gentlemen's reading room, ballroom, and bedrooms. The walls of the upstairs rooms are beautifully stenciled. The tavern's roof was raised and porches added by E. Bump in 1844.

The **Farmers' Museum,** housed in Edward Clark's gambrel-roofed stone dairy barn, features an extensive collection of tools along with craft demonstrations. All the craftspeople, including woodworkers, broom makers, spinners, and weavers, use tools appropriate to the era.

The tinsmithing exhibit has a fine collection of tinsmithing tools,

John Niro paintings related to sheet metal work, and the complete contents of a small sheet metal and tinsmithing shop, including the wagon from which the products were sold.

A large area of the barn is devoted to an exhibit called **The Farmer's Year**. It begins in March with the repairing of fences and stone walls. In April, there is spring sowing (the tools are on display); in May, planting; in June, cultivating and road mending; in July, haymaking; in August, grain harvesting; in September, hop picking; in October, threshing; in November, slaughtering; in December, preparing for winter; in January, lumbering; and in February, fixing and preparing tools.

Upstairs, there are exhibits on plastering, heating, woodworking, coopering, house framing, trapping, wildfowling, shoemaking, shooting, broom making, soapmaking, basket weaving, cheese making, and button making.

Happy Times, an exhibit of nineteenth-century rural amusements, includes the Cardiff Giant, a hoax perpetrated by George Hull in 1869 to confound people who believed there had been giants on earth.

There are many special events throughout the season, including Sheep Dog Invitational Trials, Kite Build and Fly Day, Draft Horse Day, Morris Dancers at the Museum, Antique Fire Muster Day, Balloon Day, Spinners All, and the Annual Autumn Harvest Festival.

Across the road from the Farmers' Museum & Crossroads Village is **Fenimore House**, an imposing stone mansion fronting Lake Otsego. It was built in the 1930s by Edward Clark on the site of the Fenimore cottage (demolished in 1932) and farm that once belonged to James Fenimore Cooper.

Like the museum, Fenimore House is administered by the New York State Historical Association, whose headquarters are in the house. It is now a museum featuring a very fine collection of American folk art and, of course, Cooper memorabilia.

In the first-floor library, there is an interesting collection of bronze busts by J.H.I. Browere, who made plaster life masks of leaders of the early Republic. The busts were cast from these masks. Those on exhibit include Thomas Jefferson, John Adams, Alexander Hamilton, James and Dolly Madison, and DeWitt Clinton.

The library also displays paintings of Judge William Cooper, the founder of Cooperstown, and James Fenimore Cooper, his famous son. Several paintings illustrate scenes from Cooper's *Leather-Stocking Tales*, such as *The Last of the Mohicans*, *The Spy*, and *The Prairie*.

The folk art collection on the second floor consists of naïve paintings, fireboards, weather vanes, ships' figureheads, embroidered pictures, and samplers. Among the most interesting naïve paintings are those of the local gentry, their families, and especially, their children done by itinerant painters.

A room of photographs by Smith and Telfa, Cooperstown photographers, illustrates the history of photography and shows the life, work, and celebrations of the town and the Lake Otsego region. An unusual exhibit illustrates phrenology, the popular nineteenth-century pseudo-science.

On the lower level is an exhibit on American textiles that presents the evolution of cloth from handwoven articles to machine-made products. Among the items illustrated are the makings of cloth from flax, silk, wool, and cotton. Household inventories of family linens from 1825, 1855, and 1890 show the change from handmade items to machine-made bedding and linen. A collection of quilts and samplers is also on display.

A **gift shop and bookstore** on the first floor features books on American art and handicrafts and on the history of New York State.

SIDE TRIPS

The other museum to see at Cooperstown is the **Baseball Hall of Fame and Museum**. According to tradition, Abner Doubleday, a Civil War general and West Point graduate, invented the game of baseball in 1839, and it was first played in Farmer Phinney's Cooperstown pasture. The museum was dedicated in 1939, when baseball was 100 years old.

The Hall of Fame is a high-ceilinged, paneled room hung with bronze plaques for each player, giving his name, team, years of play, and a summary of his career. Another room celebrates the **Great Moments of Baseball** such as pitcher Sandy Koufax's perfect game.

The second floor is devoted to the origins of baseball, the evolution of uniforms, and information on all-star games. The third floor features displays on Casey Stengel and Babe Ruth and much baseball memorabilia. Whether you're a die-hard fan or not, you're sure to enjoy this fine tribute to our national pastime. Located on Main Street. Open daily, 9:00 A.M. to 9:00 P.M., May to October; 9:00 A.M. to 5:00 P.M., November to April. Adults, $4.00; children 7-15, $1.50. (607)547-9988.

Old Bethpage Village Restoration

Recreation of a nineteenth-century
farming village

Address: Old Bethpage Village Restoration, Round Swamp Road, Old Bethpage, NY 11804
Telephone: (516)420-5280
Location: 37 miles east of New York City, Exit 48 from Long Island Expressway, Exit 39 from Northern State Parkway, Exit 31 from Southern State Parkway
Open: Tuesday to Sunday, 10:00 A.M. to 5:00 P.M., March to November; 10:00 A.M. to 4:00 P.M., December to February; closed Thanksgiving, Christmas Day, and New Year's Day
Admission: Adults, $3.00; children, $1.50; reduced rates for Nassau County residents; group rates available
Restaurants: Reception Center, cafeteria
Shops: Reception Center Gift Shop, gifts
Facilities: Cassette tour tapes in four languages, picnic area

WHERE TO STAY
Motels/Hotels, Plainview: Holiday Inn, Sunnyside Boulevard at Fairchild Avenue, 11803, (516)349-7400, $$$; Pickwick Motor Inn, at Long Island Expressway Exit 48, 11803, (516)694-6500, $$$; Howard Johnson's Plainview Plaza, 150 Sunnyside Boulevard, 11803, (516)349-9100, $$$–$$$$
Motels/Hotels, Hicksville: Astro Motor Inn, 828 South Oyster Bay Road, 11801, (516)433-1900, $$
Camping, Montauk: Hither Hills, c/o Long Island State Park and Recreation Commission, P.O. Box 247, Babylon 11702, (516)668-2554
Camping, Wading River: Wildwood, c/o Long Island State Park and Recreation Commission, P.O. Box 247, Babylon 11702, (516)929-4314

Camping, Patchogue: Watch Hill on Fire Island National Seashore, 120 Laurel, 11772, (516)597-6633

HISTORY

Old Bethpage Village recreates a typical Long Island farming community in the 1800s. The town of Old Bethpage never actually existed, but its more than forty-five structures are authentic historic structures from communities on Long Island.

Dutch and English farmers began settling Long Island in the 1640s. By 1700, Long Island was controlled by the English and was dotted with small villages. Fishing and farming were the primary occupations on the peaceful island until the mid-1800s, when towns started growing into commercial and industrial centers.

In 1962, Nassau County acquired the former Powell Farm for the development of a nineteenth-century village. The buildings reflect the variety of pre–Civil War architectural styles native to the island. As architecturally worthwhile Long Island structures become available, they are moved to the site, carefully restored and furnished, and then opened to the public. Landscaping, fencing, and farmlands recreate pre–Civil War conditions.

In this living village, farmers dress in nineteenth-century outfits, grow crops, tend animals, and do their chores; storekeepers run the shops; and craftsmen are hard at work.

TOUR

A leisurely stroll through the village takes at least three hours. Cassette tours, in four languages, are available at the **Reception Center**.

The **Schenck Farmhouse** was home to the Schencks, prosperous Dutch farmers from Manhasset. The farmhouse, which was owned by the Schenck family for almost 200 years, was built around 1730. It is one of few remaining structures on Long Island using Dutch construction methods such as the massive first-floor ceiling joists spanning thirty-two feet, round-butt shingles, and the large jambless stone fireplace. Restored to its 1760 appearance, the house is furnished with English and Dutch antiques.

A fisherman named Joseph Conklin owned the 1820 **Conklin House**. The simple one-and-a-half-story house and small barn reflect Conklin's involvement in fishing, clamming, crabbing, lobstering, and eeling. A roadway made of clamshells, a common Long Island paving material, runs near the home.

The **Layton Store-House**, built in 1865 in Norwich, was both a general store and the home of John M. Layton. Items sold in the store included pottery, bonnets, cloth, baskets, dolls, school slates, books, tinware, lighting devices, sausage grinders, and tools. The living quarters are furnished in early Victorian style.

The **Luyster Store** is a one-room weatherboard-sided building dating from 1820. The inventory in John Luyster's East Norwich store included flour, molasses, nails, buckets, eggs, lamp oil, and tallow, and much of his stock was stored in barrels in the basement.

In the **Bach Blacksmith Shop**, a working blacksmith uses traditional methods and tools. William Bach, Sr., who built the plank-sheathed building in 1865, and his son, William, Jr., operated the Hicksville shop for almost 100 years, from 1865 to 1960.

The **Cooper House** is named for Peter Cooper, who lived in it from 1813 to 1818, but the house dates back to the late 1600s. Originally constructed as a one-room house, it was enlarged during Cooper's ownership. It has been restored to its 1815 appearance. Cooper, who was an inventor and mechanical wizard, founded New York City's Cooper Union Institute, a tuition-free art and technical school.

The **Powell Homestead** is the only building in the village on its original site. Thomas Powell purchased the land from the Indians in 1695. His grandson, Joshua Powell, built the original house in 1750. The rear wing was added in the 1850s by Joshua's grandson, Richard, who had seven children. Some of the furniture in the house has been in the Powell family since colonial times. The **Powell Farm** is complete with barns, pastures, animals, apple and pear orchards, smokehouse, outhouse, pigpen, and carriage shed.

The **Williams Farmhouse** was built in the early 1820s in New Hyde Park. A typical New England two-story farmhouse, it was home to Richard Williams and his family of ten. In 1853, the house passed to Richard's son, Henry, who was a master house carpenter. Henry used the carriage shed as his shop, and a built-in cabinet in the sitting room is an example of his work. Much of the furniture and accessories belonged to the Williams family, and this house contains more original family possessions than any other home in the village.

Originally a saltbox, the **Lawrence House** was built in the late 1700s in College Point; in the early 1800s, it was remodeled into a gambrel-roof structure. It has been restored to its 1820s' appearance. The Lawrences were prosperous farmers and real estate owners, and their Federal-period furnishings reflect their status. A distinctive feature of the house is the eighteenth-century wood-paneled fireplace wall.

The three-room **Ritch House** was built in 1810 in Middle Island. The house is named for one of its owners, Lewis Ritch, a hat maker. His **shop**, which displays such hat-making equipment as blocks, bodies, and hatboxes, is right next to the house. A hatter's shop is a rarity among craft shops in restored villages and is well worth a visit.

Noon Inn was operated as an inn in East Meadow from 1845 until 1913. However, it was built as a single-family home in 1840. Furnishings are country style.

A Greek Revival country cottage built in Hempstead in 1839 is known as the **Kirby House**. Richard Kirby was a tailor and Methodist minister. One room of the house is set up as his tailoring shop.

The **Benjamin House** is a one-and-a-half-story gambrel-roof building in the late Federal country style. It was erected in 1829 in Northville on property owned by the Benjamin family for over 100 years. William Benjamin, who built the house, farmed and was a Congregational clergyman.

District No. 6 School House was built in 1826 near Manhasset Valley Park. The building is a typical small rural schoolhouse, complete with wooden benches, a wood-burning stove, plastered walls, and wainscoting. Parents paid a fee for their children to attend (free schooling was not mandatory in New York until 1867).

Manetto Hill Methodist Church (1857) served farm families in Manetto Hill, later renamed Plainview. It was a circuit church, where services were conducted only when a visiting pastor was available. The small and simple Greek Revival–style church was heated by a wood-burning stove.

The **Hewlett House**, a two-and-a-half-story gambrel-roof dwelling, dates back to the American Revolution. However, this house from Woodbay has been restored to its appearance in 1840, when it was occupied by Lewis Hewlett, great-grandson of George Hewlett, who settled in Hempstead in 1657.

The small **shoemaker shop** was built by the Hedges family in 1750. It is restored to its 1820 appearance. Its eighteenth-century hewn and braced oak framing is still visible in the interior.

Landscaping in the village reflects horticulture practices of the early 1800s, a time when little formal planting was done. There are kitchen and flower gardens and crops in the field.

Many special events are held at Old Bethpage, including town meetings and militia drills in April, sheep-shearing in May, horticulture exhibitions and a painting exhibit in June, an Independence Day celebration in July, Civil War Camp in August, muster days in September, and the Long Island Fair and the 1840 presidential election in October. The latter is a reenactment of the 1840 election.

SIDE TRIPS

Old Bethpage Village is located on Long Island, just thirty-seven miles from New York City. Beaches on Long Island's North and South Shores as well as the area's many recreational, historic, and cultural sites make it a popular vacation spot.

Bethpage State Park is a nearly 1,500-acre park that offers golf, tennis, hiking, biking, and other activities. Located east of Bethpage Parkway, (516)249-0700.

Recreation of a nineteenth-century village

Address: P.O. Box 1819, Rochester, NY 14603
Telephone: (716)538-6822
Location: On Flint Hill Road (George Street), 1 mile west of the village of Mumford; 20 miles southwest of Rochester, New York Thruway Exit 46 or 47
Open: Daily, 10:00 A.M. to 5:00 P.M., second Sunday in May to third Sunday in October; weekends, 10:00 A.M. to 4:00 P.M., spring and fall
Admission: Adults, $6.75; children 6 to 14, $3.00; people in wheelchairs, free; group rates available
Restaurants: Depot Cafeteria and Tavern
Shops: Flint Hill Country Store, gifts; PRL Junction, village-made crafts, books; Gallery of Sporting Art Museum Store, reproductions
Facilities: Picnic areas, Gallery of Sporting Art, trolley rides, partially accessible to handicapped

WHERE TO STAY

Inns, Mumford: Genesee Country Inn, 948 George Street, 14511, (716)538-2500, $$
Bed and Breakfast, Caledonia: Annindale, 165 Spring Street, 14423, (716)538-4593, $

Inns, Rochester: Rose Mansion & Gardens, 625 Mount Hope Avenue, 14620, (716)546-5426, $$

Motels/Hotels, Rochester: Hilton/Rochester, 175 Jefferson Road, 14623, (716)475-1910, $$$; Rowntowner Motor Inn, 800 Jefferson Road, 14623, (716)475-9190, $$; Marriott Thruway, P.O. Box 9912, West Henrietta Road, 14623, (716)359-1800, $$$; Red Roof Inn, 4820 West Henrietta Road, 14467, (716)359-1100, $; Howard Johnson's, 3350 West Henrietta Road, 14623, (716)475-1661, $$–$$$

Camping, Bergen: Southwest Rochester KOA, Route 19, 14416, (716)494-1550

Camping, Leroy: Frost Ridge Recreation Area, Conlon Road, 14482, (716)768-9730

Camping, Springwater: Holiday Hill Campground, 14560, (716)669-2600

HISTORY

Genesee comes from the Iroquois word *gennishey,* meaning beautiful valley. The Iroquois named the river that flows from Pennsylvania northward to Lake Ontario. The region known as Genesee country, in western New York, is bounded by the Finger Lakes, the Niagara frontier, and Lake Erie.

Genesee country was inhabited by the Senecas, an Iroquois tribe. They rebuffed attempts by French Canadians to settle this area and during the Revolutionary War joined the British in raids on frontier communities. In retaliation, General George Washington sent General John Sullivan and nearly a third of the Continental army in 1779 to attack Iroquois strongholds in the Genesee area. The Iroquois fled, and soon after white settlers from New England started arriving in the fertile valley. They cleared the land for farming, and merchants and tradesmen soon followed.

Although the first half of the nineteenth century was not an easy time for these early New York settlers, the land was rich and especially good for raising wheat. With plenty of hard work, settlers on the Genesee frontier prospered.

The Genesee Country Museum is the realization of a dream of John L. Wehle, chairman of the Genesee Brewing Company. In 1966, Stuart Bolger was hired as museum director to recreate a nineteenth-century Genesee frontier town. The buildings needed to form a village were obtained from the various colonies that made up the Genesee frontier and were moved to the 125-acre site near Mumford.

Opened in 1976, the year of the Bicentennial, the museum portrays the everyday life of a rural western New York village in the early nineteenth century. All buildings are original, though not on original sites. Most furnishings and artifacts in the buildings have also been gathered from the Genesee area.

TOUR

You enter the village through the **Tollhouse**. This 1850 structure belonged to the Rochester and Hemlock Lake Plank Road Company, which built some of the almost 3,000 miles of plank road in New York State. Tolls for passage on the roads were collected here, and the building was also home to the toll collector and his family.

Facing the **village green** is the 1836 **Foster-Tufts House**, a sophisticated two-story colonial-style frame with a side ell, built by Charles Foster.

The two-story brick Federal-style **McKay House** was built in 1814. Its owner, John McKay, was a wealthy settler from Pennsylvania. The house reflects his prosperity in its size, design, and furnishings.

A one-and-a-half-story frame, **Amherst Humphrey House** was built near the Genesee Turnpike in the 1790s. Humphrey was pathmaster of his road district and, eventually, overseer of highways. The mantels, the house's five fireplaces, and the rest of the interior millwork and trim were intact when the house was acquired for the village.

A printer and a bookbinder work in the two adjoining small buildings from Caledonia, dating from 1820 and 1840.

The village's **Drugstore** is a small Greek Revival building from Tyrone built around 1840. It is equipped with all the ingredients necessary for a pharmacist to measure and mix medicine.

Other village shops include an 1840 **dressmaker's shop** from Roseboom; an 1802 **cooper shop** from Stafford; an 1825 **bookseller shop** from Rush, where books, prints, and stationery may be purchased; an 1830 **blacksmith shop** from Elba; and an 1840 **tackle shop** from Mumford, which was famous for its fishing streams (a fly-tying business was unusual for the nineteenth century).

The **Pioneer Farmstead** is representative of a first-generation Genesee Country farmstead. The **log cabin** was built around 1800 in Scottsville, and the early nineteenth-century **barn** and **smokehouse** are also built of logs. The farm includes pastures, cornfields, orchards, gardens, and of course, animals. Open-hearth cooking, candle making, and soap making are demonstrated here.

Genesee Village recreates all the services needed by its citizens: an 1822 one-room **schoolhouse**, an 1845 **physician's office**, the 1848 **Hasting's Law Office**, the 1824 **Delancey Stow Insurance Office**, and several **churches**. Other village businesses include the 1848 **Altay Store**, a general store; the 1820 **boot and shoemaker's shop**; the 1834 **post office store**; the 1860 **tinsmith shop**; and the 1870 **gunsmith's shop**.

A well-stocked **Trading Post**, which also served as an inn for drovers, comes from Riga Center. Its inventory is based on account books from the Tyron Trading Post near Irondequoit Post.

Hosmer's Inn was used as a granary in recent years until it was acquired by the village. This Georgian-style 1814 building has been restored to its former glory. The inn originally stood alongside the Ontario and Genesee Turnpike near Avon, and was known for its good food and pleasant accommodations. A brick-floored kitchen is on the ground floor; the first floor includes a taproom, a public dining room, a ladies' dining room, and a ladies' sitting room.

Not every building at Genesee is a typical small-town building. One exceptional structure is the **Hamilton House**, a fifteen-room Victorian Italianate villa found in Campbell. The villa, which has a two-story carriage house and an icehouse, was built in 1870 by J. D. Hamilton, who was in the tannery business. Another unusual home is the **Octagon House**, built in 1870 and occupied by Erastus Hyde, a physician who also headed a spiritualist colony in Lily Dale.

The **Shaker Building**, the birthplace of George Eastman, the father of modern photography, is a simple house built in 1847 in Waterville.

The reconstructed **brewery and hop house** was built in Rochester in 1870. The **Romulus Female Seminary**, a private school where young ladies studied the arts, language, and literature, was built in Romulus in 1855.

There's an abundance of attractive, authentic gardens in the village. Both in what is grown and in the arrangement, they reflect careful research.

The **Great Meadow**, near the entrance to the village, has a Victorian bandstand in its center. Buildings surrounding the meadow include the **Flint Hill Country Store**, a gift store; the **Depot Cafeteria and Tavern**, for food and drink; **P. & L. Junction**, a store featuring the work of village craftsmen; the **Carriage Barn**, displaying a collection of horse-drawn vehicles; and the **Gallery of Sporting Art**, which has an outstanding collection of paintings, prints, and bronze sculptures relating to wildlife and hunting.

A free **trolley** makes regular rounds of the village daily during July and August and on weekends in the spring and fall. Of special note among many special events are the Highland Gathering, Horse Competition Weekend, and Nineteenth-Century Games Day, all in June; the Independence Day Celebration, Herriott Trained Animal Circus, and Recreation of the Battle of Gettysburg in July; and the Antique Fire Apparatus Muster, Barbershop Music Festival, Old Time Fiddler's Fair, and Black Powder Shoot in August.

SIDE TRIPS

The Genesee Country Museum is only twenty miles from Rochester, where you'll find the **International Museum of Photography**. This museum has an important collection of photographic art and technology. It is in the mansion of George Eastman, founder of the Eastman Kodak Company, 900 East Avenue, Rochester, 14607, (716)271-3361. Open Tuesday to Sunday, 10:00 A.M. to 4:30 P.M. Admission: adults, $2.00; students, $1.00; children 5 to 12, 75 cents.

The **Susan B. Anthony House** is a National Historic Landmark. The famous suffragette wrote *The History of Woman Suffrage* in this house, which has been restored to its late nineteenth-century appearance. 17 West Madison Street, Rochester, 14610, (716)235-6124. Open Wednesday to Saturday, 1:00 to 4:00 P.M. Admission: adults, $1.00; children, 50 cents.

PENNSYLVANIA

Restoration of the 1830s Harmony Society community; NR, NHL

Address: 14th and Church Streets, Ambridge, PA 15003
Telephone: (412)266-4500
Location: On Route 65, 18 miles northeast of Pittsburgh
Open: Tuesday to Saturday, 9:00 A.M. to 5:00 P.M.; Sunday, noon to 5:00 P.M.; closed Mondays, Christmas, New Year's Day, Thanksgiving, Good Friday, Easter, and election days
Admission: Adults, $3.00; senior citizens, $2.00; children 6 to 17, $1.00; group rates available. Luncheons and dinners available to tour groups by reservation only.
Shops: Gift Shop in the Carriage House
Facilities: Picnic area, accessible to handicapped

WHERE TO STAY
Motels/Hotels, Coraopolis: Holiday Inn–Airport, 1406 Beers School Road, 15108, (412)262-3600, $$$–$$$$; Ramada Inn, 1420 Beers School Road, 15108, (412)264-8950, $$; Sheraton Inn Airport, 1160 Torn Run Road Extension, 15108, (412)262-2400, $$$
Motels/Hotels, Beaver Falls: Beaver Valley, Big Beaver Boulevard, 15010, (412)843-0630, $; Best Western Conley's Motor Inn, Big

Beaver Boulevard, 15010, (412)843-9300, $$; Holiday Inn, Route 18, 15010, (412)846-3700, $$

Camping, Hookstown: Racoon Creek State Park, RFD 1, Box 900, 15050, (412)899-2200

Camping, Industry: Orchard Grove Campsite, RFD 1, Tuscarawas Road, 15052, (412)495-9957

Camping, Evens City: KOA Pittsburgh North, Route 1, Box 280A, 16033, (412)776-1150

HISTORY

Old Economy is a restored village maintained and operated by the Pennsylvania Historical and Museum Commission. It is located in the Pittsburgh suburb of Ambridge.

Economy was the third and final location of the Harmony Society, a pietistical group of German Protestants founded by George Rapp (1757–1847). After emigrating from Germany, Rapp and his followers located first at Harmony, Pennsylvania, from 1804 to 1814 and then moved to New Harmony, Indiana, from 1814 to 1824. They returned to Pennsylvania and established Economy in 1825, which was their central community until the society dissolved in 1905.

A Lutheran offshoot, the Harmonists were a millennialist sect who considered themselves among the chosen people of God. They expected the imminent return of Jesus Christ to establish the kingdom of the godly on earth for a thousand-year reign of peace. The group practiced celibacy, were pacifists, and lived communally.

Like other German Pietists, they were a practical group who excelled in agriculture, crafts, and light industry. They sold their products— crops, beer, wine, whiskey, and cloth—and built an economic surplus for the community. They were excellent furniture makers and carpenters. Manufacturing cloth eventually replaced farming as their chief industry.

In 1824, Father Rapp sent David Shields to Pennsylvania to find property suitable for the group. Shields found a 3,000-acre tract of land on the Ohio River, which the society purchased. Rapp decided to call the village Economy, a Greek term that meant living as a family unit. The town was laid out in a grid arrangement of streets with houses at the center. A formal garden was surrounded by the principal buildings. Factories and farm buildings were located on the outskirts, and fields ringed the town.

By the time the Harmonists moved back to Pennsylvania, they were no longer accepting new members, and because they practiced celibacy, they did not produce any. Therefore, when a schism in 1832 claimed one-third of the membership, it was a serious blow. The schism was caused by Bernard Muller, who called himself Count Maximillian de

Leon. He arrived in Economy in 1831 and was initially believed by Father Rapp to be the Messiah. After staying for several months, Count de Leon left to form his own, more liberal community, taking many Harmonists—and their valuable personal property—with him. Leon and his group founded a short-lived communal settlement called Phillipsburg, the present site of Monaca, Pennsylvania.

Despite these losses of people and property, the Harmony Society's cloth mills were very successful, and the society became a financial power. It invested in oil and railroads; bought land; developed the town of Beaver Falls; and backed many local businesses.

By the time George Rapp died in 1847, the society's membership had become middle-aged, and their mill operation was becoming outdated by the technological advances of the Industrial Revolution. In 1880, the average age of the membership was about seventy, and the society was experiencing financial problems because of bad investments. The society liquidated all its capitalist ventures and paid its debts in 1894. In 1905, the last three living members dissolved the 100-year-old group.

In 1915, the state of Pennsylvania took over the five-and-one-half acres of land that constitute the present museum and turned it over to the Historical and Museum Commission. In 1937, Charles Stotz and Edward Stotz, Jr., began restoration work; they were later aided by the Works Progress Administration.

TOUR

A visit to Economy presents a study in sharp contrasts between the nineteenth-century Rappite community and the industrialism of Pittsburgh and its suburbs. Smoke from steel mills and factories, expressway traffic, and other aspects of modern life seem incongruous with the fenced-in village. You get the sense that the Industrial Revolution surrounded the community site, nearly enveloping it.

The museum is well administered, with authenticity the rule; many of the artifacts on display were made and used on the site. Because of the communitarian nature of the society, the buildings are impressively large. It is interesting to compare Economy with its sister community, New Harmony, Indiana (see page 221).

The center of the original 20-acre town has been restored to its 1830s' appearance. Seventeen buildings, many of them two-story brick and Federal style, have been preserved; they constitute the administrative, cultural, and economic center of the town. Many other original Rappite buildings stand outside the restored area, are privately owned, and used as homes.

The **Feast Hall**, built in 1829 and one of the largest buildings in the village, was used for several purposes. It housed a museum, established by the Harmonists in 1826, that contained art, Indian relics, botanical specimens, and stuffed animals, all used for teaching purposes. Another room has a wooden Franklin printing press that the society used to print six religious books.

The second floor of the building is entirely occupied by a room large enough to hold 1,000 people that was used for *Liebesmahl* (love feasts). On most religious holidays, all the members of the society gathered in the room, with men on the right and women on the left, to eat a meal of stew, noodles, bread, fruit, salad, beer, and wine. After the meal, a religious service that included music was held.

Fearing fire, the Harmonists did not permit a kitchen in the Feast Hall. Cooking was done nearby in the **Feast Kitchen**, a separate one-story frame building. Meals for as many as 800 people at a time were prepared here; the large-scale functional design of this kitchen is remarkable.

A series of shops produced necessities for the community. The **Cabinetmaker's Shop** is a one-story building; this is where the furniture, doors, moldings, and mantels for society buildings were made. A carpenter in residence uses the tools and methods employed by Rappite craftsmen.

The **Utility Building** is an unpainted frame building used as a firehouse. All the men of the society were considered members of the fire department. An 1826 pumper engine, made by the society, had to be filled by bucket brigade.

The large **Granary** held a year's supply of grain on the upper three and a half floors; the first floor was used for stockpiling food. Although the Harmonists were expecting the millennium, they were well prepared for the fire, disease, and starvation that were to precede it. The granary is constructed of huge chestnut beams, and the first floor is half-timbered.

Only the first floor of the large two-story brick **tailor's shop** is open to tourists. The first floor also houses a **shoemaker's shop**, a **barber's shop**, a **hat shop**, and a **weaving exhibit**. The tailor and the shoemaker were responsible for the appearance of the members, who wore clothes supplied by the society. As members filed into church each Sunday, the tailor and shoemaker would check their attire; if they noted signs of wear or shabbiness, the craftsmen would ask the person to come to the shop to be measured for a replacement.

Underneath the tailor's shop is a large vaulted stone **wine cellar** where the homemade wine was aged in large casks both for the Harmonists' own use and for sale.

The society sold shoes, hats, flour, whiskey, farm products, and cloth to the public. Distribution of goods to the 120 households that made up the Harmony Society was also handled at the **Store**. During the community's most prosperous years, 1825 to 1850, the store took in $100,000—brisk business by nineteenth-century standards.

The store, in addition to several other functional rooms, includes the **doctor's office**, furnished with some pieces that belonged to Dr. Johann Muller. Dr. Muller was also the town's pharmacist, taught school, conducted the orchestra, was in charge of the museum, operated the printing press, and tended the botanical garden. What a loss when this jack-of-all-trades left in the 1832 schism!

Rappites lived in groups of three to eleven people; they ate, cooked, and slept in the houses they shared. Love feasts were the only meals taken communally. The houses followed uniform design. The necessary doors, windows, sashes, precut lumber, and bricks were delivered to each building site and quickly assembled. A man headed each household, and the house was known by his name.

Baker House is a typical Harmonist household. The first floor has a large living room, where the members ate and relaxed. It is simply furnished with Harmonist-made tables, chairs, and a corner cupboard containing Harmonist pottery. It also has a kitchen and bedrooms with rope beds and large wardrobes.

Each house also had a shed. The **Baker House Shed** has been reconstructed on its original site. Its four rooms were used for food storage, tool and wood storage, as a chicken house, and as an outhouse. All food was drawn from the store except vegetables, which were grown in each household's kitchen garden. The **Baker House Kitchen Garden** has been restored with appropriate vegetables, flowers, and herbs.

Economy's restored **formal garden** at the center of town has boxwood-edged paths dividing it into quarters. The large **pavilion** was designed by Frederick Rapp, George's adopted son. The orchestra played in the pavilion where villagers strolled through the garden admiring the flowers. A thatched-roofed **grotto** made of rough stones stands in the southeast corner. The interior is decorated like a Greek temple, and under a large dome is a gold lily, said to have had religious significance for the Harmonists.

The **Great House** consists of two separate structures: the **George Rapp House**, built in 1826, and the **Frederick Rapp House**, which dates from 1830. The central structure and two wings of George Rapp's house have twenty-five rooms. It is furnished more elegantly than other Harmonist homes. Although equality was one of the tenets of the religion, the Rappites wanted their leader, whom they considered a prophet, to live in a house appropriate to his position. The great house faced the main street so that visitors could see "what a united brethren could do," according to George Rapp.

Rapp's **study** was the office in which the society's business was conducted. George and Frederick Rapp shared the responsibility of the business operations of a community of 750 people. Rapp also used the office for his religious duties, which included listening to members' private confessions of sins.

Frederick Rapp's two-story house is a separate structure, but connected. Frederick Rapp, who was born in 1775 as Frederick Reichert, was adopted by George Rapp in 1803. Trained as a stonemason, Frederick was responsible for the planning and architecture of the three Harmonist communities and was also interested in the museum and the orchestra.

Here, too, the furniture and decorations are elegant. There are both American and Harmonist pieces, carpeting, and wallpaper. Some of Frederick Rapp's possessions, including his surveyor's compass, a microscope, musical instruments, and books, are displayed.

The **carriage house** contains a carriage made for George Rapp in 1834. The **gift shop** is also in this building.

Outside the museum grounds are sixteen square blocks containing many privately owned Rappite buildings. Notable are the **Harmonist Church**, built in 1824 and located at 270 15th Street, and the 1828 **St. John's Lutheran Church**, located on Church Street between Creese and 14th Streets. Six hundred Rappites are buried in unmarked graves in the **Harmonist Cemetery** at Church and 11th Streets.

Many special events are held annually at Old Economy. There are workshops in textiles, basket making, old-fashioned cooking, and painting. Several dinner-lecture programs are offered by Harmonist specialists. Traditional crafts are demonstrated on summer weekends. A *Kunstfest,* or craft festival, takes place in June; an *Erntefest,* or harvest festival, in September; and a candlelight Christmas program in December.

SIDE TRIPS

Twenty-five miles north of Old Economy is **Harmony**, the site of the first Rappite community in the United States. Harmony is located on Routes 19 and 68. George Rapp purchased 4,000 acres from Dettmar Basse in 1804, and in 1805, the Harmony Society was formed. The Harmonists built a town of over 100 houses along with vineyards and apple orchards. In 1815, they sold Harmony to Abraham Ziegler, a Mennonite, for $127,000 and moved to Indiana. Many of the original Harmonist structures are located around the central square, including the **Frederick Rapp House** and the **church**. The **Harmonist Cemetery** has 100 people buried in it, but there is only one gravestone, that of Johann Rapp, George's son.

The **Harmony Museum** is in an 1809 Harmonist building at Main and Mercer Streets. It contains objects owned and used by the society's members, including a one-handed clock. Open Tuesday to Sunday, 1:00 to 4:00 P.M., June 1 to October 1, (412)452-7341.

**Restoration of mid-eighteenth-century
German religious community; NR, NHL,
HABS**

Address: 632 West Main Street, Ephrata, PA 17522
Telephone: (717)733-6600
Location: On Route 222 and 322, about 12 miles northeast of Lancaster
Open: Tuesday to Saturday, 9:00 A.M. to 5:00 P.M.; Sundays, noon to 5:00 P.M.; closed Thanksgiving, Christmas, New Year's Day, Easter, and election days
Admission: Adults, $2.50; groups and senior citizens, $1.75 each; children 6 to 17, $1.00
Shops: Gift Shop, reproductions, crafts, books
Facilities: Reception Center, amphitheater, picnic area

WHERE TO STAY
Inns, Ephrata: Smithton, 900 West Main Street, 17522, (717)733-6094, $$
Motels/Hotels, Ephrata: Dutch Gardens, 230 North Reading Road, 17522, (717)733-8638, $
Inns, Strasburg: Historic Strasburg Inn, Route 896, 17579, (717)687-7691, $$$
Motels/Hotels, Strasburg: Red Caboose Lodge, P.O. Box 102, 17579, (717)687-6646, $$. Sleep in a converted railroad caboose.
Resorts, Lancaster: Americana's Host Town, 30 Keller Avenue, 17601, 1-800-228-3278, $$–$$$$; Host Farm and Corral, 2300 Lincoln Highway East, 17602, (717)299-5500, $$$$ (modified American plan)
Motels/Hotels, Lititz: Willow Valley Farms Inn, 2416 Willow Pike, 17602, (717)464-2711, $$; Sheraton-Lancaster Resort, Oregon Pike, 17604, (717)656-2101, $$; Treadway Resort Inn, 222 Eden Road, 17601, (717)569-6444, $$–$$$$
Inns, Lititz: General Sutter Inn, 14 East Main Street, 17543, (717)626-2115, $$
Camping, Denver: Hickory Run Campground, RFD 2, Greenville

Road, 17517, (215)267-5564; KOA Lancaster Reeding, Route 3, 17517, (215)267-2014
Camping, New Holland: Spring Gulch, RFD 2, 17657, (717)345-3100; County Haven Campsite, RFD 2, 17557, (717)354-7926

HISTORY

Conrad Beissel, a German mystical Pietist and founder of the utopian community at Ephrata, had been influenced in Germany by the preaching of the Pietists and the mystical books of Jacob Boehme. After being exiled from Germany for his unorthodox religious views, Beissel came to Pennsylvania in 1720, where he initially lived as a hermit.

A revelation caused Beissel to establish a cloistered community at Ephrata. His followers, inpired by his leadership and preaching, separated from the Dunkard Church, with which he had previously been affiliated, and followed him to the banks of Cocalico Creek. This religious communal society, founded in 1732, was based on the medieval concept of service to God through self-denial, meditation, and a life of extreme simplicity. It has been called one of the most thorough experiments in applied mysticism.

Along with his converts, who were called brethren and sisters, Beissel fasted, grew a long beard, and preached celibacy to the prolific Pennsylvania Dutch population. Wives and husbands deserted their spouses to join him. People came from Europe to join the settlement of Seventh-Day German Baptists at Ephrata.

The community was composed of three orders: monastic brotherhood, monastic sisterhood, and married householders. The householders were craftsmen who lived nearby, worshiped at Ephrata, and supported the community's economy.

The cloistered orders spent their time in labor, meditation, and worship. They slept on narrow wooden planks eighteen inches wide, with only wooden blocks for pillows. They conducted midnight services that never lasted less than two hours and sometimes continued until dawn. Some people were said to fast for seven days at a time and to sleep only three or four hours out of twenty-four. The Ephratan diet consisted of bread, roots, greens, milk, butter, and cheese; usually there was only one meal a day. The solitary (the cloistered orders) wore white hooded habits; and for a time, the householders wore a similar habit of gray.

Between 1735 and 1749, the society constructed its log and stone buildings as its people remembered them in their Rhenish homeland. These structures were distinguished by many-storied gable ends; multiple rows of dormers on steep, graceful roofs; small, widely separated casement windows; and narrow central chimneys. They are rare examples of European-style medieval architecture in America. Their utter plainness spoke of spiritual, as opposed to material, beauty. Narrow hallways were to remind residents of the strait and narrow path, and doorways were low to inspire humility.

The community's economic life was not highly organized in the early years. Enterprise was concerned solely with supplying the barest material necessities. The members grew their own vegetables and grains. They manufactured wool and linen cloth for their clothes. Contributions to the community were on a voluntary basis and could consist of land, labor, money, or produce. Beissel managed the funds, keeping the settlement in holy poverty.

However, he believed in trying to alleviate the poverty he saw outside of his community. In 1732, even before the community was formally established, Beissel had a granary and bakehouse built, partly for the use of his followers but always available to the needy free of charge. He also started a free school for neighborhood children. The community offered clothing and housing to those in need.

In September 1777, 500 wounded soldiers from the Battle of Brandywine were brought to Ephrata. The community turned their buildings on Mount Zion, a hill rising above Cocalico Creek, into a camp hospital in which they cared for the sick. These buildings were later burned to arrest the spread of typhus fever, which killed both soldiers and Ephratans. A monument in the Mount Zion Cemetery marks the graves of many soldiers who died at Ephrata.

By 1740, the two celibate orders had grown to about seventy members each and the brethren, under the priorship of Israel Eckerling, wanted to establish the society on a better economic basis. They began by laying out extensive orchards (over 1,000 fruit trees) and even a small vineyard. In an effort to produce items for sale, brethren worked at weaving, shoemaking, and tailoring; and the sisters worked at spinning, sewing, quilting, embroidering, preparing household remedies, and making wax candles and paper lanterns. Ephrata industries, which were under the supervision of the four Eckerling brothers, included a gristmill, sawmill, paper mill, bakery, flaxseed oil mill, tannery, and printing press.

After meeting with much economic success, the cloistered members began holding secret worship services. During this time, Beissel lived apart from the community at the edge of the cloister property. In 1745, he reasserted his leadership, indicating his disapproval of the business enterprise. He enjoined the community to turn away from the worldly preoccupations and return to the monastic and meditative life. Most of the community members agreed with Beissel, except for the Eckerlings and some of their followers who were banished from the community. Beissel then disbanded the entire industrial establishment. Unfilled orders and contracts were canceled, and the horses, wagons, and oxen were sold. The orchard and vineyard were uprooted. The mills and craft operations were used only to supply the community's own needs.

Endeavors not banned by Beissel were writing music and printing books. The legacy left by the Ephratans includes hymns written by Beissel and his followers; *Frakturschriften,* the hand illumination of manuscripts; and a sizable quantity of hymnals, religious tracts, and theosophical dissertations published by the cloister press. From 1745 to the 1790s, the brethren printed books in both German and English, which the sisters embellished with their calligraphic art. These publications are considered among the rarest and most precious of early American documents. Ephrata's press also printed $25 million of Continental currency.

The most ambitious work of the cloister press was the translation and publication in 1748 of the 1,200-page *Martyr's Mirror,* a history of persecuted Christians. Printed for the Mennonites, it was the largest book produced in colonial America. It took fifteen printers three years to complete 1,300 copies.

Beissel died in 1768 and Peter Miller, whom Beissel had chosen as his successor shortly before he died, became the Ephratans' leader. The community was declining; old members were dying, and there were no new ones to replace them. Ephrata's communal celibate orders became extinct about 1800; the householders continued to use the cloister buildings until 1934.

The remaining buildings have been restored and are administered by the Pennsylvania Historical and Museum Commission.

TOUR

The tour of the Ephrata Cloister includes thirteen buildings, ten of which are original to the site and restored; one building is reconstructed, and two are original structures that have been moved to this site. Guides explain the history and customs of this unique community as they take you through the saron, sala, and cabin. The rest of the tour is self-guided.

Purchase your admission tickets at the **Reception Center**, and begin your tour there with the slide show and museum displays of printing and *Frakturschriften,* including a copy of *Martyr's Mirror.* There is also a wooden communion service, thought to be a gift from George Washington for the cloister's care of soldiers wounded in the Battle of Brandywine.

Next is the **Stable**, a 1968 reconstruction of an eighteenth-century building. It is used for housing small livestock and farm equipment.

The **Barn** is an eighteenth-century structure that was moved to Ephrata. It is used to demonstrate carpentry methods.

The 1743 **Sisters' House**, also called the **saron**, is an outstanding example of medieval German architecture. A three-story building, it was originally occupied by married householders. In 1745, it was remodeled to accommodate the celibate sisterhood. Each floor is designed with a central kitchen joined on either side by a common workroom and sleeping cells. The cells are small, provided only with wooden plank beds and wooden block pillows. Meals were eaten in the refectory, which is furnished with simple tables and benches. A room in which the sisters practiced the art of *Frakturschriften* contains a display of that work. The interior is typically very plain, with white walls and wooden plank floors.

Sisters led an austere life, dividing their time between work and prayer: private prayer, from 5:00 to 6:00 A.M., work from 6:00 to 9:00 A.M., prayer from 9:00 to 10:00 A.M., work from 10:00 A.M. until noon, a church service from noon to 1:00 P.M., work from 1:00 to 5:00 P.M., private prayer from 5:00 to 6:00 P.M., a vegetarian meal at 6:00 P.M., singing or *Frakturschriften* school from 7:00 to 9:00 P.M., sleep from 9:00 P.M. to midnight, service from midnight to 2:00 A.M., and sleep from 2:00 to 5:00 A.M.

The **Meetinghouse**, or **saal**, which adjoins the saron, was built in 1741. Church services were held on the lower floor of this two-story building; singing and writing schools were upstairs. There are four original benches and some original candlesticks inside. Framed *Frakturschriften* hang on the walls.

In Ephrata, the Sabbath was on the seventh day, Saturday. The service was an informal meeting consisting of singing and extemporaneous discourses. Many of the hymns were written by Beissel himself. He also prescribed a unique method of choral singing; visitors commented that its falsetto intonation created an otherworldly effect. No other instruments were used. The service also included communion, and sometimes foot washing.

The meetinghouse refectory was used for love feasts. Normally vegetarians, the Ephratans would eat lamb stew and bread at a feast. Any member could initiate a love feast at any time by inviting other members to this meal. Everyone ate out of the same bowl.

The small community **Bakehouse** is probably the oldest building at Ephrata; it was erected prior to the founding of the cloister. Bread baked here was distributed free to the needy. The building is now the site of a candle-making demonstration.

Adjoining the old bakehouse is the **Beissel Cabin**, a small clapboard-sheathed log house built in 1748. This hermit's cabin is sparsely furnished with benches and tables made at Ephrata and is heated by a 1756 five-plate stove. Beissel was a hermit for part of his life, and even after founding the cloister, he spent a great deal of time alone.

The **Almonry** (a place where alms were given out) is a large three-story stone building where male travelers or the homeless could find free shelter. Women in need of shelter would spend the night in the Sisters' House. This tradition of hospitality was common in European convents. The squirrel-tail ovens, located to the side and rear of the almonry's large fireplace, were used for baking bread.

A two-story frame cabin has been furnished as a typical **Householders Cabin**; however, most of the householders would have lived away from the cloister. The cabin has been restored to look as it would have around 1800; the furnishings are simple but not as stark as those in the saron.

In the **Weaver's Shop**, built around 1750, there is a cloth-processing exhibit. This building is architecturally interesting because it is one of the few remaining colonial, half-timbered structures. The construction consists of a pegged timber framework chinked with stone. The interior walls are mud-plastered, and the outside is clapboarded. The ceiling beams, which extend to the outside of the building, are particularly unusual.

The **Printshop** contains a press built in Philadelphia and brought to Ephrata in 1804. It is the oldest American-made press still in operation.

The **Hill House** is a mid-eighteenth-century cabin. It shows the domestic life of a celibate member of the cloister society who chose to live as a hermit.

The **Graveyard** is surrounded by a rebuilt stone wall. Many of the graves are above ground. Conrad Beissel and Peter Miller are buried here. Here is a translation of the German inscription on Beissel's gravestone:

> Here rests offspring of the love of God, Friedsam (Beissel was known as Father Friedsam Gottrecht at the Cloister), A Solitary. But later became leader, guardian and teacher of Solitary and of the congregation in Christ in and about Ephrata. Born at Eberback in the Palatine. Called Conrad Beissel. Fell asleep July 6th Anno 1768. Aged according to his spiritual age, 52 years, but according to his natural 77 years and 4 months.

After visiting the cemetery, walk over to the **Academy**. This building dates from 1837, new by Ephrata standards. A private academy was operated by the church until the time of the Civil War, when it was leased to the township and used as an elementary school until 1926. The two-story building with a belfry displays schoolroom furniture of the 1840s. A separate building houses a gift shop that offers a good assortment of reproductions, crafts, and books.

On summer Saturday nights, a musical drama is presented in Ephrata's amphitheater. *Vorspiel* depicts the way of life of the eighteenth-century communal society; the music was composed by the Ephratans. Performances are at 9:00 P.M., and there is a preperformance tour from

6:30 to 8:15 P.M. Adults, $4.00; children 6 to 18, $1.50, (717)733-4811.

There is also an Apple Dumpling Festival in October and a Christmas candlelight tour.

SIDE TRIPS

Ephrata is located in Lancaster County, Pennsylvania, home of many Amish farmers, who do indeed drive horse-drawn buggies on the roads. These plainly dressed people adhere to a simple way of life that forbids such modern inventions as electricity and cars. They do not encourage, nor do they benefit from, busloads of people driving past their farms. Taking pictures of the Amish is especially offensive because graven images are forbidden by their religion. Out of respect for the Amish, we will not recommend any of the organized tours. Only designated tourist sites are included here.

The city of **Lancaster** was founded in 1718 and served as the country's capital for a single day, September 27, 1777. On that day, the Continental Congress was fleeing the British in Philadelphia and held a meeting in Lancaster. Ninety-minute narrated walking tours of the historic downtown area are available at 15 West King Street, Lancaster, (717)392-1776.

The **Heritage Center** displays folk art and crafts produced in Lancaster County, including furniture, clocks, quilts, needlework, silver, pewter, and Fraktur, the illuminations made by Ephratans. Penn Square, King and Queen Streets, Lancaster, (717)299-6440. Open Tuesday to Saturday, 10:00 A.M. to 4:00 P.M., May to mid-November. Admission: adults, $1.25; children, 75 cents.

Wheatland was the residence of President James Buchanan. The 1828 Federal mansion has been restored to the period of Buchanan's occupancy, 1848 to 1868. Located 1½ miles west of Lancaster on Route 23, (717)392-8721. Open daily, April to November, 10:00 A.M. to 4:15 P.M. Admission: adults, $3.00; students, $2.00; children 6 to 11, $1.00.

Railroad buffs must visit the **Railroad Museum**, which traces the history of the railroad from the steam engine to the present. East of Strasburg on Route 741, P.O. Box 15, Strasburg 17579, (717)687-8628. Open Tuesday to Saturday, 9:00 A.M. to 5:00 P.M.; Sunday, noon to 5:00 P.M. Admission: adults, $2.00; senior citizens, $1.50; children 6 to 17, $1.00.

Farmers markets sell not only fruits and vegetables but also Pennsylvania antiques and crafts. They're well worth a visit. **Meadowbrook Market**, 5 miles northeast of Lancaster on Route 23, is open Friday and Saturday, (717)291-4723. **Southern Market**, 102 South Queen Street, Lancaster, is open on Saturday, (717)392-9652; and **Park City**

Market, 3 miles west of Lancaster on Route 30, is open Thursday, Friday, and Saturday, (717)299-9043.

The **Strasburg Steam Railroad** offers a forty-five minute, nine-mile round trip to Paradise, Pennsylvania, in late nineteenth-century coaches pulled by antique locomotives. Daily, May to October; weekends, November to April. P.O. Box 96A, Route 741, Strasburg 17579, (717)687-7522. Admission: adults, $3.75; children 2 to 11, $1.75.

See also Hopewell Village, page 102, and Hagley Museum and Library, page 59.

PENNSYLVANIA

**Restoration of an 1820s iron-making
community; NR, HABS**

Address: RFD 1, Box 345, Elverson, PA 19520
Telephone: (215)582-8773
Location: 6 miles south of Birdsboro on Route 345, 10 miles from the
Morgantown interchange on the Pennsylvania Turnpike, via Route
23 East and 345 North
Open: Daily, 9:00 A.M. to 5:00 P.M., until 6:00 P.M., late June to
Labor Day; closed Christmas and New Year's Day
Admission: Free
Facilities: Visitors' Center, wagon rides, picnic area, accessible to
handicapped

WHERE TO STAY
Motels/Hotels, Reading: Dutch Colony Motor Inn, 4635 Perkiomen
Avenue, 19606, (215)779-2345, $; Holiday Inn–North, North 5th
St. Highway, 19605, (215)929-4741, $$
Motels/Hotels, Wyomissing: Sheraton Berkshire Inn, Woodland and
Van Reed Roads, 19610, (215)376-3811, $$; Luxury Budget Inn,
Route 422 at Papermill Road, 19610, (215)378-5105, $; Reading
Motor Inn, 1040 Park Road, 19610, (215)372-7811, $$

Camping, Elverson: French Creek State Park, RFD 1, Box 448, 19520, (215)582-1514
Camping, Denver: Dutch Cousins Campsite, RFD 3, Hill Road, 17517, (215)267-6911; Cocalico Creek Campground, RFD 2, 17517, (215)267-2014

HISTORY

Although colonial iron production began slowly in the seventeenth century, Pennsylvania had many of the natural resources needed for iron making: iron ore in abundance, large forests from which charcoal fuel could be made, rich deposits of limestone for use in the separation of impurities from the iron, and numerous streams for powering waterwheels. By the Revolutionary War, Pennsylvania had become the most important iron-producing colony, with well over fifty operating furnaces and forges.

Mark Bird, the son of an ironmaster, owned thousands of acres of land in Berks and Chester Counties. In 1771, he built Hopewell Furnace on French Creek in southern Berks County, five miles from a forge he inherited from his father.

Operating a furnace and cutting down trees required a large number of workers who lived near their work. Family-owned iron plantations usually consisted of several thousand acres of woodlands, the ironmaster's mansion, tenant homes for as many as 100 people, a company store, blacksmith shops, barns, and of course, the furnace.

The British Iron Act of 1750 limited the American iron industry to the production of pig and bar iron that could be reworked by British forges into finished products and exported to the colonies. Mark Bird, like most ironmasters, resented the act and British interference in the business interests of the colonies. He became prominent in the revolutionary movement. He was elected to the state assembly and served as colonel of the Second Battalion of the Berks County Militia.

During the Revolutionary War, Bird was the deputy quartermaster general of Pennsylvania. His ironworks supplied cannon and shot to the Continental army. After the war, the new government was unable to pay off all its debts, including its debt to Bird. This loss, along with damage to Hopewell by floods and fire, led to Bird's economic ruin.

In 1788, Hopewell Furnace was auctioned off. It passed through several hands and was eventually purchased by Daniel Buckley and his brothers-in-law, Thomas and Matthew Brooke, in 1800. The two families owned and operated the furnace until 1883.

By the mid-1830s, after an unpromising start complicated by economic slowdowns, natural disasters, and litigation over title to the land, Hopewell Furnace had become highly profitable. Technological changes made by the Buckley-Brooke partners improved productivity.

According to an 1832 Treasury Department report, Hopewell Furnace employed 168 men with 800 dependents, owned 84 horses, and produced 1,000 tons of pig metal and 700 tons of castings.

Clement Brooke, a son of one of the original partners, was resident manager and ironmaster from 1816 until 1848 and is credited with Hopewell Furnace's economic success. He made many improvements to the property and built Hopewell Furnace into a self-contained village, a company town.

Hopewell Furnace produced cast-iron stoves, which had replaced the open fireplaces traditionally used for cooking and heating. Other products included iron housewares, wheels, mill screws, clock weights, hammers, grindstone wheels, and prison bars. Products were shipped overland by wagons until the opening of the Schuylkill Canal in 1825, after which they were shipped by boat. In the early 1840s, shipping by rail began.

The panic of 1837 brought bank failures and a depression to American business. Hopewell Furnace's markets shrank, and although the operation remained viable, it began slowing down. Large-scale stove-plate casting ended at Hopewell in 1844. Clement Brooke retired in 1848.

Industry was undergoing rapid changes because of coal and steam. Cold-blast, charcoal-fueled iron furnaces like Hopewell's had to compete with coke and hot-blast anthracite furnaces that were less expensive to run. In an attempt to modernize Hopewell, the company built an anthracite furnace in 1853; but it was a failure, and Hopewell returned to traditional methods. Business generally declined except for a brief resurgence during the Civil War. Hopewell Furnace was shut down permanently June 15, 1883.

Hopewell was a deserted village until 1935, when the federal government became interested in using the area in a New Deal conservation program. Louise Clingan Brooke, a descendant of the Buckley-Brooke partners, sold 4,000 acres to the government for about $100,000. Two Civilian Conservation Corps camps were established. They were regarded as a recreational park, and trails were built and French Creek dammed to create Hopewell Lake. When National Park Service historian Roy E. Appleman was sent to survey the site, he became interested in restoring the furnace town. Thanks to his efforts, the furnace was restored to its condition during its most prosperous period, from 1820 to 1840.

In 1938, the secretary of the interior designated the area as Hopewell Village National Historic Site within the National Park System. In 1946, the federal government separated the historic and scenic areas. About 5,000 acres, including Hopewell Lake, were deeded to Pennsylvania, and 848 acres were set aside for the historic site.

TOUR

What remains of Hopewell Furnace today is a picturesque village-plantation hidden away along a wooded side road. The huge furnace is no longer lit, but the exhibits help one imagine the around-the-clock heat, noise, and dirt that accompanied the manufacturing of iron.

Begin with the **Visitors' Center**, which has a ten-minute audiovisual presentation of background information on Mark Bird and iron making. Then start your self-guided tour at the **Charcoal House** and **Cooling Shed**.

Most of Hopewell's 5,000 acres were wooded. It took an acre of hardwood forest, cut and burned to create charcoal, to fuel a day's operation of the furnace. Colliers hauled the charcoal by wagon to the two-part charcoal house and cooling shed. There it was unloaded, completely cooled, and stored for later use.

The crumbling stone ruins of the 1853 **anthracite furnace** are all that remains of the failed attempt to modernize Hopewell's operation. Although sulfur ore had been discovered in Hopewell mines, the shipping costs of the other necessary ores were prohibitive. By 1859, the furnace was sold and Hopewell returned exclusively to its charcoal furnace. Charcoal was made at the **charcoal hearths**, a large circular clearing where from 25 to 50 cords of wood were piled in mounds, covered with leaves, and set on fire. (At its height, the furnace burned 7,000 cords of wood a year.) *Coaling*, as this process was called, took from ten days to two weeks. The smoldering fire had to be constantly monitored by colliers, who often lived in huts near the hearths. A good collier could produce a yield of 35 to 40 bushels of charcoal per cord of wood.

Hopewell Furnace was built in 1771. Its stack is thirty-two-and-a-half feet high and seven feet wide at its widest point, tapering to one-and-a-half feet at the top. The outside wall is of limestone; the interior is lined with sandstone. Fluid slag and iron ran down and collected on the hearth at the bottom of the furnace. The lighter-weight slag floating on the iron was drawn off, and every twelve hours, the molten iron was tapped for casting.

French Creek provided the fast-flowing water necessary to propel the **waterwheel** that drove the blast machinery to keep the furnace fire hot. The reconstructed twenty-two-foot wheel exudes a feeling of quiet power.

Between the charcoal house and the furnace was the **bridge house**, where ingredients for charging the furnace for the next few hours were stored. Workers called *fillers* charged the furnace about every half hour with 15 bushels of charcoal, 400 to 500 pounds of ore, and 30 to 40 pounds of limestone.

The restored **Buckley and Brooke Office Store** is a two-story stone building with a wooden lean-to shed on the east side. Workers at Hopewell did not receive cash wages; instead, their accounts at the store were credited with the amount they earned. A worker's credit could be used to make purchases at the store, to pay bills to the company, or to pay for purchases made elsewhere that had been ordered through the store, or could be drawn as cash.

The store's inventory included shoes, fur hats, cloth, whiskey, coffee, tea, rice, flour, sugar, chocolate, cheese, molasses, pork, beef, and tools. Hopewell workers were not required to shop at the store, and prices were competitive. The store was viewed as a convenience rather than a monopoly.

Hopewell Furnace's products—finished cast-iron goods and bars of pig iron that were sold to other foundries—were made in the **Cast House**. Exhibits in the Cast House describe the progression of casting technology. Other buildings related to iron production are the **blacksmith shop**, which is completely equipped and functioning, and the **barn**, which now houses a collection of horse-drawn vehicles.

Because Hopewell Furnace was in a fairly isolated location, the company built **tenant houses** for its married employees and their families. Four original houses remain; they are of whitewashed stone with shingle roofs and wooden trim painted red. The two-story stone **boardinghouse** was used by single men.

The most imposing house at Hopewell Furnace is the mansion, also known as the **Big House**. Its northwest wing was built around 1771, and large additions were made in 1802 and 1820. The big house was home to the owner and his family, along with their servants and some workers. The basement dining room was the dining area for the single men of the community. Business was conducted in the second-floor study, and traveling businessmen slept on the third floor. The Victorian furnishings in the rooms open for viewing were acquired from the Brooke family.

Outbuildings include the **springhouse**, which supplied drinking water and stored perishables, the **smokehouse**, and the **bake oven**.

Beginning the last week of June and continuing through Labor Day, guides and craftspeople demonstrate and explain carpentry, blacksmithing, molding and metal casting, open-hearth cooking, weaving, and spinning. Special celebrations are held on the Fourth of July, Establishment Day (first Sunday in August), and Fall Festival (last Sunday in September).

SIDE TRIPS

French Creek State Park, the recreational portion of the Hopewell property purchased by the federal government, surrounds the historic site on three sides. The heavily wooded 7,339-acre park preserves this area's outstanding natural beauty. It has three lakes, a swimming pool, fishing, boating, hiking trails, picnicking, hunting in season, horseback riding, and environmental education programs, as well as several camping areas. French Creek State Park, RFD 1, Box 448, Elverson, 19520, (215)582-1514.

The **Daniel Boone Homestead** honors the American pioneer, who was born in a log cabin on this site in 1734. At that time, Berks County was at the edge of the wilderness. The cabin in which Boone was born to Quaker parents was replaced by a two-story stone structure sometime in the eighteenth century. The grounds include a blacksmith shop, smokehouse, barn, and log cabin. There is a lodge for overnight accommodations. RFD 2, Box 162, Birdsboro, 19508, (215)582-4900.

Visit **Valley Forge**, a National Historic Park. The 2,255-acre park commemorates the winter of 1777–1778, when George Washington's bedraggled Continental army camped here while British troops occupied Philadelphia. The park includes a **Visitors' Center**, the colonial-style **stone house** that was Washington's headquarters, a **bakehouse**, **soldiers' huts**, **fortifications**, and **parade grounds**. Located 3 miles west of Pennsylvania Turnpike Interchange 24. Superintendent, Valley Forge, 19481, (215)783-7700.

See Ephrata Cloister, page 94, and Hagley Museum and Library, page 59.

PENNSYLVANIA

Old Bedford Village

Replica of an 1850 village

Address: P.O. Box 1976, Bedford, PA 15522
Telephone: (814)623-1156 or (814)623-1157
Location: On Route 220, 3 miles south of the Pennsylvania Turnpike at Bedford Exit 11
Open: Daily, 9:00 A.M. to 5:00 P.M., second Sunday in April to last Sunday in October; weekends only in November

Admission: Adults, $4.50; senior citizens, $3.25; children 6 to 12, $3.00; group rates available

Restaurants: Ye Olde Tavern, soft drinks in the bar; Visitors' Center, cafeteria

Shops: Many craft shops throughout the village; The Barn, crafts and souvenirs

Facilities: Visitors' Center, 40 buildings, picnic pavilion, accessible to handicapped

WHERE TO STAY

Resorts, Bedford: Bedford Springs Hotel, Bedford Road, 15522, (814)623-6121, $$$$ (modified American plan). This 1804 mountain resort was known for its mineral springs; the hotel was the summer White House of President James Buchanan from 1856 to 1860.

Motels/Hotels, Bedford: Econo Lodge, Route 220, 15522, (814)623-5108, $; Quality Inn, RFD 2, Box 171, Route 220 Business, 15522, (814)623-5188, $; Crinoline Courts, RFD 2, Route 220 Business, 15522, (814)623-9511, $; Midway, RFD 2, Route 220 Business, 15522, (814)623-8107, $; Penn Manor, Route 220 Business, P.O. Box 71, 15522, (814)623-8177, $

Camping, Shellsburg: Shawnee State Park, Route 30, P.O. Box 67, 15559, (814)733-4218

Camping, Imler: Blue Knob State Park, RFD 1, Box 230A, 16655, (814)276-3576

HISTORY

Fort Bedford, on the Raystown River, was erected during the French and Indian wars for the British troops who were advancing on the French at Fort Duquesne. British Brigadier General John Forbes, with his 7,500 soldiers and 1,000 wagoners, made a wagon road west of Bedford. Known as Forbes Road, it became a major route of westward migration.

Fort Bedford was the first British fort in America to be captured by American rebels. In 1769, Captain James Smith and a party of eighteen men attacked the fort and liberated the American prisoners. By the onset of the Revolutionary War, Fort Bedford was already in ruins.

The town of Bedford began as a village that grew up around the fort. Surveyed in 1761, Bedford was laid out in 1766. In 1771, it became the county seat for a large part of western Pennsylvania. During the Revolutionary War, Indians repeatedly attacked this frontier town.

As migration moved farther west, traffic on Forbes Road decreased, and Bedford became a quiet farming town and resort area. Old Bedford Village was built for the Bicentennial to recreate a pioneer Pennsylvania town during the 1790s. It is a nonprofit corporation and is governed by a board of directors.

TOUR

One enters Old Bedford through a **covered bridge**, which was moved ten miles to the site. Old Bedford is craft-oriented, with demonstrations and numerous shops. Costumed guides in each building offer a limited amount of information on the building and its contents. The antique furnishings used in the buildings throughout the village are of local origin.

The **Biddle House** is a two-story log house that was moved from Dutch Corner. Built in 1782, it is the oldest house in the village. An unusual but stunning stone double fireplace—one fireplace for cooking and one for heating—dominates the house.

The **Kegg-Blasko House** was originally two houses; they were later combined into a two-story log house with a front porch. Because the house was once occupied by a cobbler, it features an exhibit of cobbler's tools. The Kegg part of the house dates from 1768; the Blasko side, from 1775.

A one-story brick house is occupied by the **Pewter Shop**, where a small number of antique pewter articles are on display. Demonstrations of the pewterer's craft are conducted here.

A one-room stone schoolhouse dating from 1854 now serves as a **Basket Shop**, where visitors can watch basketmaking demonstrations.

An unusual feature of the **wheelwright's shop** is that it is constructed of vertical logs with their bark still in place.

Two blacksmiths man the forge at a **Blacksmith Shop** set up in a barn.

A two-story log house, the **Fisk House** (1840), is now a leather shop.

One of the most interesting buildings is an **Octagonal Schoolhouse** built by Quakers in 1851 and used as a public school. The white frame structure, which originally housed eight grades with the teacher's desk and blackboard in the center, was used in nearby Fisterberg until 1932.

Plays and musicals are presented on the stage of the **Old Bedford Village Opera House**, which is a log structure.

The reconstructed **Toy Shop** features antique toys and a toy-making demonstration. The **Feather House** next door dates from about 1800 and is now used as a bakery.

The **Printshop** has a wooden press from the Ephrata Cloister in Lancaster County (see page 94). The Ephrata colony produced some of the earliest and most beautiful illuminated manuscripts on this continent, as well as Continental currency, the money produced by the colonies to pay the Continental soldiers during the Revolution. Examples of the Ephratans' fine printing work are on display.

Ye Olde Tavern, a two-story stone and log building, is a reproduction of the Pendergrass Tavern, built in 1750 in nearby Bedford. The tavern was also used as a courthouse when the circuit court came to Bedford. From a cage bar, a guide sells root beer and birch beer to thirsty tourists.

The **Hemming House** (1812) is a log building now known as the **furniture and undertaking shop**. Wooden tables, quilt racks, and small wooden objects are made there.

A two-story log house originally located in Pennsylvania Hollow, the 1790 **Shaffer House** is the site of a patchwork and quilting demonstration. Visitors are invited to try their hand at quilting.

The **Knisely School** is a one-room red schoolhouse built in 1869. All eight grades attended classes there from October through February. (Children were not needed to do farm chores during the winter months.)

The 1850 **Clouse House**, a two-story log house, is now a pottery shop. The kiln is in a shed behind the house.

Other craft-oriented shops are the **candle shop, doll house, clock shop, gun shop, weaving shop**, and **tinsmith shop**. Rounding out the village are the **jail, store and post office, church, farmhouse**, and **sawmill**.

The **barn** serves as a craft shop on the upper level and a souvenir shop on the lower level. Pottery, quilts, candles, pewter, books, and period toys are available, but these items are not necessarily made in the village.

Annual festivals at Old Bedford Village include a May Day celebration, Settler's Day celebration in mid-June, an arts and crafts festival in early July, Children's Day in mid-July, a bluegrass festival in early August, Pioneer Days on Labor Day weekend, a pumpkin festival at the end of October, and an old-fashioned Christmas celebration in December.

SIDE TRIPS

In July and August, the Bedford Springs Hotel hosts the annual **Bedford Springs Festival for the Performing Arts**, six weeks of music, dance, poetry, and song performed by acclaimed artists. In addition to concerts, there are master classes, lectures, and open rehearsals. Call (412)391-5460 for information.

A four-by-six-block area of downtown Bedford has been designated a **national historic district**. It includes many eighteenth-century buildings. The **Frazer Tavern** dates from 1768 and is the oldest standing structure in Bedford. The **Espy House**, built in 1771, served as President George Washington's headquarters when he brought the army to western Pennsylvania to quell the Whiskey Rebellion in 1794.

The **Tourist and Resort Bureau** is in the **Anderson House** (1814), 137 East Pitt Street. This building was once owned by Dr. John

Anderson, founder of the Bedford Springs Hotel. Information on the Bedford County–area attractions and accommodations and a walking tour map of the historic district are available. The bureau is open year-round, from 8:30 A.M. to 5:00 P.M., P.O. Box 1171, (814)623-1771.

In **Fort Bedford Park and Museum**, adjacent to downtown Bedford, there is a reconstruction of the original British fort built in 1758. The fort is open daily, 9:00 A.M. to 5:00 P.M., May 1 to October 28. The museum displays tools and household artifacts of pioneer Pennsylvania, Indian artifacts, rifles, and an original Conestoga wagon. Admission: adults, $2.00; senior citizens, $1.50; children, $1.00.

Shawnee State Park is a 3,800-acre park at the foot of Allegheny Mountain. It offers facilities for swimming, fishing, and boating in its 451-acre lake, in addition to picnicking, hiking, and camping. Shawnee is in Schellsburg, 8 miles west of Bedford along Routes 30 and 31, (814)733-4218.

Other Bedford County attractions include fifteen **covered bridges**.

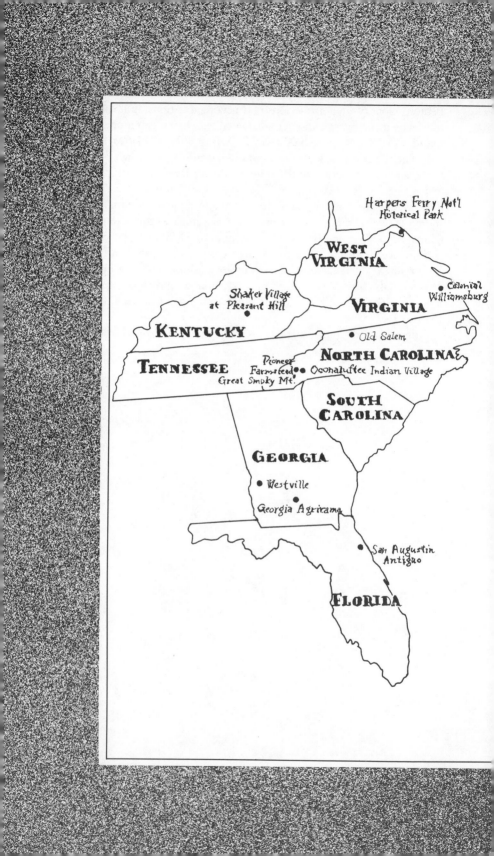

Harpers Ferry Nat'l
Historical Park

**WEST
VIRGINIA**

Shaker Village
at Pleasant Hill

Colonial
Williamsburg

VIRGINIA

KENTUCKY

Old Salem

NORTH CAROLINA

TENNESSEE

Pioneer
Farmstead
Great Smoky Mt.

Oconaluftee Indian Village

**SOUTH
CAROLINA**

GEORGIA

Westville

Georgia Agrirama

San Augustin
Antiguo

FLORIDA

South and Southeast

FLORIDA
    San Augustin Antiguo, St. Augustine

GEORGIA
    Georgia Agrirama, Tifton
    Westville, Lumpkin

KENTUCKY
    Shaker Village at Pleasant Hill, Harrodsburg

NORTH CAROLINA
    Oconaluftee Indian Village, Cherokee
    Old Salem, Winston-Salem
    Pioneer Farmstead, Great Smoky Mountains
    National Park, Oconaluftee

VIRGINIA
    Colonial Williamsburg, Williamsburg

WEST VIRGINIA
    Harpers Ferry National Historical Park,
    Harpers Ferry

San Augustin Antiguo

**Restoration/reconstruction of the
eighteenth-century Spanish colonial
settlement; NR, NHL, HABS**

Address: Historic St. Augustine Preservation Board, P.O. Box 1987,
St. Augustine, FL 32084
Telephone: (904)824-3355
Location: 38 miles south of Jacksonville
Open: Daily, 9:00 A.M. to 5:00 P.M.
Admission: Adults, $2.50; children 6 to 18, $1.25; families, $5.00;
group rates available
Restaurants: Benet House, ice cream parlor
Shops: Benet Store, a museum store with reproductions and craft
items
Facilities: Carriage tours, outdoor drama

WHERE TO STAY
Resorts, St. Augustine: Ponce de Leon, P.O. Box 98, Ponce de Leon
Boulevard, 32084, (904)824-2821, $$
Inns, St. Augustine: Kenwood Inn, 38 Marine Street, 32084,
(904)824-2116, $–$$

Motels/Hotels, St. Augustine: Days Inn, 2800 Ponce de Leon Boulevard, 32084, (904)824-3383, $; Howard Johnson's East, 338 San Marco Avenue, 32084, (904)824-3301, $; Monterey, 16 Bayfront, 32084, (904)824-4482, $; The Palms, 137 San Marco Avenue, 32084, (904)824-6181, $; Quality Inn Historic Area, 2500 Ponce de Leon Boulevard, 32084, (904)824-2883, $$

Camping, St. Augustine: North Beach Camp Resort, 2300 Coastal Highway, 32084, (904)824-1806; St. Augustine Beach KOA, Route 5, Box 95, 32084, (904)471-3113; Ocean Grove, RFD 5, Box 16K, 32084, (904)471-3414; Anastasia State Park, 5 Anastasia Park, 32084, (904)471-3033; Siesta Campground, Route 7, Box 253 A1B, 32084, (904)824-4071

HISTORY

St. Augustine is the oldest permanent European settlement in North America and the nation's oldest continuously occupied city. On September 8, 1565, fifty-two years after Florida's discovery by Ponce de León, Don Pedro Menéndez de Avilés arrived in the Spanish territory with 700 colonists. He named the colony St. Augustine because Florida had first been sighted on St. Augustine's Day, August 28.

The expedition, ordered by King Philip II of Spain, was intended to settle the territory and drive out the French, who had been encroaching on the Spanish claim and threatening Spanish treasure fleets along Florida's shorelines.

Although Menéndez was highly successful on both counts, St. Augustine's status as a permanent Spanish colony and military base was constantly challenged. In 1586, Sir Francis Drake pillaged and burned the town; and in 1668, Captain John Davis, a pirate, plundered the homes and killed many people. In 1670, the English settled Charleston in the Carolinas, and England and Spain agreed to respect each other's possessions.

Castillo de San Marcos, St. Augustine's star-shaped stone fortress, was begun in 1672 and took more than twenty years to complete. It was made of native shell stone, called *coquina*, and a cementlike mortar made from shell lime. The white plastered walls were thirty feet high and up to thirteen feet thick.

Carolinians attacked St. Augustine in 1702 after destroying Spain's northern missions but could not penetrate the fort, though they tried for fifty days. The Carolinians burned the entire city except for the fort and then withdrew. The settlement was rebuilt with stone.

Another attack on St. Augustine was made in 1740 by British General James Oglethorpe of Georgia, but again, the castillo withstood the assault.

Toward the end of the French and Indian wars, Spain formed an alliance with France against the British. After the British captured

Havana, Spain agreed to cede Florida in return for the Havana port. England held St. Augustine for twenty years (1763 to 1784). During the American Revolution, the Florida outpost remained loyal to England.

A treaty signed by England, France, and Spain in 1783 returned Florida to Spain. St. Augustine remained a Spanish possession until July 10, 1821, when Spain ceded Florida to the United States.

In 1836, Seminole Indians attempted to regain control of Florida, and the *castillo* was used by the Americans as a military prison. After the Seminole War ended in 1842, Florida became the twenty-seventh state in the Union.

During the Civil War, Florida seceded from the Union; and in 1861, Confederate troops took possession of the *castillo*, a federal fort. In March 1862, a Union blockade squadron demanded the surrender of St. Augustine. The small Confederate garrison withdrew, and the city was occupied by Union forces for the duration of the war.

After the war, Northern visitors began going to St. Augustine because of its mild winter climate. Henry Flagler, a cofounder of Standard Oil Company, built three luxurious hotels in the Spanish Renaissance style. But although the tourists Flagler attracted brought vitality and income to St. Augustine, older buildings were sacrificed to new construction. Fires in 1887 and 1914 also destroyed many historic buildings.

In 1959, the St. Augustine Historical Restoration and Preservation Commission was established by the Florida legislature. The group, renamed the Historic St. Augustine Preservation Board, has concentrated on preserving and restoring the city's historic section. San Augustin Antiguo, the museum village, is operated by the board.

TOUR

San Augustin Antiguo is a restored Spanish colonial village of the 1700s located within St. Augustine's restoration area. Although you'll see reconstructions of early thatch and wood buildings, the originals were burned during the many invasions the town endured. The oldest extant buildings in St. Augustine are from the eighteenth century.

Begin your tour at the **Ribera House**, 22 St. George Street, which serves as the information center. The Ribera House is a reconstruction of the home of an upper-class Spanish family. It was built on its original eighteenth-century foundation. Street-side windows are covered on the outside with wooden rejas (window grates) and on the inside by shutters. You enter the house through an arched loggia, a roofed open gallery, typical of St. Augustine–style houses. There is a Spanish garden with roses and a grape arbor off the rear loggia. On the second floor, you will find an exhibit of nineteenth-century Spanish furniture.

Casa de Gallegos, 21 St. George Street, is a reconstruction of a two-room tabby house with a walled garden. (Tabby is a type of concrete made from oyster shells and lime.) Guides demonstrate early crafts such as spinning, making soap, making fishnets, and cooking.

Casa de Gomez, 23 St. George Street, is a reconstruction of a timber frame house typical of those built in the first Spanish period (1565 to 1763). A one-room dwelling, it represents a house occupied by a Spanish infantryman in the 1760s.

The **Peso de Burgo-Pellicer Houses** are two frame houses that share a common wall. Built around 1780, they are used for demonstrations of spinning, weaving, candle making, and cabinetmaking. **Casa de Arrivos** is a restoration of a colonial home built around 1720. A practicing silversmith works in the house. The eighteenth-century tabby **Skinner Outbuilding** houses a working blacksmith and his shop.

The **Spanish Military Hospital**, 8 Avilés Street, is a reconstruction of the original hospital and pharmacy, Nuestra Señora de Guadalupe, built during the second Spanish period (1783 to 1821). The building is authentically furnished and equipped with an apothecary shop, a morgue, a doctor's office, an isolation ward, an officers' ward, and an enlisted men's ward. On the second floor, there is a museum of Florida medical history.

SIDE TRIPS

You can sightsee in St. Augustine by train, boat, or horse-drawn carriage. To arrange a tour, contact Colee's Sightseeing Carriage Tours, P.O. Box 604, (904)829-2818; Sightseeing Trains, 3 Cordova Street, (904)829-6545; or Scenic Cruise, Municipal Yacht Pier, 610 Euclid Avenue, North Beach, (904)824-1806. However, a leisurely stroll through the narrow streets that radiate from St. Augustine's central **Plaza de la Constitucien** will easily transport you back to 1598, when the town was first laid out.

The **Gonzalez-Alvarez House** at 14 St. Francis Street is often referred to as the **Oldest House**. Although its exact date is not known, it is believed to have been built between 1703 and 1727, making it the oldest Spanish residence in the country. It was originally a one-story building with coquina walls and tabby floors. It became the home of Major Joseph Peavett during the British colonial period (1763 to 1783), and Peavett added a wood frame second story, fireplace, and glass windowpanes. Open daily 9:00 A.M. to 5:00 P.M.

Another oldest, the **Old Wooden Schoolhouse**, 14 St. George Street, is believed to be the oldest school building in the United States. Records indicate it was built at the end of the first Spanish period, which lasted until 1763. It is the oldest wooden structure in St. Augustine and the only wooden building that survived the colonial period.

The **Fernandez-Llambrias House**, 31 St. Francis Street, is a restored late eighteenth-century two-story house built by the Spanish. It is a coquina structure with a second-floor balcony and a veranda in the rear. It is included in the National Register of Historic Places.

The **Ximenez-Fatio House**, also on the National Register, is at 20 Avilés Street. Built about 1800, it is a two-and-a-half-story frame house with clapboarding. Its distinctive features include gabled dormers, cantilevered wooden-frame balcony, two-story rear ell, and one-story separate kitchen. It has been restored to its appearance as a luxurious 1830 boardinghouse and is now a museum maintained by the Florida Society of Colonial Dames of America.

Restored or reconstructed buildings now used as commercial businesses include **Casa de Maria Triay** (1783 to 1821), an artist's studio and shop; **Casa de Gonzalez** (1565 to 1763), a restaurant; and the reconstructed **Casa de Josef Salcedo**, 42 St. George Street, a country store and bakery.

The Greek Orthodox Church in America has restored **Casa de Avero**, a house dating from the first Spanish period, at 41 St. George Street. Now known as **St. Photios Shrine**, it commemorates the first colony of Greeks to arrive in the New World in 1768; Greek Orthodox religious services are conducted here.

Castillo de San Marcos National Monument, on 1 Castillo Drive, was begun in 1672 and finished in 1695, replacing a succession of earlier wooden forts. The star-shaped coquina fort is the oldest masonry fortification in the continental United States. Castillo de San Marcos, later known as Fort Marion, was built by Indians, slaves, and Spanish soldiers. Based on a medieval plan, the fort has thirty-foot-high walls, a council chamber, officers' quarters, storerooms, dungeons, and watchtowers and is surrounded by a moat. It was never captured by an enemy. Open daily 8:30 A.M. to 5:30 P.M.

The **Alcazar Hotel** is one of three Spanish Renaissance–style hotels built by oil magnate Henry Flagler in 1888. It is now occupied by the **Lightner Museum**, which contains the personal collection of O. C. Lightner, founder and publisher of *Hobbies Magazine*. The **Ponce de León Hotel** has become **Flagler College**, and **Zorayda Castle**, built to resemble the Alhambra, now houses oriental art treasures.

Cross and Sword, an outdoor musical drama about the founding of St. Augustine, is presented in the **St. Augustine Amphitheater**. The play, which was written by Paul Green, is presented nightly except Sunday at 8:30 P.M. from mid-June to mid-August. On State Road 3-A1A, (904)471-1965. Unreserved seats: adults, $5.00; children, $3.00; reserved seats: adults, $6.00; children, $4.00.

Georgia Agrirama

Recreation of a nineteenth-century, post–Civil War farming community

Address: P.O. Box Q, Tifton, GA 31794
Telephone: (912)386-3344
Location: At Exit 21 at the intersection of I-75 and 8th Street; 175 miles south of Atlanta
Open: Daily, 9:00 A.M. to 6:00 P.M., June to Labor Day; Monday to Saturday, 9:00 A.M. to 5:00 P.M., Sundays, 12:30 to 5:00 P.M., after Labor Day to May 31
Admission: Adults, $3.00; children 6 to 16, $1.50; families, $8.50; group rates available
Restaurants: Snack bar in the Visitors' Center
Shops: Country Store in the Visitors' Center, gifts, reproductions, handicrafts
Facilities: Visitors' Center

WHERE TO STAY
Motels/Hotels, Tifton: Best Western Davis Brothers, 1008 West 8th Street, 31794, (912)382-7210, $; Holiday Inn, P.O. Box 1267, I-75 and Route 82, 31794, (912)382-6687, $$; Village Green, I-75 and

Route 41, 31794, (912)382-2650, $; Quality Inn, Route 1, P.O. Box
7-3, 31794, (912)386-2100, $; Ramada Inn, P.O. Box 1450, 31794,
(912)382-8500, $
Camping, Tifton: Covered Wagon Campground, P.O. Box 7097,
31794, (912)382-9700
Camping, Sycamore: Lakeview Inn & Campground, Route 1, 31790,
(912)567-3357
Camping, Adel: Reed Bingham State Park, Route 2, P.O. Box 394
B-1, 31620, (912)869-7788
Camping, Cordele: Georgia Veterans Memorial State Park, Route
280, 31015, (912)273-2190

HISTORY
Known officially as the State Museum of Agriculture, Georgia
Agrirama recreates a typical late nineteenth-century south Georgia
village and farm. This seventy-acre outdoor museum, consisting of
thirty-five restored buildings, opened in July 1976.

Serving cultural and educational as well as historical objectives,
Georgia Agrirama is governed by the Georgia Agrirama Development
Authority, a nonprofit organization created in 1972 by the Georgia
legislature. Special Living History Workshops on nineteenth-century
crafts and skills can be arranged for school groups.

During the period represented by Georgia Agrirama, 1870 to 1899,
the "new South" evolved. Following the War Between the States and
Reconstruction, Georgia, like other Southern states, underwent agricultural and industrial renewal. This museum village allows visitors to
compare and contrast aspects of late nineteenth-century Southern
farming and small-scale industry. Its distinctive features include two
farming communities, an industrial complex, and a rural small town.
Exhibits and demonstrations are staffed by guides attired in period
costumes.

TOUR
The **Visitors' Center** complex includes the **Information Center,**
housed in an 1850 log cabin, ticket office, concession stand, and the
Country Store, which features period reproductions, gifts, and handicrafts.

The **Gibbs Farmhouse** (1896) was moved to the site from Ty Ty,
Georgia. Typical of Southern farmhouses of the late 1890s, it features
the columns, railings, and steep roof of the Victorian era. Noteworthy
is the **dogtrot,** a breezeway running through the center of the house.
Also of special interest is the traveler's room on the front porch, which
was used by drummers (peddlers) and circuit riders (preachers).

The reconstructed **cane mill**, **syrup shed**, and **syrup house** contain exhibits on sugar production. After the juice was extracted from the cane by crushing, it was boiled to produce syrup. The cane syrup was then stored in barrels in the syrup house.

The **smokehouse** was used for curing and smoking pork, hams, and sausages. (The smoking of meat was a usual feature of Southern food preparation.) Buildings such as a **barn**, **chicken house**, **corncrib**, **harness house**, **hogpen**, and **seed cotton house**, dating from the 1880s and 1890s, recreate a late nineteenth-century Georgia farmstead.

The **Clark Cabin** (1886) was moved to the site from Colquitt County. The mud and stick chimney is especially interesting. The primitive furnishings are typical of the late frontier domestic environment.

The **Davis Gristmill** (1876) was moved from Warwick. It was used to grind corn into meal and grits, a cereal-like Southern dish.

The **Sawmill**, powered by an Atlas steam engine, was used in Appling County in the 1890s.

The **turpentine still furnace** represents an important enterprise in rural Georgia, the distilling of turpentine from rosin, which was readily available from plentiful pine forests. The rosin was boiled in a large copper pot; the steam passed through a condensing coil and distilled as turpentine.

The **Blacksmith Shop**, a recreated building, is the scene of smithing demonstrations.

The **printing office** features an 1888 Whitlock press.

The turn-of-the-century **train depot** was moved from Montezuma. Near the depot is the Milstead 104, a steam locomotive and tender.

The **Doctor's Office** (early 1870s) displays the instruments of a small-town physician.

The **Wesley Chapel** (1882) was moved from Dougherty County. Its pews, pulpit, and railing are original.

The **Cotton Gin House and Warehouse**, a recreated building, contains an 1896 Lummus cotton gin and rotating double-bale press that is powered by a Frick 110 steam engine. The gin is operated during the late fall ginning season.

The Agrirama features gardens and crops of sugar cane, melons, corn, peanuts, and cotton, all important agricultural products in the late nineteenth century. Children will enjoy the mules, cows, pigs, chickens, and other farm animals. Special events throughout the year include quilting workshops, exhibitions of steam-powered farm machinery, concerts of south Georgia folk music, and Christmas programs.

Westville

Recreation of a nineteenth-century, antebellum farming community

Address: P.O. Box 1850, Lumpkin, GA 31815
Telephone: (912)838-6310
Location: At the intersection of U.S. Highway 27 and State Route 27; 35 miles south of Columbus
Open: Monday to Saturday, 10:00 A.M. to 5:00 P.M.; Sundays, 1:00 to 5:00 P.M.; closed Thanksgiving, Christmas, and New Year's Day
Admission: Adults, $3.50; senior citizens, $2.50; students, $1.50; group rates available
Restaurants: Snacks available in village kitchens
Shops: Gift Shop, handicrafts and reproductions
Facilities: Picnic area, wagon rides, partially accessible to handicapped

WHERE TO STAY

Motels/Hotels, Americus: Americus, P.O. Box 543, 1005 Meadowbrook Drive, 31709, (912)924-3613, $; Best Western, P.O. Box 684, Routes 19 and 280, 31709, (912)924-4431, $–$$
Motels/Hotels, Columbus: Courtyard by Marriott, 3501 Courtyard Way, 31904, (404)323-2323, $$; Holiday Inn—Airport, 2800 Manchester Expressway, 31904, (404)324-0231, $$; Quality Inn—Martinique, 1011 4th Avenue, 31901, (404)322-6641, $
Camping, Columbus: Lake Pines Campground, P.O. Box 5487, 31906, (404)561-2154; Lake Crystal Trailer Court, 6023 Crystal Road, 31907, (404)561-3555
Camping, Fort Gaines: Cotton Hill and George P. Bagby Campground on Walter F. George Lake, P.O. Box 281, 31751, (912)768-2561

HISTORY

Westville, a recreated museum village, depicts daily life in preindustrial Georgia during the 1850s. It is a project of the Westville Historic Foundation, Inc., a not-for-profit, educational corporation.

Westville is named for Colonel John Word West, a historian who served as president of North Georgia College. The village developed from his private collection of historic buildings and artifacts. The process of moving buildings to Westville began in 1968, and the museum village opened to the public on April 2, 1970.

Although this village conveys the general atmosphere of pre–Civil War rural Georgia, visitors should be alert to some of its unique features. For example, it has one of the few extant cotton presses, the only known animal-powered cotton gin in the United States, and one of the largest displays of mid-nineteenth-century Georgia-made decorative art. Westville's demonstrations of nineteenth-century Southern crafts and work skills are particularly valuable.

TOUR

Westville, which is still in the process of acquiring historic buildings, is a fifteen-block town encompassing fifty acres.

One of the first buildings you'll see after passing through the village gates is **Stewart County Academy** (1832), with its collection of period textbooks. Academies were generally private educational institutions for students in their teens. It should be noted that unlike the New England states, Southern states did not establish common or public schools until after the Civil War.

The **Grimes-Feagin House** (1842), built in Stewart County, is a modest but comfortable dwelling. It is furnished as it would have been in a rural Southern community.

The **McDonald House** (1843) was the home of Edward McDonald, a man of wealth and social status. It is furnished with early nineteenth-century Empire-style pieces, including an ornate square piano, elaborate bedroom wardrobes, a hand-carved rosewood bed, and an oversized, very long dining room table. The Empire style (which takes its name from the Second French Empire) is more elaborate than the earlier Federal style and was popular with wealthy Americans.

Chattahoochee County Courthouse, an original two-story frame building, was the seat of county government. President Jimmy Carter's great-grandfather and grandfather served as county officials in this building. Southern political life centered on the county, in contrast with the town government prevalent in New England. Today, the courthouse is the home of Westville's educational programs.

The **Bryan-Worthington House** (1831) was built in Stewart County by Loverd Bryan, a cotton gin operator. It is in the Federal style, which was popular from 1800 through the 1830s.

The **Doctor's Office** (1845) was built by Dr. William Lewis Paullin of Fort Gaines. It displays medical and dental instruments. Physicians in small towns and rural areas were general practitioners and often among the few college graduates in a community.

The rambling, unpainted **Patterson-Marrott Farmhouse** (1850) was built in South Carolina. In its parlor, a docent demonstrates cotton spinning. The farmhouse kitchen was built separately from the main house to minimize the threat of fire. To be noted is the large open fireplace with iron frying pans, ovens, pots, and other utensils; there is also a brick oven in the chimney that was used for baking. Near the farmhouse are the mule barn, whiskey still, sugarcane mill, and syrup kettle.

The **Yellow Creek Camp Meeting Tabernacle**, built in 1840 in Hall County, is a large, open structure with a roof supported by twelve-inch-square, hand-hewn beams. It contains a pulpit, a kneeling rail, and benches. The camp meeting, peculiar to the South and the frontier, was a social as well as a religious event that attracted widely scattered families.

The **Wells House**, the oldest building in the village, was built before 1827. The interior of the original split-log house is surrounded by a two-story frame addition.

The **Adams Store**, originally located at the Lumpkin stagecoach stop, was a general store used by local farm families. It now is used as a gift shop.

The **Lawson House** (1836) is made of logs covered by boards.

The **Moye Whitehouse** (1840) is an excellent example of Greek Revival architecture. The neoclassicalism of the Greek Revival school was popular throughout the United States in the 1830s and 1840s.

The **Bagley Gin House** was built in the 1840s. This cotton gin, which is mule-driven, has a cotton screw press for baling cotton after it has been ginned. The cotton gin, invented by Eli Whitney in 1793, was essential to the Southern economy. Before its invention, little cotton was produced in the United States because the process of separating the fiber from the seeds by hand was too time-consuming. The mechanical efficiency of the gin helped to make cotton "king" in the American South. Westville's gin is one of the few remaining in the United States.

One of the major purposes of Westville is to keep alive and to demonstrate the crafts of early preindustrial America. Among the shops where crafts are demonstrated are the **blacksmith shop**, the **cabinet-maker's shop** (1836), and the **shoemaker's shop** (1838). The **pottery shop**, **pug mill**, and **kiln** are an example of a jug factory, where churns, jars, pitchers, and other items were made.

The **West House** (1850) was the residence of Colonel John Word West's grandparents.

Special events at Westville include an old-fashioned Independence

Day celebration; the Fair of 1850, held in the fall and patterned after cultural fairs of the pre–Civil War era; and Yuletide Season, December 12 to 26, featuring traditional German, English, and Scotch-Irish holiday festivities.

SIDE TRIPS

Bedingfield Inn (1836), on Lumpkin's Town Square, is a restored stagecoach inn furnished with period furniture. Open Tuesday to Sunday, from 1:00 to 5:00 P.M.; (912)838-4201. Admission: adults, $1.00; children, 50 cents.

Providence Canyon State Park, 7 miles west of Lumpkin on Highway 39C, consists of 1,108 acres of chasms, canyons, and woodlands. There is a Visitors' Center. Admission is free. For information, call (912)838-6202.

An exhibit focused on the lives of Jimmy and Rosalynn Carter can be seen at the **James Earl Carter Library of Georgia Southwestern College**. There are photographs, memorabilia, video presentations, and items donated by the family of former President Jimmy Carter. Wheatley and Glesner Streets, Americus, 31709. Open Monday to Friday, 8:00 A.M. to 5:00 P.M. when school is not in session. The rest of the year, it is open Monday to Thursday, 8:00 A.M. to 10:00 P.M.; Friday, 8:00 A.M. to 5:00 P.M.; and Sunday, 2:00 to 9:00 P.M. Admission is free.

Plains, the home of Jimmy Carter and his family, is 9 miles west of Americus via Route 280.

Shaker Village at Pleasant Hill

**Restoration of a nineteenth-century
Shaker community; NR, NHL**

Address: Route 4, Harrodsburg, KY 40330
Telephone: (606)734-5411
Location: On Route 68, 25 miles southwest of Lexington and 7 miles northeast of Harrodsburg
Open: Daily, 9:00 A.M. to 5:00 P.M., March 30 to December 1; hours vary in winter; closed Christmas Eve and Christmas Day. Riverboat rides, April 29 to October 27
Admission: Adults, $4.50; students 12 to 18, $2.00; children 6 to 11, $1.00. Riverboat rides: adults, $4.00; students 12 to 18, $2.00; children 6 to 11, $1.00. Combination village and riverboat tickets available for adults only, $7.00.
Restaurants: Snack bar, dining rooms in the Trustees' Office [reservations essential, call (606)734-5411]
Shops: Craft shops, crafts, reproductions, books
Lodging: Farm Deacon's Shop, East Family Brethren's Shop, East Family Sisters' Shop, Trustees' Office
Facilities: Library, riverboat rides, accessible to handicapped

WHERE TO STAY

Inns, Harrodsburg:　Shaker Inn at Pleasant Hill, 3500 Lexington Road, 40330, (606)734-5411, $$. Reservations are essential.

Camping, Harrodsburg:　Chimney Rock Resort, Route 152, RR1, 40330, (606)748-5252

Camping, Danville:　Pioneer Playhouse Park, Route 150, 40422, (606)236-2747

Camping, Lexington:　Clay's Ferry Campground, 8950 Richmond Road, 40515, (606)623-1569

HISTORY

On January 1, 1805, three Shaker missionaries (see the Appendix for a brief history of the Shakers) from New Lebanon, New York, traveled 1,200 miles to central Kentucky. They had heard about the Great Kentucky Revival, in which a wave of camp meetings had reawakened religious sentiments among thousands of people. After making some converts, the Shaker group gathered on Shawnee Run, a few miles from Harrodsburg.

Two years later, in 1807, a permanent settlement was established on the elevation that came to be called Pleasant Hill. In January 1809, two elders and two eldresses were sent from Union Village in Ohio to form the first ministry. In 1809, the first building in the village, the first Centre Family Dwelling, now known as the Farm Deacon's Shop, was built. Of the 270 buildings erected over the ensuing century, 27 remain today.

The Shakers were active craftspeople. They produced brooms, cooper's wares, weaving implements, shoes, woolen goods, pressed cheese, medicinal products, seeds, and herbs. By 1816, they had begun to make trading trips to New Orleans to sell their surplus goods.

Pleasant Hill's membership had increased to nearly 500 by 1820. During the course of the century, 1,500 Shakers lived in this prosperous community. Their landholdings reached approximately 7,000 acres, and they grew wheat, rye, oats, flax, Indian corn, broomcorn, and potatoes. There were also extensive fruit orchards.

The society was divided into five communal families, each numbering from 50 to 100 members and governed by two elders and two eldresses. Each family was a semiautonomous unit, with its own dwelling, shops, barns, fields, and orchards.

During the late 1850s, Pleasant Hill, like the other Shaker communities, began to experience the effects of the Industrial Revolution. Mass-produced items turned out on factory assembly lines were cheaper than the Shaker-made handicrafts. As their markets declined, so did Pleasant Hill's prosperity.

Along with a declining economy, the Kentucky Shakers faced the sectional issues generated by the Civil War. Although a border state with many Southern sympathizers, Kentucky remained loyal to the Union. The Shakers were pacifists and refused to fight. Elder Frederick Evans of Mount Lebanon persuaded President Abraham Lincoln to exempt Shakers on religious grounds. The Pleasant Hill Shakers, like their brothers and sisters elsewhere, generously fed, housed, and nursed both the Confederate and the Union troops that marched through their village. This impartiality angered their neighbors, who were also intolerant of the Shaker practice of buying and freeing slaves and accepting them into full membership in the society. The Shakers' stores of food, cattle, horses, wagons, and flatboats were often confiscated by the military.

In 1898, the Trustees' Office and hundreds of acres were sold. By 1900, three of the families had disbanded, and their vacant buildings were rented out. On September 12, 1910, the last of the property was sold and the society, four brothers and eight sisters, was dissolved. Between 1910 and 1960, the property was redivided and resold. The buildings, used for various purposes (including a bus station), were neglected, and two were destroyed by fire.

In 1961, a group of people led by Earl D. Wallace of Lexington decided to restore Pleasant Hill. They formed a nonprofit educational corporation known as Shakertown at Pleasant Hill, Inc. James L. Cogar, a former curator of Colonial Williamsburg, became Pleasant Hill's first president, and the village opened to the public in the spring of 1968.

Cogar is responsible for restoring the twenty-seven original buildings according to the principle of adaptive use. The three functional uses are exhibitions that tell the story of the life and customs of the Shaker society; education by means of seminars, symposia, and conferences; and hospitality, dining and overnight accommodations. Pleasant Hill is the only museum village in which all overnight accommodations for guests are in restored buildings.

TOUR

Shaker Village at Pleasant Hill is one of our favorite restorations. The buildings are original and architecturally impressive. The group of people who lived here is fascinating. The Shaker furniture is authentic, and the collection large and varied. The site is of medium size and do-able without courting exhaustion. The setting is picturesque, the guides knowledgeable, and the craft stores well stocked with good reproductions. Lodging and dining rooms retain an attractive and authentic atmosphere.

You'll begin your self-guided tour at the **Centre Family Dwelling**. The Centre, or First, Family was the highest rank according to the spiritual travel of the members and was given the place of honor nearest the meetinghouse. The T-shaped second Centre Family Dwelling was started in 1824 and completed in 1834. Master architect and carpenter Micajah Burnett laid out the plan of the village and designed the buildings, including this one.

The symmetry of the double doorways and two inside stairways to separate the men's quarters from the women's, along with the utter simplicity of the wide halls, white walls, high ceilings, arched doorways, wood trim, and plain wooden floors, contribute to the beauty of this outstanding building.

Burnett's design was based on early New England Shaker building styles with elements of Federal classicism. The roof has square gabled ends and three massive chimneys. There are forty rooms in this four-story Kentucky limestone building, the largest erected at Pleasant Hill; it housed 100 Shakers. It is now the major exhibition building.

All rooms contain authentic Shaker furniture from the early nineteenth century, much of it made at Pleasant Hill. There is a kitchen complete with cooking utensils, a dining room, a meeting room, an infirmary, and simply furnished sleeping rooms.

The **Meetinghouse** was the spiritual center of the community. (Shaker religious services are described in the Appendix.) The one at Pleasant Hill was built in 1820 and has the double doorways typical of Shaker architecture. The white frame building rests on a heavy limestone foundation. Roof and ceilings are supported by a series of interlocking cantilever-type trusses and overhead studdings and rafters; this construction made it possible to have a meeting room large enough to accommodate all the worshipers.

The **Farm Deacon's Shop**, built in 1809, was the first permanent structure in the village. Originally the dwelling house for the Centre Family, it was used as a tavern after 1817 and, finally, as an office for the farm deacons. The two-foot-thick walls of this two-and-a-half-story structure are built of white limestone quarried from cliffs along the nearby Kentucky River. The ash floors are original. Artifacts relating to the Shakers' herb industry are displayed on the first floor; the second floor is used for guest lodgings.

In 1833, Micajah Burnett devised a water system that provided every house and barn in the village with running water. The yellow frame **water house** contains the machinery and tanks for the first public waterworks in Kentucky.

Next to the water house is the small **Brethren's Bath House**, built in 1860. Each family was a self-sufficient unit with its own large dwelling for eating and sleeping; a craft shop for women; separate bathhouses for men, women, boys, and girls; a washhouse; and various other outbuildings.

On the first floor of the **East Family Brethren's Shop** (1845), a broom maker works in his fully equipped shop. Across the hall, a carpenter uses traditional tools. The **East Family Sisters' Shop** (1855) houses spinning and weaving demonstrations on the first floor. The second floor of each shop now accommodates overnight guests.

The **Trustees' Office**, built in 1839 by Micajah Burnett, is one of the finest examples of Shaker architecture extant. It was used by the Shakers to conduct business with the outside world and to house and feed guests. Trustees were the people appointed to transact that business. The building is of flemish-bond brick and has a single front door. As you enter it, you'll be struck by the impressive twin spiral staircases.

Today, the first floor is used as a restaurant and a registration office for overnight guests. Upstairs, there are lodging rooms. The trundle beds for children are a delight.

Pleasant Hill has two gardens: the **kitchen garden** by the Trustees' Office and the **herb garden** by the Centre Family Dwelling. You will also want to stroll over to the peaceful Shaker graveyard.

Special events at Shaker Village include demonstrations of flax working, beehive-oven baking, silk culturing, candle dipping, vegetal dyeing, basketry, cider making, and hearth cooking. There are also programs on Shaker songs. The **Shaker Heritage Weekends** held in September feature craft demonstrations, religious songs, and services.

You can take a one-hour ride on a paddle-wheel riverboat, the *Dixie Belle*, from May through October. The rides on the Kentucky River leave from **Shaker Landing**, east of the village entrance.

ACCOMMODATIONS

Normally, we would recommend other area attractions, but Pleasant Hill is a special case. It is not only a fine historic restoration of the home of a fascinating communal group, but also is one of those rare self-contained villages where you can eat and sleep as well as see the sights. Once you spot the hand-stacked fieldstone fences lining the highway and pull into the parking lot, you will not need your car again until you leave.

We encourage you to immerse yourself in the atmospheric surroundings, soak up history, enjoy the lovely bluegrass countryside, walk the lantern-lit paths at night, and feast in the charming dining rooms. We have recommended this interesting and relaxing destination to everyone from historians to honeymooners—it's ironic these celibate people created such a romantic environment. They have all enjoyed their sojourn at Pleasant Hill and remarked on its restorative value.

There are seventy-two rooms for guests in fourteen original Shaker buildings. Even though these buildings are restored to nineteenth-century standards, the guest rooms are heated, air-conditioned, and electrified and have their own bathrooms. They are charmingly furnished with reproduction Shaker rockers, beds, desks, and handwoven rugs. The Shaker pegs that are seen in all the exhibit buildings line the walls for hanging clothes. Advance reservations are essential.

The dining rooms are in the Trustees' House. Meals are moderately priced, and the Shaker and Kentucky recipes showcase American cuisine at its finest: fresh foods properly prepared and beautifully served. No alcohol is sold. Reservations are needed, especially for dinner.

Two cookbooks containing recipes used at the Trustees' House are sold in the craft shops.

Recreation of a 1750 Cherokee Indian village

Address: Cherokee Indian Reservation, Cherokee, NC 28719
Telephone: (704)497-2315 or (704)497-2111
Location: ½ mile north of Cherokee on Route 441
Open: Daily, 9:00 A.M. to 5:30 P.M., May 15 to October 25
Admission: Adults, $5.00; children 6 to 12, $3.00; group rates available
Facilities: Botanical garden and nature trail, outdoor drama, accessible to handicapped

WHERE TO STAY
Motels/Hotels, Cherokee: Cool Waters, P.O. Box 4970, Route 19, 28719, (704)497-3855, $$; El Camino, P.O. Box 482, Route 19, 28719, (704)497-3600, $$; Holiday Inn, P.O. Box 648, Route 19, 28719, (704)497-9181, $$; Indian Hills, Route 19, 28719, (704)497-9171, $$
Resorts, Maggie Valley: Maggie Valley Country Club and Motor Lodge, P.O. Box 126, Route 19, 28751, (704)926-1616, $$$$

(modified American plan); Cataloochee Ranch (a guest ranch),
P.O. Box 500, Route 1, 28751, (704)926-1401, $$$ (modified
American plan)

Resorts, Waynesville: Waynesville Country Club Inn, 28786,
(704)456-3551, $$$$ (modified American plan)

Inns, Waynesville: Piedmont Inn and Motor Lodge, P.O. Box 419,
630 Eagle Nest Road, 28786, (704)456-8636, $$$

(See Pioneer Farmstead, page 146, for accommodations in Gatlinburg,
Tennessee.)

HISTORY

The early history of the Cherokee Indians is unwritten and shrouded in
legends. We know that the tribe lived in the southern Appalachians,
occupying land that would become North and South Carolina, Virginia, Tennessee, Georgia, and Alabama for several centuries before
the Spanish explorer Hernando De Soto sighted them in 1540. This
prosperous, nonmigratory tribe was composed of hunters, fishers, traders, artists, and farmers who grew corn, beans, squash, melons, and
tobacco. They were also warriors who defended their lands against
encroachment by other Indian tribes and by the late 1700s white
pioneers who began settling in their territory. From 1756 until the turn
of the century, the Cherokee and the white settlers fought each other
over land. Losses from these battles and from smallpox introduced by
whites decimated the Cherokee and wrecked their economy.

In an attempt to prevent further war, the tribe, in 1820, established
the Cherokee Nation, a republican form of government with a thirty-
two member unicameral legislature. The nation was divided into eight
districts that sent representatives to the Cherokee national legislature
at New Echota, Georgia. During this period, the Cherokee also became
a literate people. Sequoyah invented and developed a complete Cherokee alphabet. This is the only case in American Indian records of a
system of writing invented without white involvement. As a result of
Sequoyah's work, the Cherokee adopted a written constitution and
code of law in 1828. They also established a national press.

The Cherokee constitution, which declared the tribe a sovereign and
independent nation, angered the people of Georgia. Discovery of gold
in Georgia on the edge of Cherokee territory fueled the efforts of the
federal government, under Andrew Jackson, to have the Indians
relocated. Most of the Cherokee violently opposed removal, but Elias
Boudinot and Major Ridge, two Cherokee who favored it, signed the
Treaty of New Echota in 1836. The terms of the treaty were that the
entire tribe would be moved beyond the Mississippi within two years in
return for land in Oklahoma and $5 million.

When the Cherokee did not leave voluntarily, General Winfield
Scott forced their removal. In 1838, Scott seized 17,000 Cherokee and

placed them in hastily built stockades. They were then forced to march west along the 800-mile route that came to be called the "Trail of Tears." This march, which ended in Oklahoma in March 1839, caused the deaths of 4,000 Indians.

Approximately 1,100 North Carolina Cherokee avoided removal by hiding out in the mountains. Aided by Colonel William Holland Thomas, a white trader who became their legal advisor, the Cherokee tried to take advantage of a treaty provision that allowed them to stay in their home state if they became citizens. In 1866, North Carolina finally recognized the Cherokee's right to permanent residency. Thomas had purchased 50,000 acres for the Cherokee in his name; title would revert to them when they paid for it.

In 1876, the Cherokee, having acquired even more land, were granted final title to the 65,000-acre Qualla Boundary. In 1889, the tribe incorporated as the Eastern Band of Cherokee Indians. They live in western North Carolina in the communally-held Qualla Boundary, which is a tribal-owned preserve, not a reservation held in trust by the federal government.

In 1952, the Cherokee Historical Association, a nonprofit organization formed to perpetuate the history and traditions of the Cherokee, built Oconaluftee Indian Village, a recreation of an early eighteenth-century Cherokee community.

TOUR

The village, which is located in a forested cove where Indians camped thousands of years ago, is a 30-acre site surrounded by a palisade of locust posts. There are five structures: **three 1750 dwellings, one sixteenth-century dwelling**, and a **council house**. Cherokee men and women wearing traditional dress work at their crafts throughout the village.

After a brief orientation, an Indian guide leads a tour group to a beadwork demonstration. The women use the same type of imported Venetian beads white traders introduced to create sashes worn by chiefs.

Proceeding down the winding, shaded path, you'll find women making pottery with local clay. Coil and ball methods are explained by the guide; no potter's wheel is used. The construction of blowguns from green river cane is demonstrated by Indian men. Particularly interesting is the basket-weaving demonstration, in which original Cherokee designs and native dyes and materials are used. You will also see members of the tribe grinding corn, making arrowheads, and carving wooden masks, tomahawks, and various tools. The process of making a Cherokee canoe is slow and laborious; the interior of a yellow poplar tree trunk is burned out with hot coals. These long-lasting dugouts, which could transport ten to twelve men, were communally owned.

In finger weaving, the weaver manipulates up to forty-eight threads without using a loom of any kind. Belts, straps, and other decorative items are made in this manner.

Because the Eastern Cherokee were not migratory, they lived in houses, not tepees or wigwams. A small stucco-like house is representative of a home lived in by the Eastern Band of Cherokee in the sixteenth century, a time predating the arrival of Europeans in this region of America. The walls are made from woven river cane cut into strips and tightly interlaced with small saplings, then covered with a plaster of river clay. There are no windows, chimneys, or doors; a fire burns in the middle of the dirt floor.

The 1750 houses are built of logs with mud chinking. They have fireplaces, chimneys, and earthen floors. In one of these eighteenth-century log cabins, the animal skins hanging on the walls emphasize the Cherokee's hunting way of life.

The **Squareground**, a small outdoor amphitheater, is a ceremonial ground. In the sand-floored center is a tree stump with an umbrella top covered with branches; this is where sacred ceremonies, which could last several days, were performed. Drums, tom-toms, and rattles were used in these religious rituals. Masks were worn by dancers to identify the type of dance—for example, a bear mask for a hunt dance.

Religious, civil, and marriage ceremonies were performed in a seven-sided wooden building known as a **council house**. The sacred fire of the Cherokee was kept here, and once a year, all fires in the village were relighted from it. The walls are of woven oak splints covered with clay. The roof is conical, with a hole in the peak to allow for smoke to escape. The sand-floored structure has seven sets of risers, one for each Cherokee clan. Marriage within a clan was forbidden. A husband joined his wife's clan, and children belonged to their mother's clan.

Adjacent to the village is the **Cherokee Botanical Garden and Nature Trail**, where more than 150 species of plants native to the Great Smokies are grown.

SIDE TRIPS

The Cherokee Historical Association sponsors *Unto These Hills*, an outdoor dramatization of the Eastern Cherokee story beginning with the arrival of De Soto in 1540 and culminating with the removal of almost all the Cherokee on the infamous Trail of Tears to the West. This stirring drama, performed by descendants of those people, is presented daily except Sunday from mid-June to late August at 8:30 P.M. The **Mountainside Theater** is adjacent to Oconaluftee Indian Village. P.O. Box 398, Cherokee, 28719, (704)497-2111. Tickets are $6.50 and $8.50 for adults; $4.00 for children under 12.

The modern **Museum of the Cherokee Indian** is located on Route 441 and the Mountainside Theater Road. In its collection are clothing, wooden masks, handwoven baskets, 2,000-year-old pottery, and stone weapons. In six minitheaters, multimedia slide and tape shows trace the story of the Cherokee from ancient times to the present. A special display is devoted to Sequoyah, the inventor of the Cherokee alphabet. The museum is open year-round from 9:00 A.M. to 5:30 P.M., September to mid-June, and from 9:00 A.M. to 8:00 P.M. from mid-June to August. For information, call (704)497-3481. Admission: adults, $3.00; children, $1.50.

You won't want to miss the **Qualla Arts and Crafts Mutual, Inc.**, an outstanding Indian-owned and -operated arts and crafts cooperative featuring a stunning collection of handmade baskets and beautiful jewelry. Items sold here are of the highest quality. Located on Route 441 North at the entrance to the Mountainside Theater. Open all year. For information, call (704)497-3103.

The city of Cherokee is located at the entrance to the very popular **Great Smoky Mountains National Park**, which encompasses more than 500,000 acres along the Tennessee–North Carolina border. The park is especially known for its lush flowering plants, including dogwood, mountain laurel, wild lilies, orchids, azaleas, and rhododendrons. Activities include fishing, bicyling, bird-watching, camping, and hiking along 800 miles of trails, including a 72-mile section of the Appalachian Trail.

Old Salem

Restoration of an eighteenth-century Moravian community; NHL, NR

Address: Drawer F—Salem Station, Winston-Salem, NC 27108
Telephone: (919)723-3688
Location: South of business district on Old Salem Road
Open: Monday to Saturday, 9:30 A.M. to 4:30 P.M.; Sundays, 1:30 to 4:30 P.M.; closed Christmas Day
Admission: Adults, $6.00; children 6 to 14, $3.00; family plan, $18.00. Old Salem and Museum of Early Southern Decorative Arts: adults, $8.00; children 6 to 14, $3.00; family plan, $23.00. Museum of Early Southern Decorative Arts: adults, $3.50, children 6 to 14, $1.75. Admission to individual Old Salem buildings also available. Group rates available.
Restaurants: Salem Tavern dining rooms, Mayberry Restaurant
Shops: T. Bagge Community Store, museum store with Moravian and museum reproductions; Salem Gift and Book Store, gifts, books, film
Facilities: Reception Center, picnic area, guided tour for handicapped available

WHERE TO STAY

Motels/Hotels, Winston-Salem: Hilton Inn, Marshall and High Streets, 27101, (919)723-7911, $$–$$$; Stouffer Winston Plaza, 425 North Cherry Street, 27102, (919)725-3500, $$$; Hyatt, 300 West 5th Street at Cherry and Marshall Streets, (919)725-1234, $$$; Ramada Inn—Downtown, 128 North Cherry Street, 27101, (919)723-8861, $$; Holiday Inn—Central, 127 South Cherry Street, 27101, (919)725-8561, $$
Motels/Hotels, Clemmons: Tanglewood, P.O. Box 1040, 27012, (919)766-0591, $$
Camping, Clemmons: Tanglewood Park, P.O. Box 1040, 27012, (919)766-0591
Camping, High Point: Oak Hollow Family Campground, 1400 Oakview Road, 27260, (919)869-6711

Camping, Mocksville: Lake Myers Campground, Route 1, P.O. Box 90, 27028, (704)492-7736

HISTORY

The Moravians, who founded Salem in 1766, trace their faith to the Bohemian Protestant martyr, Jan Hus. Hus died at the stake in 1415 because of his unrelenting opposition to corruption in the Roman Catholic Church. A faithful band of his followers known as *Hussites* sought refuge in Moravia, a province in present-day Czechoslovakia. In 1457, they formed a society known as *Unitas Fratrum* (Unity of Brethren), renounced the authority of Rome, and began to ordain their own ministers.

Despite persecution, the Unity flourished, spreading across Moravia, Bohemia, and into Poland until the Counter Reformation and Thirty Years War (1618 to 1648) destroyed all but a remnant of the group and forced its members into exile.

Pietism, the "religion of the heart," was kept alive by the distinguished educator and Moravian bishop of the *Unitas Fratrum,* John Amos Komensky, (1592–1670), also known by his Latin name, Comenius. The Moravians who eventually emigrated to the New World incorporated many of Comenius's educational ideas into their efforts to convert the Indians to Christianity.

The brethren followed the rule that the spirit of love should be constantly maintained toward all the children of God, regardless of race or creed. In their daily lives, the brethren strove to preserve purity and simplicity. Like other Protestant denominations, the Moravians, as members of the Unity were commonly called, turned to America as a place where they could practice their beliefs free from persecution and whose Indian tribes offered unlimited opportunities for missionary activity.

By 1740, the brethren had founded a successful colony at Bethlehem, Pennsylvania. Their reputation as industrious, law-abiding people attracted the attention of a British nobleman, Earl Granville, who approached the Moravian leaders with an offer of land. In 1753, a 98,985-acre tract was purchased in what is now Piedmont, North Carolina. The Carolina purchase was named *der Wachau* after the Austrian estate of Count Nicholas Ludwig von Zinzendorf, an important patron of the sect. The settlement came to be known as *Wachovia.*

Salem was planned as Wachovia's trade center, a town where economic development and architectural details would be regulated as strictly as people's lives. Construction began in 1766, and by the spring of 1772, most of the major buildings had been completed, and early settlers and the government of Wachovia proceeded to move in.

The Moravian beliefs combined pietistic behavior with a zeal for commerce. A person's work and the profit it yielded were considered essential to spiritual growth. Whether a candlemaker or tinsmith, a Moravian craftsman should develop his skills to the utmost in order to glorify the divine taskmaster.

The guild system was the way that the brethren accomplished their many objectives. A Salem youth began his apprenticeship, with elaborate ceremony, at about the age of fourteen and with rare exceptions remained in that status for a full seven years. The guild system yielded high-quality products that were sold for profit.

Because the Moravians did not separate church and state, the business of running the town and enforcing the rules of the congregation was vested in three main boards or committees. The duties of the *Aufseher Collegium* (board of overseers) were to superintend trade, enforce zoning laws and building codes, discipline wayward apprentices and masters, control community accounts, and allocate funds for capital-improvement projects. The board, which was made up mostly of laymen and was concerned primarily with secular matters, also turned a harsh eye on tradesmen accused of immoral conduct. Matters of a strictly spiritual nature were referred to the Elders Conference. Another important body was the Congregation Council, which dealt mainly with issues involving all members of the community.

The Moravian "choir" system arose out of the belief that a close association of persons of like age, sex, or marital status promoted spiritual growth. There were choirs for married people, children, single brothers, single sisters, older boys, older girls, widows, and widowers. Some of the choirs—single brothers, widows, single sisters—lived in their own choir houses. All choirs worshiped together on a regular basis.

The choir system was closely linked with a sense of shared life and property, but by the time of Salem's founding, the brethren were allowed greater latitude in their economic lives. They were free to live in their own homes, though the church's leasehold system retained a right to the land on which the houses stood, and could also choose their own building styles. In the early days, only confirmed Moravians were allowed to live in or own houses in Salem.

Moravians were allowed to use alcohol and tobacco in moderation, but dress codes were severe, particularly for women. Each sister wore an ankle-length dress and, at church services, a traditional *Haube* (head covering). However, the colors of their clothing were the gayest that could be wrung from their homemade dyes.

As the area surrounding Wachovia grew more populous, the highly regimented congregation system of Salem lost much of its appeal. Gradually, the old rules were either relaxed or abandoned; and by the middle of the nineteenth century, Salem had ceased to function as a congregation town. Today, only the church, an active Protestant denomination, remains as a Moravian entity.

Although the original Salem ceased to exist, many of its buildings remained standing. But the founding of a new town, Winston, on its northern borders in 1849, the growth of Winston's tobacco and textile industries, the merger of Winston and Salem in 1913, and the gradual spreading of the city until it all but engulfed the old Moravian town led to its deterioration and near extinction.

In the spring of 1950, a broad-based, nonprofit organization known as Old Salem, Inc., brought together Moravians and non-Moravians in an effort to preserve the historic town. More than fifty buildings have now been restored or reconstructed on their original sites, recreating another era in the heart of a bustling metropolis.

TOUR

Although only nine buildings are used as museums at Old Salem, they are set in a sixteen-block area of Moravian-built eighteenth- and nineteenth-century buildings, many of which are now private homes. To ensure an authentic appearance, more than a hundred nonconforming structures within the congregation town limits were demolished when restoration efforts began. Almost all the existing buildings, even those privately owned, have been restored, reminiscent of Williamsburg. Even though admission is charged to enter museum buildings, you are free to stroll the brick paths through the restored area at any time, eat at the Salem Tavern, or shop in museum stores.

Salem was a congregational community, strictly planned by Moravian church leaders. The site for Salem ("peace" in Hebrew) was chosen because of its good water supply, proper drainage, and southern exposure. The principal structures, which included houses for the single brothers, single sisters, a community store, and a tavern, were built around an open square.

Salem is architecturally interesting because of the number of large eighteenth-century buildings that show strong European influence. Houses sit flush with the sidewalks and have half-timbered walls, tile roofs, central chimneys, and symmetrically placed windows.

After viewing the slide show on Moravian history at the **Reception Center**, begin your tour at the town square, which was originally farmland. Later, it was used for grazing sheep, but it eventually came to resemble a New England commons. The only major building on the square is the **Market-Fire House**, built in 1803. This reconstructed brick firehouse contains an exhibit of early fire-fighting equipment.

The northern, half-timbered portion of the **Single Brothers' House** dates from 1769; the southern, brick portion was added in 1786. Because the lime needed for mortar was scarce in Wachovia, oak timbering was used in 1769 to reinforce the house's brickwork. By 1786, when the addition was built, lime was more plentiful, and the community used brick in all its building projects.

Typically, a Salem boy entered the Moravian guild system at four-teen. He left his home, moved into the Single Brothers' House, and began a seven-year apprenticeship under one of the master craftsmen. After achieving journeyman status, he continued to live with the single brethren until he married. At that time, he moved into his own home and started his own business.

The Single Brothers' House was not only a residence but also contained the shops of the master craftsmen. The restored building contains craft shops stocked with appropriate tools, and craftspeople demonstrate and explain their work. These shops include a **tin shop, gun shop, dye shop, weaver's room, shoemaker's shop, tailor's shop, potter's shop, cooper's shop,** and **joiner's shop.** The productivity of the brothers, along with the high quality of their products, was a major factor in the economic success of Salem.

The **Boys' School,** a brick building erected in 1794, also faces Salem's square. Built by master builder Johannes Gottlob Krause, it is noteworthy for the artistry that appears in the pattern of the brick masonry on the west gable, the coved cornices, and the belt course of brick on the east gable. Until 1896, the school was attended by boys aged six to fourteen; but in that year, it became the home of the Wachovia Historical Society. Collections of artifacts acquired by Mora-vian missionaries were displayed here until the 1950s, when Old Salem, Inc., restored the building and assumed management of the collection. Exhibits in the **Wachovia Museum** now relate directly to the history of Wachovia: Moravian pottery, church history, Moravian music, ironwork, lighting devices, and a restored classroom. Moravians placed great emphasis on education, and the boys' curriculum included geometry, Latin and English grammar, geography, history, penman-ship, and German.

North of the square is the **Miksch Tobacco Shop**. This 1771 building was the first privately owned house in Salem. Matthew Miksch not only lived in but also operated a tobacco business from this house. The house was built of logs, but because the brethren disapproved of plain log houses on their main street, it (like others) was covered with clapboards. Originally, the house had two rooms, but Miksch added a third room at the back and a loft.

The **Winkler Bakery** was built in 1800 for a baker named Thomas Butner. In 1808, Christian Winkler acquired the shop. Bread is still being baked in the wood-fired domed brick bake oven attached to the south side of the building. Eighteenth-century baking processes are used to produce European-style white bread, Swedish rye, whole wheat, and Moravian sugar cake and sugar cookies. All these products are sold at the bakery, and the aroma of fresh-baked bread permeates the restored area.

South of the square is the **John Vogler House**, which was built in

1819. This house has many Federal characteristics and thus represents a departure from Salem's Germanic architectural tradition. Vogler was an accomplished silversmith who also dabbled in clock making, gunsmithing, jewelry making, and silhouette making. Seventy percent of the furniture in the house belonged to the Vogler family. One room is used as a Vogler family museum, with their silver, guns, and artwork exhibited. Another room is used for Vogler's silversmithing shop, and many of his spoons, ladles, and snuffboxes are displayed.

The **Schultz Shoemaker Shop** was built in 1827. Samuel Schultz originally operated his business from his 1819 home but decided to construct a separate building adjacent to it. This home and shop are typical of those owned and operated by married craftsmen. The shop displays the tools and products of early nineteenth-century shoemaking.

The **Vierling House** was built in 1802 and was the last and largest masterwork of Johannes Krause. Unique features of this brick Georgian house are the exposed-stone foundation and the herringbone gable patterns. Krause was commissioned to build the house by Dr. Samuel Benjamin Vierling, the most renowned of Salem's early physicians. It was in this house that Dr. Vierling practiced the professions of physician, surgeon, and apothecary. He is said to have performed mastectomies, skull trepans, and other major operations in his apothecary. The restored house contains both living quarters and medical offices.

The **Tavern Museum** (1784) is a plain three-story brick building with a veranda. Taverns to accommodate travelers were a high priority of the congregation town, and this one had a fine reputation for its food and drink. Among the prominent Revolutionary War figures who stopped at Salem was George Washington, who spent two days at this tavern in 1791.

The first floor has a **Publick Room** where the ordinary (a standard meal at a fixed price) was served each day. Across the hall is a **Gentlemen's Room** for the more elite clientele. It is furnished with private tables and Windsor chairs instead of long tables and benches. Cooking was done in the twin fireplaces of the large kitchen. There are several sleeping rooms in addition to the innkeeper's bedroom, with its canopy bed.

Salem Tavern (1816), where today's visitors can stop for a meal, was originally a boardinghouse built as an adjunct to the main tavern building. The outside is restored to its 1816 appearance; the inside has been adapted for dining in a hospitable tavern atmosphere.

Gardens were part of the early congregational town plan. Each family maintained its own garden to supply vegetables for the table. A landscaping program has restored many gardens to various time periods: the **Treibel** and **Miksch Gardens**, 1759 to 1761; **Eberhardt Garden**, 1814; **Levering Garden**, 1820; **Leinbach Garden**, 1822; **Cape Fear**

Bank Garden, 1847; and **Anna Catharina Garden**, 1772. There is also an arboretum of native trees near the Museum of Early Southern Decorative Arts.

Operated by Old Salem, Inc., the **Museum of Early South Decorative Arts** was founded by Frank L. Horton, Old Salem's first director of restoration, during the 1950s. Ten rooms representative of the early South have been removed from their original locations and reassembled in the museum. They are decorated with furniture, paintings, metalwork, pottery, and glasswork produced by Southern craftsmen. A large part of the collection was donated by Mr. Horton and his mother, Mrs. Theo Liipfert Taliaferro. The museum emphasizes the products of craftspeople used in the three principal cultural regions of the Old South: the Chesapeake, the Carolina low country, and the back settlements during the years between 1640 and 1820.

God's Acre, founded in 1779, is the graveyard for Salem's Moravian congregation. Long rows of identical gravestones attest to the sect's belief in equality. People were buried with their fellow choir members rather than with their families. A large square is provided for each choir: married women and widows, married men and widowers, single men and boys, and single women and girls. An Easter sunrise service has been held in God's Acre every year since 1772 and attracts thousands of visitors.

Salem Academy and College, a four-year liberal arts college for women, is an outgrowth of a girls' boarding school operated by the Moravians. The first building for the school was erected in 1805 and has been restored to its 1837 appearance and now serves as a dormitory. College buildings are not open to tourists.

The **Home Moravian Church** was built in 1800. Although it has undergone many interior renovations, its exterior looks much as it originally did. This church has been occupied continuously by the Moravian congregation since 1800.

Two shops are operated at Old Salem. One is in the southern half of the restored 1775 **T. Bagge Community Store** and the other, the Salem Gift and Book Store, is in an 1850 addition to the 1810 **Inspector's House**. The shops carry reproductions made by the village's working craftsmen, including pottery, candles, quilts, wooden toys, tinware, and needlework kits. There is also a fine selection of books, many of them about Moravians.

Many educational and special events are held at Old Salem throughout the year. There are classes or lectures on weaving, blacksmithing, paper cutting, vegetable and flower gardening, nineteenth-century architecture, rifles, early laundry techniques, rug hooking, beehive-oven baking, and ice creams of the colonial period. Concerts are scheduled throughout the year.

SIDE TRIPS

Historic Bethabara ("house of passage" in Hebrew) is the site of the first Moravian settlement in North Carolina. Archaeological research has uncovered the foundation walls and cellars of many of the original buildings. The 1756 **palisade**, a fort that gave refuge to outlying settlers in times of trouble, has been reconstructed. The 1788 **Gemein Haus** (Congregation House), a fine example of Moravian architecture, the 1782 **potter's house**, and the 1803 **brewer's house** have all been restored as exhibit buildings. The **Visitors' Center** contains exhibits on the early settlers, including many artifacts found on the site. Nature trails lead to the Moravian graveyard. called **God's Acre.** Located at 2147 Bethabara Road. Open Monday to Friday, 9:30 A.M. to 4:30 P.M. and Saturday and Sunday, 1:30 to 4:30 P.M., from Easter to Thanksgiving. For information, call (919)924-8191. Admission is free.

Two of Winston-Salem's major industries are tobacco and beer. The R. J. Reynolds Tobacco Company, Cherry Street and Reynolds Boulevard, offers free tours of its plant Monday to Friday, 8:00 A.M. to 10:00 P.M. For information, call (919)773-2000. Guided tours of the Stroh Brewing Company's plant, Route 525 at Barnes Road, are conducted Monday to Friday, 9:00 A.M. to 4:00 P.M. For information, call (919)788-6710, extension 375. Admission is free.

A museum of American art now occupies the former estate of Richard J. Reynolds, founder of the R. J. Reynolds Tobacco Company. **Reynolda House**, Route 67 and Reynolda Road, is open Tuesday to Saturday, 9:30 A.M. to 4:30 P.M., and Sunday, 1:30 to 4:30 P.M. For information, call (919)725-5325. Admission: adults, $4.00; senior citizens, $3.00; students, $2.00.

Tanglewood Park is a 1,000-acre public resort in Winston-Salem. Its facilities include golf courses, tennis courts, a lodge, cottages, campsites, restaurants, swimming, and riding trails. It is open year-round and can be reached by exiting at Clemmons from I-40 West. P.O. Box 1040, Clemmons, 27012, (919)766-0591. Admission is $1.00 per vehicle.

Pioneer Farmstead

Recreation of a 1900 pioneer homestead

Mailing Address: Superintendent, Great Smoky Mountains National Park, Gatlinburg, TN 37738
Telephone: (615)436-5615
Location: In North Carolina, at Oconaluftee Visitor Center, in Great Smoky Mountains National Park; on Route 441, 2 miles north of Cherokee, North Carolina, near the Blue Ridge Parkway
Open: Daily, 8:00 A.M. to 4:30 P.M.; 8:00 A.M. to 7:00 P.M. in summer
Admission: Free
Facilities: Visitors' Center, accessible to handicapped

WHERE TO STAY

Motels/Hotels, Gatlinburg: Best Western Twin Island, P.O. Box 648, 539 Parkway, 37738, (615)436-5121, $$; Bon Air Mountain Inn, 950 Parkway, 37738, (615)436-4857, $; Brookside Resort, Roaring Fork Road, 37738, (615)436-5611, $$; Edgepark-Whaley, P.O. Box 484, 4550 River Road, 37738, (615)436-4164, $$$; Holiday Inn, P.O. Box 353, Airport Road, 37738, (615)436-9201, $$–$$$; Howard Johnson's, P.O. Box 408, Gatlinburg Parkway,

37738, (615)436-5621, $$; Hemlock Resort, P.O. Box 749, 37738, (615)436-5043, $$

Camping, Gatlinburg: Big Creek, Cataloochee, Balsam Mountain, Deep Creek, and Smokemont Campgrounds, Great Smoky Mountains National Park, 37738, (615)436-5615. For camping reservations, write to Ticketron, P.O. Box 2715, San Francisco, CA 94126. For information, call (615)436-5615

(See Oconaluftee Indian Village, page 133, for accommodations in Cherokee, North Carolina.)

HISTORY

After colonists settled the tidewater coastal areas of the South, they began to move westward. When they encountered such great mountain ranges as the Alleghenies and the Appalachians, they followed rivers and streams, searching for passages to the lands in the West. By the late 1700s, white pioneers, mainly English, Scotch-Irish, and Irish, first entered the area now known as Great Smoky Mountains National Park. This land, which straddles the southern Appalachian region, was occupied by Cherokee Indians for centuries (see Oconaluftee Indian Village, Cherokee, North Carolina, page 133).

Life for white settlers in the Oconaluftee River valley was primitive and hard. They battled with Indians over territory, and because of their isolation, they had to learn to be self-sufficient. Gradually, many forested areas became fields and pastures. Subsistence farming was often supplemented by hunting, trapping, and timbering. In remote mountain areas, the frontier characteristics, including old customs and speech patterns, persisted for a long time.

In the early 1900s, this rural pattern was radically altered by the arrival of logging companies. Sawmills began cutting down one of the finest spreads of lumber in the United States. Logging not only altered the beauty of nature, but also disrupted the economy of the mountaineers, who began to lose their self-sufficiency along with their isolation.

A movement to create a national park in the vicinity of the Tennessee–North Carolina border began around the turn of the century but foundered. A $5 million gift from John D. Rockefeller, Jr., provided the impetus for purchasing the 515,000 privately owned (85 percent by lumber companies) acres for the proposed park. On June 15, 1934, Congress authorized the Great Smoky Mountains National Park. Sixty percent of the original spruce, fir, hemlock, oak, and walnut trees had already been lost to the lumber companies, but the remainder was preserved.

The mountaineers whose land had been purchased left the area, leaving their buildings behind. The National Park Service preserved some of these historic structures and moved some of them to Pioneer Farmstead, near Oconaluftee Visitors' Center in Oconaluftee, North

Carolina. These buildings and the demonstrations performed in them interpret life in the southern Appalachians. There is another collection of buildings just across the state line in Cades Cove, Tennessee, along with several other historic buildings scattered throughout the park. Of the 1,500 pioneer structures still standing when the park was established, 88 remain. Visitors can easily walk the Pioneer Farmstead area; however, the Cades Cove structures are distributed along an eleven-mile loop drive.

TOUR

The Pioneer Farmstead, set in a small clearing surrounded by heavily wooded mountains, consists of about a dozen authentic structures moved from their original locations throughout the park. It recreates a 1900 pioneer mountain farmstead.

The Oconaluftee **Visitors' Center,** which is housed in a modern building, has exhibits on the daily life of the pioneers, their tools, crafts, and skills. There is also a remarkable painting of a local pioneer woman at age 100 called *Aunt Winchester, Matriarch of the Smokies.*

The **two-story log house** with two stone chimneys was built by a master craftsman, John Davis. When we visited, a costumed woman was cooking potatoes and other vegetables in the kitchen fireplace.

A **meat house** was essential to the pioneers' winter food supply. Soon after the first frost, usually in November, hogs were butchered. The meat, arranged in layers, was placed on a shelf at the far end of the building and each layer was covered with a thick coating of salt. After the meat was cured, it was hung from poles to keep it dry and inaccessible to rodents. Bear meat and venison might also be found in a meat house.

Another food-storage building was the **apple house**, a two-story wooden structure with a stone base. Summer apples were stored on the upper floor; winter apples on the lower. The thick stone walls prevented freezing.

Corn, the Indians' gift to the pioneers, was stored in the small, one-story **corncrib**. Corn kept the livestock fed and was the staple of the pioneer diet.

Chickens, kept in the **chicken house**, were another item of the pioneers' diet. Poultry provided meat, eggs, and feathers for bedding. A low, overhanging roof supported by stilts is the **barn**'s most unusual feature. Other buildings include a **gear shed**, where farm implements were stored; a **springhouse**, which protected the water source and contained a cooling trough for storing perishables; and a **blacksmith shop**.

A garden, usually tended by a pioneer woman and her children, was the family's source of corn, beans, cabbage, lettuce, onions, peppers, potatoes, turnips, and pumpkins. The **farmstead** also includes a pigpen, a bee gum stand (a collection of hollow black gum trees inhabited by bees), and a sorghum mill (an ox- or horse-powered two-roller mill that squeezed the juice from sorghum cane). Molasses was made from the boiled-down sorghum juice.

Nearby is the **Mingus Mill**, where the corn was ground into meal. The mill, named for John Jacob Mingus, believed to be the valley's first white settler, is on its original site.

Demonstrations of milling, weaving, shake splitting, muzzle loading, and blacksmithing are conducted each summer at Pioneer Farmstead and Cades Cove. Molasses made from sorghum cane is demonstrated in the fall.

See Oconaluftee Indian Village, page 133, for a description of facilities in the Great Smoky Mountains National Park.

VIRGINIA

Colonial Williamsburg

**Restoration of the eighteenth-century
capital of the English colony of Virginia;
NR, NHL, HABS**

Address: The Colonial Williamsburg Foundation, P.O. Box C, Williamsburg, VA 23185

Telephone: (804)229-1000

Location: On Colonial Parkway and Route 132, 40 miles west of Norfolk, 50 miles east of Richmond

Open: Daily, 9:00 A.M. to 5:00 P.M.

Admission: 10-Admission Ticket: adults, $9.00; children 6 to 12, $4.50; 18-Admission Ticket: adults, $13.00; children 6 to 12, $6.50; Patriot's Pass (unlimited admission to all Colonial Williamsburg buildings for one year): adults, $20.00; children 6 to 12, $10.00

Restaurants: Visitors' Center, cafeteria and grill; The Cascades, Chesapeake Bay country cuisine; Williamsburg Inn, gracious dining rooms; Williamsburg Lodge; Christiana Campbell's Tavern, restored tavern for brunch and dinner; Josiah Chowning's Tavern, restored tavern serving lunch and dinner; King's Arms Tavern, restored tavern; A Good Place to Eat, sandwiches and snacks; Golf Clubhouse Grill, light lunch

Shops: Tarpley's Store; Prentis Store; Greenhow Store; Geddy Silver-

150

smith Shop; Golden Ball, silver jewelry; Colonial Post Office, reproduction maps and prints; McKenzie's Apothecary, candles, spices, herbs; Grocer's Shop, food products; Raleigh Tavern Bakery, cake, breads; Craft House, Williamsburg reproductions; bookstore in Visitors' Center, books, films, records; gift shops in lobbies of Williamsburg Inn, Williamsburg Lodge, and The Cascades

Facilities: Visitors' Center, bus transportation, craft demonstrations, Rockefeller Folk Art Center, hotels and motels, adjacent to the College of William and Mary, accessible to handicapped

WHERE TO STAY

Motels/Hotels, Williamsburg: Williamsburg Inn and Colonial Houses, Francis Street, 23185, (804)229-2141; for reservations, 1-800-446-8956; in Virginia, 1-800-582-8976; $$$$. The inn, operated by Colonial Williamsburg, is one of the nation's most distinguished hotels. Colonial Houses consist of 26 colonial homes in the historic area that are operated as guest facilities. The Motor House, P.O. Box B, 23189, (804)229-1000; for reservations, 1-800-446-8956; in Virginia, 1-800-582-8976; $$. Large motel near Visitors' Center operated by Colonial Williamsburg. The Williamsburg Lodge, South England Street, 23189, (804)229-1000; for reservations, 1-800-446-8956; in Virginia, 1-800-582-8976; $$$-$$$$. Operated by Colonial Williamsburg. Fort Magruder Inn and Conference Center, 6945 Pocahontas Trail, 23187, (804)220-2250, $$$. Best Western Patrick Henry Inn, York and Page Streets, 23189, (804)229-9540, $$$. King William Inn, 824 Capitol Landing Road, 23189, (804)229-4933; for reservations, 1-800-446-1041; $. Ramada Inn—East, P.O. Box 519, 315 York Street, 23189, (804)229-4100, $$$. Williamsburg Westpark, P.O. Box HN, 1600 Richmond Road, 23189, (804)229-1134, $$.

Camping, Williamsburg: Williamsburg Campsite, Route 9, P.O. Box 274, 23185, (804)564-3101; Fair Oaks Holiday Trav-L, Route 9, P.O. Box 294A, 23185, (804)565-2101; Jamestown Beach Campsite, P.O. Box CB, 23187, (804)229-7609; Indian Village Campground, 1811 Jamestown, 23185, (804)229-8211; First Settlers Campground, P.O. Box BE, 23187, (804)229-4900; Safari-Colonial Campground, Route 4, Box 341C, 23185, (804)565-2734

HISTORY

Already well known for the College of William and Mary, which is named in honor of the British sovereigns, Williamsburg has many claims to significance in American history. In 1699, it became Virginia's second capital, replacing Jamestown, the first permanent English settlement in the New World, where colonists had faced continual famine, fire, and Indian raids since its founding in 1607.

Williamsburg was both an outpost of the powerful British Empire in the New World and an ideological training ground for those who would help to lead America to independence. The magnificently restored Royal Governor's Palace (1720) was the official residence of the king's representative in Virginia, a royal colony. While the Governor's Palace affirmed the majesty and dominion of the Crown, the House of Burgesses, composed of elected representatives of Virginia's counties, broadcast the fledgling efforts of Americans to govern themselves.

Williamsburg eventually became a center of revolutionary activity. Here George Washington, Patrick Henry, George Wythe, Thomas Jefferson, and other Founding Fathers began the struggle that would lead to the birth of a new nation. It was at Williamsburg that Patrick Henry, protesting British taxation without representation, gave his famous speech with the cry, "Give me liberty, or give me death!"

At Williamsburg on May 15, 1776, the Virginia Convention passed a resolution urging the Continental Congress to declare the colonies free and independent of Great Britain and to create a national confederation. Acting on that resolution, Richard Henry Lee proposed in Philadelphia that Congress declare the colonies "absolved from all allegiance to the British Crown." Congress adopted Lee's resolution on July 2 and approved the Declaration of Independence on July 2.

Meanwhile, on June 12, 1776, the Virginia Convention at Williamsburg adopted George Mason's Virginia Declaration of Rights, which later became the basis for the first ten amendments of the Constitution of the United States.

In 1781, Williamsburg surrendered its role as Virginia's capital when the offices of the new commonwealth were moved to Richmond to be more convenient to the state's growing population and be better protected from enemy attacks.

Williamsburg is also significant in the history of restoration in the United States. Colonial Williamsburg is one of the finest historical restorations not just in the United States but in the world.

Colonial Williamsburg is the name identifying all the activities of the Colonial Williamsburg Foundation, a nonprofit educational organization. Among its activities are the restoration and interpretation of the historic sections of Williamsburg, the development of an extensive educational and cultural program based on Williamsburg's historical significance, the management of visitor accommodations and services, and the operation and maintenance of the Abby Aldrich Rockefeller Folk Art Center, Carter's Grove Plantation, and Bassett Hall, the home of Mr. and Mrs. John D. Rockefeller, Jr.

The concept of restoring Williamsburg originated with the Reverend Dr. W. A. R. Goodwin, rector of the Bruton Parish Church. In 1926, Goodwin discussed the idea with John D. Rockefeller, Jr., who agreed to provide financial support. It was decided to restore the extant buildings to their appearance during the colonial era. Important buildings such as the Governor's Palace and the Capitol, which no longer existed, were painstakingly researched and recreated.

Today, the historic area of Williamsburg covers 173 acres of the original town, based on the 1699 street plan. It is a mile long, with the Wren Building of the College of William and Mary at the western boundary and the Capitol at the eastern end; the average width is one-half mile. The area includes the buildings fronting on the three major streets of the city: Duke of Gloucester, Francis, and Nicholson Streets. Within or adjacent to this area are eighty-eight restored houses, shops, taverns, public buildings, and dependencies. In addition to the Governor's Palace and the Capitol, more than fifty structures have been rebuilt on their original sites. Ninety acres of gardens have been planted in eighteenth-century style.

TOUR

Without doubt, Williamsburg is the crown jewel of America's restored museum villages. The quality and breadth of its restoration and its visitors' programs attract thousands of visitors each year. Indeed, many of the other restored villages and communities that are described in this book owe their inspiration and design to Colonial Williamsburg.

Because Colonial Williamsburg is large and complex, you should begin your tour at the official **Colonial Williamsburg Information Center**. This is a scene of often hurried activity, but you will nevertheless find the time used here to orient yourself well spent. Here you will find complete details on what to see and do, ticket sales, an orientation film, and cultural and historical exhibits. Information is available on accommodations, dining, special activities and programs, and travel attractions throughout tidewater Virginia. A guide for handicapped visitors is also available. Historic Area buses provide transportation for ticket holders.

Because of the size of the Williamsburg restoration, the site description follows the major streets and comments only on the buildings open to the public. But on each street you will also see a number of privately owned restored buildings.

The **Capitol**, one of the major landmarks, is a careful recreation of the first building that served as Virginia's capitol from 1704 until it was destroyed by fire in 1747. A second Capitol was completed in 1753, which incorporated the surviving walls of the first Capitol but was a different architectural style. In 1780, Virginia's government moved to Richmond.

Under the supervision of Henry Cary, a leading colonial architect, the foundations of the Capitol were laid in 1701, and construction was completed in 1705. The architecture is a simplified version of the Renaissance style. Note the round and arched windows and cupola.

Since the Capitol was built during Queen Anne's reign, her coat of arms is emblazoned on its tower.

The building's H-shaped design reflects the composition of the colonial government, which was headed by a royal governor appointed by the British crown. One wing housed the elected House of Burgesses on the first floor and their committee rooms on the second. Among the distinguished Americans who served as burgesses were George Washington, Patrick Henry, Richard Henry Lee, and Thomas Jefferson. The Capitol's other wing housed the General Court Room and the Council Chamber. The Council consisted of the governor and his appointees. A costumed guide notes that burgesses met in a rather austere setting that contrasts with the more elegant Council Chamber.

Be sure to see the portraits of Edmund Pendleton, John Robinson, and Patrick Henry in the Conference Room and the large painting of George Washington by the famous American artist Charles Willson Peale that hangs in the hallway.

The **Public Records Office** was built in 1747. To safeguard the records from fire, the one-story building was constructed with sloping chimney caps, plastered window jambs, interior brick partitions, and a masonry floor. The building also served as office of the secretary of the colony.

The **Pasteur-Galt Apothecary Shop**, built in 1760 and now one of Colonial Williamsburg's craft shops, was the shop of physicians Dr. William Pasteur and his partner, Dr. Minson Galt. The shop is marked with the mortar-and-pestle sign of the apothecary and the snake-entwined staff of the physician. It contains exhibits of the ointments, herbs, medicines, and elixirs of the colonial period. The room at the rear contains the doctors' apparatus and surgical instruments.

The **Raleigh Tavern**, a reconstruction on the north side of Duke of Gloucester Street, was named for Sir Walter Raleigh, who encouraged English settlement in North America and popularized the use of tobacco in Europe. Colonial taverns were places of public receptions, meetings, and dining. Among the prominent persons who dined or met at the Raleigh were George Washington, Peyton Randolph, John Marshall, Thomas Jefferson, and the Marquis de Lafayette.

At the **Raleigh Tavern Bakery**, costumed bakers make bread and cakes according to colonial recipes in two large red brick, dome-shaped ovens.

The **Golden Ball** is a reconstruction of a jeweler's shop that stood on the site from 1727 to 1907. The shop was first owned by James Craig. Displays in the shop feature eighteenth-century jewelry and silver. Both eighteenth-century reproductions and contemporary jewelry can be purchased, including silver, pewter, and replicas of pieces in the Williamsburg collection. As in most of the craft buildings, a costumed artisan is at work.

Wetherburn's Tavern is located on property purchased by Henry Wetherburn in 1738. The restored white frame building, used continuously for the past 200 years, has been variously a tavern, store, girls' school, guesthouse, and inn. It is now leased as an exhibition building by Colonial Williamsburg. The detailed inventory of Wetherburn's estate was used as a guide in furnishing it. Added information came from archaeological excavations of the site, which uncovered 192,000 artifacts such as glass, pottery, porcelain, and bottles.

The **printing office** was owned in the eighteenth century by William Parks, publisher of the *Virginia Gazette*, which first appeared in 1736. Site excavations unearthed pieces of type, bookbinder's ornaments, and other artifacts related to printing. The privately owned site, leased by Colonial Williamsburg, is the location of the **printing shop, post office**, and **bookbindery**, which are craft shops. Of particular interest are the demonstrations of the printing press and bookbinding.

The **Market Square Tavern,** at the intersection of Queen and Duke of Gloucester Streets, is operated as a hostelry of the Williamsburg Inn. Among the tavern's famous guests were Thomas Jefferson and Patrick Henry. Of special interest is the **Great Room**, with its naturally finished original pine paneling. The tavern has an attractive garden planted with the trees, flowers, and herbs that were popular in the eighteenth century.

Chowning's Tavern, which was opened in 1766 by Josiah Chowning, is operated by Colonial Williamsburg as an eighteenth-century tavern, or *ordinary*. It serves luncheons and dinners featuring such popular period fare as brunswick stew, Welsh rabbit, oysters, clams, and draft ale. Behind the tavern is a delightful garden shaded by an arbor of scuppernong grape vines.

The **Magazine and Guardhouse**, a substantial red brick, octagonal building, is a well-known landmark. The magazine, erected in 1715 by Governor Alexander Spotswood, was used as an arsenal for the weapons, powder, and ammunition needed to defend the colony. It now houses a display of weapons of the French and Indian wars, including flintlock muskets, the standard arms of British and colonial troops.

The **Courthouse**, built in 1770, was used by Williamsburg and James City County until 1932. The red brick T-shaped building features arched windows, a white octagonal cupola, and overhanging pediments. As the chief government agency in colonial Virginia, the county court had wide judicial and executive powers.

The **James Geddy House and Silversmith Shop**, a two-story L-shaped structure, was built in 1750. From 1760 to 1777, it was home to James Geddy, one of Williamsburg's leading silversmiths. Today, it is used for craft displays and demonstrations and includes a collection of watches and watchmaker's tools.

The **Bruton Parish Church**, at the corner of Duke of Gloucester

Street and Palace Green, has been used as a place of worship since 1715. During the colonial era, the Church of England, or Anglican church, was established as the official religion. Today, the Bruton Parish Church functions as an Episcopal church, the contemporary American descendant of the Anglican church. Arched doors and windows reflect the architectural style of Anglican churches of the eighteenth century. The west gallery was reserved for students from William and Mary. The churchyard contains tombstones marking the graves of members of the congregation who died during the colonial period.

Merchants Square, located between the restored area of Colonial Williamsburg and the campus of the College of William and Mary, is an attractive shopping and commercial area that conforms to the architectural style of the colonial city. More than thirty distinctive specialty shops offer antiques, books, gifts, clothing, souvenirs, and food. The **Scribner Book Store** carries a wide assortment of books on Virginia's colonial heritage; the **Bookpress Ltd.** features antiquarian books, prints, and maps.

The **College of William and Mary**, located at the western end of Duke of Gloucester Street, is one of America's oldest institutions of higher learning. Among its famous graduates were Thomas Jefferson and John Marshall. Through the efforts of the Reverend James Blair, Episcopal commissary for Virginia, a royal charter issued in 1693 authorized the establishment of the college. The first building was completed in 1700.

When it was first established, the College of William and Mary had the mission of seeing "that the Church of Virginia may be furnished with a seminary of ministers of the Gospel." However, the original religious objective was tempered. In 1779, the original classical curriculum and the three original departments of grammar, philosophy, and theology were broadened to include more modern subjects such as mathematics, science, law, and history; and the college began to prepare educated gentlemen to be lawyers, physicians, and politicians.

The **Wren Building** was named for Christopher Wren, the noted English architect whose style influenced its design. The building retains its 1716 appearance.

The **Chapel** was built in 1732. Several prominent Virginians, including John and Peyton Randolph, are entombed in its crypt.

The **President's House**, built in 1733, continues to be the official residence of the college's presidents. The **Brafferton Indian School**, built in 1723, was used as a boarding school for young Indian boys during the colonial era.

Bassett Hall, an eighteenth-century house that was the Williamsburg home of Mr. and Mrs. John D. Rockefeller, Jr., looks as it did when the Rockefellers restored and furnished the house in the mid-

1930s. Tours are conducted daily from 10:00 A.M. to 5:00 P.M. Admission is $5.00 for adults, $4.00 for young people 13 to 17, and $3.00 for children 6 to 12. Tour reservations are required.

The **DeWitt Wallace Decorative Arts Gallery**, on Nassau Street, opened in 1985. It displays high-quality art objects, furniture, silver, ceramics, textiles, and paintings from the Williamsburg collection. The modern, 62,000-square-foot museum is entered through the lobby of the reconstructed **Public Hospital** of 1773, the last major public building of eighteenth-century Williamsburg to have been reconstructed.

The **Public Gaol**, a restored exhibition building, is located on the north side of Nicholson Street. It was built under the supervision of Henry Cary and completed in 1704. Debtors' cells were added in 1711, and the keeper's quarters were added in 1722. It was used by the colony until 1780 and served as the city jail of Williamsburg until 1910. In 1933, it became part of Colonial Williamsburg.

Anthony Hay's Cabinetmaking Shop was purchased by Anthony Hay in 1756; the shop's addition was built around 1770. The reconstructed building houses two operating craft shops. The cabinetmaker uses the cherry, walnut, and mahogany woods so popular in the eighteenth century to produce handmade furniture. In the second shop, musical instruments of the period such as harpsichords and guitars are handcrafted.

The **Peyton Randolph House** is the imposing home of the distinguished statesman who served both colonial Virginia and the early American Republic. From 1766 to 1775, Randolph was speaker of Virginia's House of Burgesses. He was elected president of the Continental Congress in 1774. The western section of the house was built by Sir John Randolph, Peyton Randolph's father, in 1715. In 1724, a one-and-a-half-story house next door was purchased; a middle two-story addition was then built to join the two houses. The house was reconstructed in 1940.

Robertson's Windmill is an operating craft shop. The mill's lower chamber contained machinery to screen and sack flour and meal; the upper chamber held the shaft and millstones that ground the grain. The mill was wind-powered, by sails lashed to wooden frames.

The **Brush-Everard House**, a restored frame town house built in 1717, is an exhibition building. It was built by John Brush, a Williamsburg gunsmith and armorer, as his residence and shop. The property was purchased by William Dering, an artist and dancing master, in 1742. It was then owned by Thomas Everard, a politician who was auditor of Virginia and mayor of Williamsburg. Everard enlarged the house by adding two wings that formed a U-shaped design.

The reconstructed **Governor's Palace**, which resembles a Georgian-style English country manor, is a splendid structure that recalls the power and majesty of the British Empire. Designed by Henry Cary and completed in 1720, it was the residence and official headquarters of seven royal governors of Virginia until the outbreak of the American Revolution in 1775. It then served as the official mansion of the Commonwealth of Virginia's first two governors, Patrick Henry and Thomas Jefferson.

The palace was destroyed by fire in 1781. Reconstruction of the building, begun in 1931, was based on archaeological excavations, which unearthed the foundations, and research that included the use of Thomas Jefferson's 1779 floor plan, records of the House of Burgesses, and a copper plate of the palace found in the Bodleian Library at Oxford University.

A visit to the Governor's Palace is a delightful experience, especially for children, who come face to face with American history. Visitors are met at the front entrance by a liveried footman. A guide accompanies visitors through the palace as they encounter the governor's staff—the clerk of the council, the butler, and household servants. On one of our visits, a youngster eagerly accepted the assignment of presenting a petition to the governor's secretary.

For those interested in the palace's architecture and furnishings, there is a separate architectural tour. Of particular interest is the first-floor entry hall, with its collection of firearms and swords.

The formally designed palace garden features both native American and European trees and plants. As in many of the Williamsburg gardens, holly and boxwood are prominent.

The **George Wythe House** is a restored exhibition building that was once the home of George Wythe (1726–1806), a leading scholar and lawyer. A member of the House of Burgesses, Wythe served as the colony's attorney general and was a signer of the Declaration of Independence. In 1779, he was appointed as professor of law at The College of William and Mary. Among his famous students were Thomas Jefferson and John Marshall, a chief justice of the U.S. Supreme Court whose landmark decisions established many of the precedents for the country's legal system.

The **garden and yard area** is the location of an **orchard** and such reconstructed frame dependencies as the **kitchen, laundry, smoke-house, stable,** and **chicken house.** Among the crafts demonstrated in the dependency buildings are basketmaking, spinning, and weaving.

The **Craft House** will interest visitors wishing to purchase heirloom furniture, silver, brass, pewter, and glass reproductions of the Colonial Williamsburg collection. The display rooms are arranged in the manner of a large colonial house. Living and dining rooms are on the first floor, and bedrooms are above. Wallpaper in colonial patterns and paint in the popular colors of the period are available, as are gifts, souvenirs, and books. Open Tuesday to Saturday, 9:00 A.M. to 9:00 P.M.; Sunday and Monday, 9:00 A.M. to 5:00 P.M.

The **Abby Aldrich Rockefeller Folk Art Center** is a museum and gallery given to Colonial Williamsburg in 1939 by Mrs. John D. Rockefeller, Jr. The museum, with a collection of over 1,800 art objects, was designed to further the knowledge and appreciation of American folk art. The rotating exhibits include primitive paintings, wood carvings, weather vanes, and other early American art objects. Open daily, 11:00 A.M. to 7:00 P.M. Admission is by donation.

Christiana Campbell's Tavern, on Waller Street, is a reconstructed early eighteenth-century building now operated as a restaurant by the Colonial Williamsburg Foundation. It specializes in seafood, steaks, and colonial fare.

SIDE TRIPS

Williamsburg itself and the historic tidewater Virginia area, which includes Jamestown and Yorktown, offer a wide range of attractions and accommodations to visitors.

The **Old Country, Busch Gardens**, located in Grove, 4 miles east of Williamsburg on Highway 60, is a theme park that features seventeenth-century facsimile European villages: the English Bambury Cross, a Scottish town, the French *ville* of Acquitaine, a German *burg*, and a small Italian *città*. The Old Country has a range of amusement rides, concerts, and shows. Ethnic food of the various countries is featured in the cafes and restaurants. For information, phone (804)253-3350. Admission is $13.95.

Two miles farther east on Highway 60 is **Carter's Grove Plantation**, an 800-acre estate with a 200-year-old mansion house. Open to the public from 9:00 A.M. to 5:00 P.M., March through November and during the Christmas season. Tickets are $6.00; with a Colonial Williamsburg admission ticket, $4.00. Also on exhibit are the seventeenth-century remains of **Wolstenholme Towne**, an archaeological exhibit on the early colonial period. Highway 60 is a 7-mile scenic country road that winds through woodlands, meadows, marshes, and streams. It begins 1 mile past the Williamsburg Lodge on South England Street.

Jamestown, on Jamestown Island south of Williamsburg, was the location of the first permanent English settlement in North America, founded in 1607. It was Virginia's capital until 1699 and is part of the historic triangle of tidewater Virginia that also includes Williamsburg and Yorktown. Administered by the National Park Service, the U.S. Department of the Interior, and the Association for the Preservation of Virginia Antiquities, Jamestown has a **Festival Park**, with replicas of the first fort, an Indian dwelling, and the ships used to transport the colonists across the Atlantic. For further information, contact the Superintendent, Colonial National Historical Park, P.O. Box 210, Yorktown, VA 23690. The phone number is (804)898-3400.

Yorktown was the scene of the last major battle of the American

War for Independence. On October 19, 1781, British General Charles Cornwallis surrendered to General George Washington, commander of the Continental army. Earlier, in 1691, Yorktown was established as one of Virginia's four official ports; its major export was tobacco.

Colonial National Historical Park, administered by the National Park Service, consists of 4,500 acres, including the battlefield area. **Yorktown Battlefield and Visitors' Center** is open daily from 8:30 A.M. to 5:30 P.M. You can drive the 7-mile **Battlefield Tour**, which includes **Moore House**, where the surrender terms were negotiated, and the 9-mile **Allied Encampment Tour**, which features **Washington's Headquarters** and the **French Cemetery**. For information, call (804)898-3400. Admission is free.

Harpers Ferry National Historical Park

Restoration of a mid-nineteenth-century village; NR

Address: P.O. Box 65, Harpers Ferry, WV 25425
Telephone: (304)535-6371
Location: On Route 340, near the Virginia and Maryland borders
Open: Daily, 8:00 A.M. to 5:00 P.M.; closed Christmas Day and New Year's Day. Conducted walks, demonstrations, and living history demonstrations from June to August only
Admission: Free
Shops: National Park Bookstore, books on Civil War and regional history
Facilities: Visitors' Center, hiking trails

WHERE TO STAY
Inn, Harpers Ferry: Hilltop House, P.O. Box 806, Ridge Street, 25425, (304)535-6321, $$
Motels/Hotels, Harpers Ferry: Cliffside Inn, Route 340, P.O. Box 786, 25425, (304)535-6302, $$

Camping, Harpers Ferry: Canal Campground of Maryland, Route 3240, P.O. Box 581, 25425, (301)834-9240; Harpers Ferry KOA, Route 3, P.O. Box 1300, 25425, (304)535-6895

HISTORY

Harpers Ferry's location has contributed to its role in history. The town is situated at the confluence of the Shenandoah and Potomac Rivers on a point of land where Virginia, Maryland, and West Virginia meet in the Blue Ridge Mountains. Early nineteenth-century buildings climb the hills from the banks of gray and green merging waters. Steep tree-covered cliffs look down on the town. Here is how Thomas Jefferson described Harpers Ferry in his *Notes on the State of Virginia:*

The passage of the Patowmac through the Blue Ridge is perhaps one of the most stupendous scenes in Nature. You stand on a very high point of land. On your right comes up the Shenandoah, having ranged along the foot of the mountain a hundred miles to seek a vent. On your left approaches the Patowmac in quest of a passage also. In the moment of their junction they rush together against the mountain, rend it asunder and pass off to the sea. The first glance of this scene hurries our senses into the opinion that this earth has been created in time, that the mountains were formed first, that the rivers began to flow afterwards, that in this place particularly they have been so dammed up by the Blue Ridge of mountains as to have formed an ocean which filled the whole valley; that, continuing to rise, they have at last broken over at this spot and have torn the mountain down from its summit to its base. The piles of rock on each hand, but particularly on the Shenandoah, the evidence marks of their disruptions and avulsions from their beds by the most powerful agents in nature, corroborate the impression. But the distant finishing which nature has given the picture is of a very different character. It is a true contrast to the former. It is as placid and delightful as that is wild and tremendous. For the mountain being cloven asunder, she presents to your eye, through the cleft, a small catch of smooth, blue horizon, at an infinite distance in that plain country, inviting you, as it were, from the riot and tumult roaring around to pass through the breach and participate in the calm below. Here the eye ultimately composes itself; and that way, too, the road happens actually to lead. You cross the Patowmac above the junction, pass along its side through the base of the mountain for three miles, the terrible precipice hanging in fragments over you, and within about 20 miles reach Fredericktown and the fine country around that. This scene is worth a voyage across the Atlantic.

Thomas Jefferson, *Notes on the State of Virginia,* 1785

It was not its beauty but its economic opportunity that lured Peter Stephens, the first white settler, to the area in 1733. Stephens, who was a trader, operated a ferry across the river. In 1747, a millwright and architect named Robert Harper purchased Stephens's ferry operation. In 1763, the Virginia General Assembly established the town of "Shenandoah Falls at Mr. Harper's Ferry" and gave Harper the exclusive right to maintain a ferry across the Potomac River. This ferry continued to operate until 1824, when the Wager family, Harper's descendants, built a double wooden span across the river, which they operated as a toll bridge until 1839.

George Washington decided Harpers Ferry would be a good location for a second national armory. In 1796, the government purchased 118 acres from the Wager family, and construction of the U.S. Armory and Arsenal began in 1799. Muskets, rifles, and pistols were manufactured in the twenty workshops and offices that made up the U.S. Musket Factory, which was located along the Potomac. A privately owned company, Hall's Rifle Works, produced breech-loading rifles for the government. Hall's business occupied nine buildings along the Shenandoah River.

Harpers Ferry gradually became an industrial transportation center linking the east-west Potomac routes with the north-south routes. In 1833, the Chesapeake and Ohio Canal reached Harpers Ferry.

It was the U.S. Armory that drew John Brown to Harpers Ferry. Brown, a 59-year-old abolitionist who believed that violence was the only way to end slavery, decided to arm an uprising of slaves. At midnight on Sunday, October 16, 1859, John Brown, leading eighteen men who called themselves the "Provisional Army of the United States," captured the bridge watchman, and crossed the covered bridge into Harpers Ferry. Without resistance, the raiders seized the Shenandoah bridge, Hall's Rifle Works, and the Federal Arsenal, barricaded the B & O bridge across the Potomac, cut telegraph wires, and took prisoners—all in the space of two hours.

John Brown intended to set up a free-black stronghold in the mountains of Maryland and Virginia. A native of Connecticut, he had studied military strategy in Europe. He intended to create an army of liberated blacks who would forcefully end slavery.

After his initial success at Harpers Ferry, Brown's plans began to deteriorate. Brown's raiders stopped the 1:20 A.M. Baltimore train, but then allowed it to go through. News of the raid spread quickly. Militia companies from Virginia and Maryland were sent to Harpers Ferry where they captured or killed several raiders. U.S. marines commanded by Colonel Robert E. Lee and Lieutenant J. E. B. Stuart, both of whom were destined to win fame as generals of the Confederacy, recaptured the Federal Armory on Tuesday, October 18. Brown and his remaining raiders, along with their hostages, had barricaded themselves in the Armory's fire engine house, and were soon captured.

When it was all over, ten raiders had been killed, five were captured, and four escaped. Four townspeople, one marine, and a free black named Heyward Shephard were dead. Shephard was the baggagemaster on duty at the train station the night of the raid. When he tried to investigate the unusual commotion outside, he was shot. Ironically, the first victim of John Brown's violent attempt to free blacks was a free black.

Brown was tried and found guilty of murder, treason, and conspiring with slaves to cause insurrection. He was hanged at nearby Charles Town on December 1, 1859. Although Brown's unsuccessful raid did not free any slaves except those set free in the will of the murdered town's mayor, the widely publicized event dramatized the strong and divergent positions on the slavery issue that would lead to the Civil War.

On the day of his execution, Brown wrote, "I, John Brown, am now quite certain that the crimes of the guilty land will never be purged away but with blood. I had, as I now think, vainly flattered myself that without very much bloodshed it might be done." Less than a year and a half later, the Civil War began. Union armies marched off to face their Confederate adversaries singing the verse, "John Brown's body lies a moldering in the grave but his soul goes marching on."

Harpers Ferry's position was considered geographically strategic to both the Union and the Confederacy. Struggles to occupy the town and control the railroads were continuous and resulted in the town being passed back and forth between the two occupying forces several times.

When the Civil War began, Harpers Ferry was in Virginia; it was only later that West Virginia seceded from Virginia and became a state in 1863. On the day that Virginia seceded from the Union, April 17, 1861, the Armory became an immediate military target. When several companies of Virginia militia started marching toward the 100 Union troops guarding the Armory, Lieutenant Roger Jones decided to torch the Armory and Arsenal, burning some 15,000 arms by the time the Virginia militia entered the town. Confederate troops were able to confiscate and ship to Richmond the Armory's ordinance stock, machinery, and tools. When they withdrew in June, the Confederates burned the remaining Armory buildings.

Constant military occupation and loss of employment at the Arsenal left Harpers Ferry in ruins, physically and economically. Devastating floods in the late 1800s added to the demise of the once flourishing industrial town.

Harpers Ferry is now part of a national historical park operated by the National Park Service. The town has been restored to the way it was in 1859, when John Brown made his midnight raid.

TOUR

In 1859, Harpers Ferry was a thriving industrial center. Many factories, powered by water, lined the river banks. Today, the restored buildings and many privately owned structures are typically three-story brick or stone buildings grouped closely together on the river banks and rising picturesquely up steep High Street.

Touring begins at the visitor's center in the **Stagecoach Inn** on Shenandoah Street. The two-and-a-half-story inn was built in 1826 as a private residence but was operated as an inn by Major James Stephenson from 1830 to 1837. During the Civil War, the building was used by the federal government as a military warehouse and quarters for troops.

Shenandoah Street had been part of the Charles Town & Smithfield Turnpike Co.'s toll road in the 1830s. The street has been restored to its 1833 macadamized finish, which consists of small broken stones compacted into a solid layer.

The **Philip Coons Building**, a three-story stone building erected in 1846, which once had shops downstairs and residences upstairs, now is used for rest rooms. The **McCabe Marmion Building**, another three-story edifice built in 1845, has a blacksmith shop.

Across Shenandoah Street are the **Provost Office** and a **Dry Goods Store** in an 1812 building that was used as quarters for the Master Armorer until 1858. The 1858 brick building next door was to be the new quarters for the Master Armorer. However, it was occupied by John E. P. Daingerfield, the Paymaster's clerk at the time of the raid, and Daingerfield was taken hostage. The building is now a gun museum with exhibits on the history of gunmaking.

The **Civil War Museum**, in an 1839 building, focuses on the war's effect on Harpers Ferry. Constant troop movements, battles to occupy the strategic town, shellings from the bulwarks on nearby cliffs, occupation or burning of buildings, all combined to wreak havoc on the once prosperous town.

The **John Brown Museum** in another 1839 building focuses on the story of John Brown and his raiders. A movie on the raid is also shown here.

Across from the museums is **Arsenal Square**, where the foundations of two of the original buildings have been excavated. The buildings were burned in 1861, at the start of the Civil War.

John Brown's Fort is the ironic name given to the small one-story 1848 Armory fire engine house and watchman's office. During the raid, Brown originally held hostages here. Later, he and his followers barricaded themselves there. When the marines' demand for surrender was turned down by Brown, they battered down the engine house door and took the raiders captive. The engine house was the only Armory building to survive the Civil War. In 1891, it was displayed at the

Chicago World's Fair, where it met with little interest. It was returned to Harpers Ferry and placed at various locations until 1963, when the National Park Service moved it to its present location on Shenandoah Street, not far from its original location on Potomac Street.

Walk to the **Point**, where you can see the Shenandoah and the Potomac Rivers actually merge their green and gray waters. Then standing in West Virginia, you'll see Maryland on one side and Virginia beyond the ridge on the other.

Armory employees relaxed over a drink in the 1839 **Whitehall Tavern** on Potomac Street next to the 1856 **Post Office**. In the **Confectionary** on High Street, built in 1845 and enlarged later, townspeople could buy Frederick A. Roeder's breads, cakes, and rolls. There is a **Pharmacy** in an 1813 building.

A **bookstore**, operated by the Harpers Ferry Historical Association, is in a small brick building that dates from 1845. Its collection of Civil War books is especially good.

Harper House, a stone house built on the side of a hill, is the oldest house in town. Robert Harper began building the house in 1775, but the Revolutionary War delayed completion until 1782. Unfortunately, Harper died that year without ever occupying it. The house was used as the town's tavern until 1803 and served such prominent guests as George Washington and Thomas Jefferson. It is restored as a tenant house of the 1850s with families living in crowded conditions on each level.

Stone steps, cut out of rock at the turn of the nineteenth century, lead to **St. Peter's Catholic Church**, which was built in 1896, and the ruins of **St. John's Episcopal Church**, which was built in 1852 and served as both a Confederate barracks and as a hospital during the Civil War.

Armory employees usually lived nearby, and one worker's house, built between 1822 and 1831, survives. It is located near **Jefferson Rock**, the shale rock where Thomas Jefferson is said to have stood in October 1783 while admiring the view he described in his *Notes on the State of Virginia*.

A footbridge leads to **Virginius Island**, a thirteen-acre island in the Shenandoah River that was a thriving industrial area in the 1800s. At the time of John Brown's raid, water supplied the power to a cotton factory, flour mill, saw mill, machine shop, iron foundry, and a blacksmith shop. Flooding was a continual problem and industry was especially hurt by the devastating flood of 1870. Now, only ruins remain in the heavily forested area.

At Harpers Ferry, the restoration and the town flow into each other. Most of the restored buildings are in the **Lower Town**. Buildings along High Street are historically and architecturally similar to restored buildings but are privately owned and used as businesses.

In the **Upper Town** near Filmore Street are a cluster of restored brick buildings built in the mid-1850s for armory officials, including the superintendent and the paymaster, and their clerks. Unused armory dwellings became campus buildings of Storer College, a normal school for the education of free blacks. The college remained in operation until 1955. Now the buildings are used as a training center for National Park Service employees.

Harpers Ferry National Historic Park includes large tracts of land along the rivers. There are marked hiking trails in all areas, and we chose to hike in Maryland Heights because of the Civil War ruins and batteries along the trail. A magnificent view of Harpers Ferry and the converging rivers from Overlook Cliff, a sheer shale cliff, is well worth the climb.

Loudoun Heights, another part of the park, also figured in Civil War battles. The 2,000-mile Appalachian Trail, which extends from Maine to Georgia, runs through Loudoun Heights.

SIDE TRIPS

Exciting white-water rafting is available on the swift rapids of Shenandoah, Potomac, and Tygart Rivers from April to October. A variety of guided tours are offered by Blue Ridge Outfitters, P.O. Box 456, Harpers Ferry, 25425. For information, call (304)725-3444.

Antietam Battlefield, maintained by the National Park Service, is just across the state line in Sharpsburg, Maryland. It was the site of a major Civil War battle. On September 17, 1862, General Robert E. Lee invaded the North, pitting 41,000 Confederate troops against the 87,000 Union troops under General George B. McClellan. Intense fighting resulted in Union losses of 12,410 and Confederate losses of 10,700; it has been called the bloodiest day of the Civil War. Although the battle was not decisive, it was considered a strategic victory for the Union because the Confederate troops withdrew. British aid to the Confederates was withheld pending the outcome of this battle. The Visitors' Center is open daily, 8:30 A.M. to 6:00 P.M., June to August; to 5:00 P.M., rest of year. Antietam Battlefield is located north of Sharpsburg, on Route 65. For information, write to P.O. Box 158, Sharpsburg, MD 21782; telephone (301)432-5124. Admission is free.

Hikers and bikers can take the **C & O towpath** along the banks of the canal in the **Chesapeake and Ohio Canal National Historical Park**. The construction of the Chesapeake & Ohio Canal, which was supposed to provide an economical shipping route from Georgetown to Pittsburgh, was begun in 1828 and ended in the 1850s, when it had reached Cumberland, Maryland, a distance of 185 miles. The National Park Service maintains the towpath and walk-in campgrounds along the route. The campground at Sharpsburg, with thirty tent sites, is open all year. The address for all the campgrounds maintained by the park is P.O. Box 4, Sharpsburg, MD 21782. For information, telephone (301)739-4200.

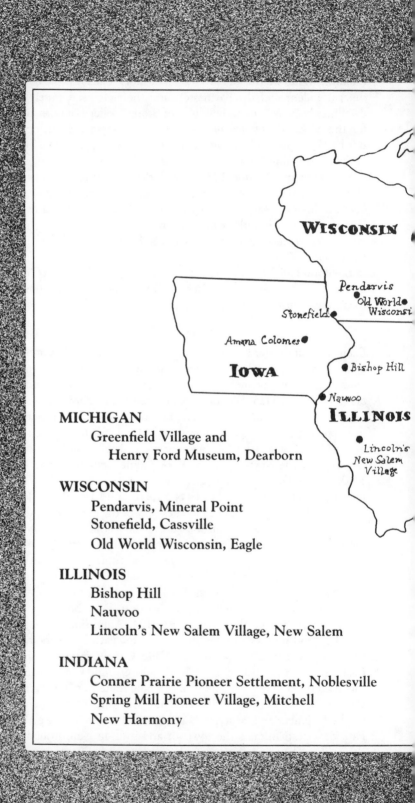

MICHIGAN

Greenfield Village and
Henry Ford Museum, Dearborn

WISCONSIN

Pendarvis, Mineral Point
Stonefield, Cassville
Old World Wisconsin, Eagle

ILLINOIS

Bishop Hill
Nauvoo
Lincoln's New Salem Village, New Salem

INDIANA

Conner Prairie Pioneer Settlement, Noblesville
Spring Mill Pioneer Village, Mitchell
New Harmony

Midwest

MICHIGAN
Greenfield Village and Henry Ford Museum

OHIO
Hale Farm and Western Reserve Village
Zoar Village State Memorial
Roscoe Village
Schoenbrunn Village State Memorial

INDIANA
Conner Prairie Pioneer Settlement
Spring Mill Pioneer Village
New Harmony

IOWA
    Amana Colonies

OHIO
    Schoenbrunn Village State Memorial,
      New Philadelphia
    Hale Farm and Western Reserve Village, Bath
    Zoar Village State Memorial, Zoar
    Roscoe Village, Coshocton

**Recreation of an American village from
colonial times to the modern era; NR**

Address: P.O. Box 1970, Dearborn, MI 48124
Telephone: (313)271-1620 or 1-800-835-2246, extension 218
Location: 15 miles west of Detroit, ½ mile south of Route 12, 1½ miles west of Southfield Road on Oakwood Boulevard
Open: Daily, 9:00 A.M. to 5:00 P.M.; closed Thanksgiving, Christmas Day, and New Year's Day
Admission: For Greenfield Village: adults, $8.00; children 5 to 12, $4.00; senior citizens, $7.00. For Henry Ford Museum: adults, $8.00; children 5 to 12, $4.00; senior citizens, $7.00. Two-day admission for both village and museum: adults, $15.00; children 5 to 12, $7.00; senior citizens, $13.00.
Restaurants: In Henry Ford Museum: American Cafe, cafeteria; Corner Cupboard, snacks. In Greenfield Village: Eagle Tavern, Main Street Lunch Stand, Riverfront Restaurant, Picnic Lunch Stand.
Shops: In Henry Ford Museum: Museum Store. In Greenfield Village: Museum Store, Museum Craft and Christmas Store, Sir John Bennett Jewelry Store, Suwanee Park Riverfront Store.

Facilities: Carriage tours, sleigh rides in winter, steamboat rides, Model T Ford rides, steam train ride, merry-go-round, foreign language interpreters and literature, picnic areas, accessible to handicapped

WHERE TO STAY

Motels/Hotels, Dearborn: Dearborn Inn, Colonial Homes, and Motor House, 20301 Oakwood Boulevard, 48124, (313)271-2700 or 1-800-221-7236, $$$. Traditional hotel built by Henry Ford for his guests, now operated by the Edison Institute; its dining room is very good. Dearborn Motor Lodge, 2211 South Telegraph Road, 48124, (313)278-0140, $; Fairlane Gold Key Inn, 21430 Michigan Avenue, 48124, (313)565-0800, $$; Holiday Inn, 22900 Michigan Avenue, 48124, (313)278-4800, $$; Travelodge, 23730 Michigan Avenue, 48124, (313)565-7250, $; Hyatt Regency Dearborn, Michigan Avenue at Fairlane Town Center, 48126, (313)593-1234, $$$$

Camping, Monroe: Sterling State Park, 2800 State Park Road, 48161, (313)289-2715

Camping, New Hudson: Haas Lake Park, 25800 Haas Road, 48165, (313)437-0900

Camping, Ypsilanti: KOA Detroit/Greenfield, 6680 Bunton Road, 48197, (313)482-7722

HISTORY

Greenfield Village and the Henry Ford Museum are the brainchildren of one man: Henry Ford. The automobile magnate who developed the mass-produced automobile, Ford was a self-made industrialist. He regarded America as a land of opportunity and became interested in preserving its heritage.

In the early 1920s, Ford conceived of a museum that would preserve the American past. He set aside a tract of land at Dearborn, Michigan, for his museum's buildings and exhibits. Feeling that written history did not do justice to the great men who founded and shaped America, Ford thought that the way to appreciate historical figures was to reproduce their physical environment, to reinvent their times.

He began collecting machines and instruments that had been significant but were now outmoded. Once he started, his collection grew rapidly as he enlisted the aid of friends and employees. By 1925, Ford's collection had completely filled the old Dearborn tractor factory.

Soon Ford turned to collecting buildings. His plan was to create both a museum and a village. His vision included showing change from era to era. He wished to show common household items from the handicraft era through the machine stage into the rapid changes of industrialization.

Much of Ford's collection focuses on his personal heroes. Among his acquisitions were the group of buildings associated with Thomas Edison's electric light, plant breeder Luther Burbank's office, an Illinois courthouse where Abraham Lincoln practiced law, Noah Webster's house, the Wright brothers' shop, and his own childhood home and first school.

An eight-acre museum building, modeled on Independence Hall in Philadelphia, was built, and twenty-eight buildings were arranged in the village. On October 21, 1925, the fiftieth anniversary of the electric light, the Edison Institute (as Greenfield Village and Henry Ford Museum together are known) was dedicated to Thomas Edison. Ford continued to acquire large numbers of structures and objects in the years following the dedication; there are now eighty-five buildings on the 260-acre village site.

Greenfield Village is visited annually by more than a million and a half people. The Americana collection ranks with the finest in the country. Of particular merit is the transportation collection. The Edison Institute is a nonprofit educational organization.

TOUR

Greenfield Village and the Henry Ford Museum comprise the country's largest indoor/outdoor museum. The Edison Institute is not focused on or restored to a particular year or era; rather, its exhibits portray aspects of American history from colonial to modern times.

Although Greenfield Village has been criticized by historians as lacking historical perspective and of being a random collection of items lacking a central theme, Ford's selections for preservation are important, educational, and interesting. The sheer scope and volume of the Edison Institute prevent us from anything more than just listing what is in the collection; detailing the background and contents of each exhibit would require a separate book. This pleasant, huge, and varied museum is well worth a two-day visit by the entire family so that the wealth of exhibits can be savored and enjoyed.

Greenfield Village is very large, with well-laid-out streets, attractive landscaping, and beautifully restored original buildings. Its emphasis is on invention and inventors, early industrial buildings, and nostalgic views of bygone days.

The Village is organized into six distinct areas: the **Village Crafts Center**, the **Village Green**, **Historic Homes**, **Edison Area**, **Suwanee Park** and **Suwanee Island**, and the **Trades and Manufactures Area**.

The **Village Crafts Center** has ten early American craft shops and houses. In the **carriage shed**, a tinsmith makes lamps and candle holders, a pewterer molds toys and bells, and a potter forms and fires his pots.

The **Currier Shoe Shop**, an 1880s building from Newton, New Hampshire, provides the setting for a leatherworker who makes leather mugs and pitchers. The **cotton gin mill**, from Henry Ford's Georgia plantation, is the site of power-loom weaving, or mechanical knitting, demonstrations. Handloom weaving can be seen in the 1832 **Richard Gardner House**, and basketweaving is demonstrated in the 1820s **pioneer log cabin**.

The fascinating art of glassblowing can be seen in the **Sandwich Glass Plant**, and jewelry making is done in the 1878 **Grimm Jewelry Store**, which was moved from Detroit. You can have your picture taken at the facsimile **tintype studio** and buy cookies baked in the brick oven of the **village bakery**. The oldest American craft shop in the village is the **Kingston Cooper Shop**, built in Kingston, New Hampshire, in 1785 and used for barrel and bucket making. Other craft demonstrations include hand-dipping candles, reeling silk, and printing. Some crafts are demonstrated daily all year; others can be seen only during the summer. Many handcrafted items are sold in the village shops.

The **Village Green** recreates the commercial, religious, and social center of an early American town. At the head of the green stands the **Mary-Martha Chapel**, a small church built from the bricks of the childhood home of Clara Bryant, Henry Ford's wife. A charming two-story white inn (1832) known as the **Eagle Tavern** was moved from Clinton, Michigan. On the green are the **Cohen Millinery Shop**, **Smiths Creek Depot** (1858), **Elias Brown General Store** (1854), **Dr. Howard's Office** (1839), and the **Wright Brothers' Cycle Shop and Home** (1870).

The most compelling site is the 1840 **Illinois Logan County Courthouse**, where Abraham Lincoln practiced law. Some of Lincoln's personal belongings, including his hat and cane, are in the room, and his presence seems very real. A reenactment of a legal case is presented here.

The **Historic Homes** section is a street lined with picturesque buildings that span a period of three centuries. They range from simple one-room log cabins, such as the birthplace of the educator William McGuffey, to the elaborate home of Noah Webster, author of the first American dictionary.

The roots of early American architecture can be seen in the seventeenth-century **limestone cottage** from the Cotswold Hills region of England. This 1620 house is surrounded by an English-style garden and a stone fence. Also on the Cotswold property are a **forge**, a **dovecote**, and a **stable**. Early American structures include the **Plympton House**, a one-room wooden house from South Sudbury, Massachusetts; a seventeenth-century **windmill** from Cape Cod; and an **early eighteenth-century house** from Connecticut.

Homes connected with famous Americans include the **Edison Homestead** from Menlo Park, New Jersey; the **Luther Burbank Birthplace**, built in Lancaster, Massachusetts, around 1800; the **George**

Washington Carver Memorial; the **Stephen Foster Memorial**, where recordings of Foster's songs are played; and the late nineteenth-century clapboard house of Orville and Wilbur Wright from Kitty Hawk, North Carolina. Two schools, the **Scotch Settlement School**, which was the first school Henry Ford attended, and the **McGuffey School**, associated with the author of the McGuffey *Readers*, are in the area.

The **Edison Area** contains the buildings connected with Thomas Edison's invention of the electric light bulb. **Edison's Research Laboratory, Machine Shop**, and **Carpenter's Shop** were moved from Menlo Park, New Jersey. Edison developed 420 of his more than 1,000 patented inventions in the New Jersey laboratory. The lab is restored to the way it looked on October 21, 1879, when the first successful incandescent lamp was tested. On the second floor of the laboratory are many of Edison's inventions, including the phonograph, mimeograph, telephone transmitter, and radio tube.

Many of Edison's assistants lived in **Sarah Jordan's Boardinghouse** (1870), which is now adjacent to the laboratory. The boardinghouse was one of the first homes to be lit by electricity; heavy electrical cords lead to it from the laboratory. Two other Edison laboratories from West Orange, New Jersey, and Fort Myers, Florida, are in the Edison Area.

The **Henry Ford Birthplace** is a simple two-story white clapboarded farmhouse built by Henry's father, William, in Dearborn in 1860. Ford restored the house to the way it looked in his childhood. The **Bagley Avenue Brick Shed** where Ford built his first car is nearby.

The **Trades and Manufactures Area** focuses on America's transition from an agricultural society to an industrial power. Included are the **Harahan Sugar Mill, Spofford Up-and-Down Sawmill, Tripp Up-and-Down Sawmill** (1855), **Armington and Sims Machine Shop and Foundry, Richart Carriage Shop** (1851), **Macon Brick Works, Loranger Gristmill** (1832), **Plymouth Carding Mill** (1850), the **pottery**, and the **printing office**.

Suwanee Park, a turn-of-the-century family entertainment center, was added to Greenfield Village in the early 1970s. The arcade includes antique game machines and tests of skill, an authentic merry-go-round, a Victorian bandstand, and a century-old ice-cream parlor from Massachusetts. Suwanee Park is located on a lagoon, and across the lagoon lies **Suwanee Island**, with its nature trails and picnic area. It can be reached by raft during the summer. Rides are available on the steam-powered paddle-wheeler *Suwanee*, which operates on the lagoon.

In addition to steamboat rides, visitors can take a narrated horse-drawn carriage ride through the village, ride the steam railroad on a two-mile trip around the perimeter of the village, or take a riverboat ride or a Model T Ford ride. A fee is charged for each of the rides.

You'll need two days in Dearborn because it takes another day to go through the fourteen-acre **Henry Ford Museum.** The facade of the museum duplicates the exterior of Independence Hall, Congress Hall, and the old City Hall in Philadelphia. **Transportation** is the theme of the best and most complete collection in the museum. Displays include aircraft, hundreds of gleaming automobiles, horse-drawn vehicles, electric trolleys, bicycles, motorcycles, fire engines, steam locomotives, and other trains.

The museum also has a large exhibit of **American furniture and other decorative arts** dating from the seventeenth to the late nineteenth centuries. Antique merchandise and crafts—toys, pewter, millinery, guns, cameras, and mechanical musical instruments—are displayed in the **Street of Shops**.

The historical development of everyday devices such as the vacuum cleaner, stove, and refrigerator are exhibited in the **home arts section**. Dairying, plowing, planting, and harvesting machinery ranging from cotton gins to huge traction engines comprise the **agricultural collection**. The machines that helped bring about the Industrial Revolution are in the **power and shop machinery section**. A **lighting collection** traces lighting devices from fat, resin, and candles to modern electrical devices. The **communications exhibit** contains typewriters; printing presses; mimeograph, telegraph, and telegram machines; radios; and televisions.

The **Activities Center** is a marvelous hands-on area where children can manipulate wooden telephones, send telegraph codes, put on a radio headset, ride a one-wheeled bike, or play a player piano.

The second floor of the museum concentrates on the **life of Henry Ford**. Personal belongings, tools, letters, photographs, his first engine, and his first car are displayed.

Many special events are held annually: Muzzle-Loaders Festival in June; Colonial Music and Military Muster, Fire Engine Muster, and 1890s Outing in July; Bluegrass Festival in August; Old Car Festival and Autumn Harvest Festival in September; and Christmas Celebration in December.

Pendarvis

**Restoration of 1830s Cornish lead miners'
homes; State Historical Site**

Address: 114 Shake Rag Street, Mineral Point, WI 53565
Telephone: (608)987-2122
Location: In Mineral Point, Wisconsin, off State Highway 151;
Mineral Point is 131 miles from Milwaukee and 175 miles from
Chicago
Open: Daily, May 1 to October 31; 10:00 A.M. to 5:00 P.M., week-
ends and weekdays during July and August; 9:00 A.M. to 4:00 P.M.,
weekdays in May, June, September, and October
Admission: Adults, $3.00; children, $1.00; adult groups, $2.40;
senior citizens 65 or over, 20% discount
Restaurants: Walker House, Royal Inn Supper Club
Shops: Gift Shop, books, pamphlets, souvenirs
Facilities: Visitors' Center, nearby picnic and playground areas

WHERE TO STAY
Motels/Hotels, Mineral Point: The Point Motel, Highway 151
(Ridge Street), 53565, (608)987-3112, $; Dairyland Motel, 535
Ridge Street, 53565, (608)987-3141, $
Camping, Mineral Point: Harding Trailer Park and Campgrounds,
Highway 23, 53565, (608)987-3456

HISTORY

In 1827, Stephen Taylor, a nineteenth-century traveler, described Mineral Point as

> . . . a piece of land elevated about 200 feet, narrowing and descending to a point, situated in the midst of a valley, as it were—a ravine bounding the same both eastward and westward, through which tributaries of the Pekatonica River flow, uniting in a wider valley to the southward. It was upon this point that the "leads were struck," the fame of which spread, and so quickly become the center of attraction, the miners flocking to them from every quarter. . . .

By the mid-1830s, the town's population was more than 2,000. When Wisconsin became a territory in 1836, Mineral Point residents sought—optimistically though unsuccessfully—to have the territorial capital established there.

In cold weather, miners without homes lived near the mines in holes dug into the sides of hills. It was from these early miners, who "hibernated" in dugouts like badgers, that Wisconsin received its nickname, the Badger State.

The first permanent homes in the community were erected by Cousin Jacks and Cousin Jennies who arrived from Cornwall, England, during the 1830s and 1840s. The Cornishmen, among the best miners in the world, brought with them the techniques they had used in Cornwall's mines. They also brought an expert knowledge of stonecutting and masonry, which they used to build limestone houses like those they had left in England. Most of these stone and log houses, more than thirty of them, were built in a ravine along a street that became known as Shake Rag Under the Hill. (The miners' wives would shake rags to call their husbands to dinner when the men were working at nearby mines.)

Using Cornish construction methods, the miners quarried the limestone from under their houses. Only the stones on the street side of the house were dressed, or *faced,* and the face stones were cut carefully to fit together. On the sides of the house, the stone was cemented with mortar.

The rectangular houses with interior end chimneys had walls eighteen inches thick, oak floors and trim, and square, handmade iron nails. The gabled roofs were made of wooden shakes (shingles).

There were about 7,000 Cornish in the entire lead-mining region in 1850, settled in Hazel Green, Platteville, and Shullsburg, as well as Mineral Point. They were hard-rock miners, in contrast with the surface-mining Americans. The Cornish introduced the safety fuse for blasting, a slow-burning fuse that allowed miners to light it and still have ample time to get out of the mine. The Cornish probably made up no more than a fifth of the population in the lead country, but their colorful names, customs, and speech were memorable. Giants and pixies were favorite folklore characters. Anyone who lost his way was said to be *pixilated* (bewitched). The only method of avoiding a pixie spell was to wear clothing inside out. A few Cornish expressions are: *to tough pipe* (to sit down to rest and smoke a pipe); *put 'ome the door* (close the door); and *a dish o' tay* (cup of tea).

After 1847, lead production, and with it the importance of Mineral Point, declined. Some of the miners turned to farming; others joined the California gold rush or went to other mining areas. The houses along Shake Rag Alley fell into disrepair.

In 1935, Robert Neal and Edgar Hellum decided to save at least one of the log and limestone houses from destruction. They purchased a one-story cottage that they named Pendarvis, after a village in Cornwall, and began painstakingly restoring it to its 1830s appearance. They removed any additions or improvements and bought restoration materials from Cornish houses that were being demolished.

Neal and Hellum eventually restored several other houses and furnished them with antiques and mining artifacts. In 1971, the Wisconsin State Historical Society took over the site.

TOUR

Neal and Hellum's first cottage, **Pendarvis**, lent its name to the restored mining village. It now serves as the **Visitors' Center**.

Trelawny (1828), next to Pendarvis, is a two-story rectangular limestone house featuring an interior end chimney and a gabled roof.

Polperro is a three-story stone and log house built in 1828. Three families occupied Polperro, one on each floor. The low ceilings contribute to the cramped feeling inside the rather small space, where large families cooked, ate, and slept during long Wisconsin winters. The miners and their families led a very hard life in crowded conditions, and visitors can well imagine their circumstances after being inside these homes.

Tamblyn's Row is a three-unit row house. Although the three structures were built at different times, they are contiguous. When Neal and Hellum began restoring Tamblyn's Row, they were surprised to discover a *kiddlywink* (a Cornish pub), completely hidden by dirt and undergrowth, on the lower level of the building. This charming room, with its stone walls, beamed ceiling, and end fireplace, is furnished with trestle tables and Windsor chairs. Here miners once played board games and enjoyed much-earned drinks and companionship.

The end two-story log house contains a **shop** with books, souvenirs, and pamphlets related to Wisconsin history. The attractive **Cornish gardens** have ferns, daisies, and columbines in bloom.

SIDE TRIPS

Mineral Point Hill, across the road from Pendarvis, is pockmarked with abandoned surface lead diggings and remnants of once-shafted lead mines. Here you'll find the **Merry Christmas Zinc Mine**, which opened in 1906, as well as the **badger holes**. Rusting mining equipment is strewn along the path. Mineral Point Hill offers a pleasing panorama of Pendarvis.

The **Walker House**, at 1 Water Street, (608)987-2000, is a charming former hotel; it was built in 1836. Parts of the hotel have already been restored, and work is in progress on others. Its restaurant features Cornish specialties such as Cornish pasty (a dough filled with beef, potatoes, and onions) and bread pudding with ice cream and caramel.

Shake Rag Alley is an attractively designed craft area with restored buildings and many working craftsmen, including a weaver, blacksmith, potter, and stained-glass artist. The gardens and pathways are planted with pansies, impatiens, and ferns. Admission: adults, $1.75; children, $1.25.

There is also a fine weaving school with an interesting textile museum called the **Looms**. A former brewery, the Looms, located at the far end of Shake Rag Street, is open daily May to October, 10:00 A.M. to 5:00 P.M. Admission: adults, $2.00; children, $1.00.

There are many other shops in town, including a needlecraft shop and various artists' studios.

W I S C O N S I N

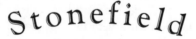

**Recreated 1890s–1900 agricultural
museum, 1890s farmstead, replica 1890s
crossroads village; State Historical Site**

Address: Stonefield, Cassville, WI 53806
Telephone: (608)725-5210
Location: Located in Nelson Dewey State Park at junction of State

Highways 81 and 133, midway between Dubuque, Iowa, and Prairie du Chien, Wisconsin, on the banks of the Mississippi River
Open: Daily, Memorial Day to Labor Day, 9:00 A.M. to 5:00 P.M.
Admission: Adults, $3.50; children 5 to 17, $1.00; senior citizens 65 and over, $2.80. Tickets sold from 9:00 A.M. to 3:30 P.M.
Restaurants: Confectionery Shop
Shops: Gift Shop, books, lead crystal, glassware, souvenirs
Facilities: Picnic area, horse-drawn carriage rides

WHERE TO STAY

Motels/Hotels, Cassville: Sand Bar Motel, P.O. Box 51, 53806, (608)725-5300, $; Eagle's Roost, 1034 Jack Oak Road, 53806, (608)725-5553, $

Camping, Cassville: Bertom Lake, Pleasant Valley, Iowa, 52762, (319)332-6696, for reservations near Cassville, Wisconsin; Nelson Dewey State Park, Route VV, 53806, (608)725-5374

Motels/Hotels, Prairie du Chien: Brisbois Motor Inn, 533 North Marquette Road, 53821, 1-800-356-5850, $; Holiday Motel, 1010 South Marquette Road, 53821, (608)326-2448, $; Prairie Motel, 1616 South Marquette Road, 53821, (608)326-6461, $

HISTORY

As you visit Stonefield, keep in mind the *crossroads village* concept. Like many small midwestern towns of the 1890s, Stonefield was a distribution and service center for nearby farm families, meeting commercial, social, cultural, religious, and educational needs. A visit to town on a Saturday or Sunday was a major event in the lives of many rural families. A village such as Stonefield, with a population of about 500, had churches, stores, a school, a post office, and a railroad depot. It was a meeting place where families could visit, renew acquaintances, and discuss politics and the economy. It was the place where the farm met the town.

Stonefield recreates life in a Wisconsin crossroads village at the turn of the century with recently constructed buildings, offices, shops, and stores in the 1890s style. The Wisconsin Historical Society plans to construct additional buildings. The buildings are furnished with authentic period pieces.

The concept underlying Stonefield is to provide visitors with a more direct experience with the past than can be permitted in museum villages, where the buildings and their furnishings need to be protected because of their age or delicate condition. Stonefield offers hands-on experience, so children as well as adults have an opportunity to get a more direct sense of the past in an unrestricted setting.

As a crossroads village, Stonefield does not represent an isolated community that is frozen in time. It illustrates a busy and active village that was at the crossroads not only geographically but also in time. As a crossroads in time, Stonefield recreates both the rural past and the transformation of the United States during the 1890s into a more technological society.

TOUR

Stonefield, in the Nelson Dewey State Park, is named for Dewey's 2,000-acre farm and estate on the bluffs of the Mississippi River. The park contains the restored **home of Nelson Dewey,** Wisconsin's first governor, the **State Farm Museum,** and **Stonefield,** which is a trust of the Wisconsin State Historical Society.

Stonefield is built around a **town square** with a bandstand. You enter the village through the **covered bridge,** and can visit the buildings on a self-guided walking tour. There are also guides at many of the buildings who provide brief descriptions and, often, craft demonstrations.

Muddy Hollow School is a typical one-room country school, where the basics of reading, writing, arithmetic, and morality were taught to the children growing up as the nineteenth century ended. The school seems permeated with the knowledge, values, and attitudes of McGuffey's *Readers,* which stressed Victorian morality, old-fashioned American patriotism, and the Puritan work ethic. The school was used until the mid-1950s.

The **Mink and Rydell Pharmacy** recreates an all-purpose small-town drugstore, which dispensed everything from drugs and patent medicines to sundries and phosphates. At the turn of the century, doctors filled their own prescriptions, and druggists sold their own concoctions. The drugstore is named for Fred Mink of Cassville and Otto Rydell of Superior, two pharmacists who donated their equipment and stock to Stonefield.

Otto's Barber Shop was a meeting place where the local men could swap stories and discuss business and politics, as well as get a shave and haircut. On display are washbasins, pitchers, razors, spitoons, and a large collection of shaving mugs that were personalized for regular customers. Two red velour barber chairs are the focus of the shop's interior.

In **Maude's Millinery Shop,** ladies' hats were designed to the customer's orders. Although many towns once had such hat shops, they were gradually replaced by more general ladies clothing stores and mail-order catalogs. The shop contains the fabrics, feathers, ribbons, materials, and models used in the millinery trade.

The impact of social and economic change is well illustrated by the contents in **Harrington's Harness and Hardware Store.** As long as horses dominated plowing and transportation, the harness shop specialized in making and selling bridles, harnesses, and saddles. When horses were replaced by tractors and automobiles, the specialized harness shop diversified into a more general hardware store. This diversification is reflected in the contents of Stonefield's hardware store: kitchen utensils, pots, pans, stoves, tools, washing machines, and other period items.

Jones Meat Market is a typical small-town butcher shop, in which the owner slaughtered, dressed, and sold meat. The market carried fresh meat, ham, bacon, fish, lard, tallow, sausage, and other items. Butcher shops were patronized by town folks; farmers raised and dressed their own meat.

Stonefield's **Farmer's Store**, the village general store, stocked items not produced on the family farm, including dry goods, leather goods, farm equipment, household appliances, kerosene, turpentine, animal feed, tea, coffee, dried beans and peas, crackers, pickles, dried fruits, and cereals. Food items arrived at the general store in bulk and were sold by the pound. In many instances, a barter system was used, with farmers trading their produce for goods.

Gastrow's Carpenter Shop was built according to the construction methods of the 1890s. Using oak timber, carpenters used handsaws and hand-boring tools to make tenon-and-mortise joints, which were pegged together with oak dowels. The shop displays carpenter's tools and also contains a wagonmaker's and cooper's shop. The cooper's shop is of particular interest because barrel making was an important occupation in the 1890s; many items were transported and stored in wooden barrels.

At **Joe Brown's Blacksmith Shop**, the craft of blacksmithing, which was so essential to nineteenth-century life, is demonstrated. Townspeople depended on the blacksmith for horseshoeing and for making nails, hinges, and other metal fixings. The blacksmith fashioned these items from scratch with the use of fire, forge, and hammer.

P. & V. Livery Stable boarded horses and operated and rented horse-drawn carriages. It consists of a frame barn and office. There are two horse-drawn buses for visitors.

The **Town Square Bandstand** was the major gathering place for concerts, patriotic celebrations, and political rallies. Many towns had their own bands, which performed at weekly concerts.

Influenced by German immigrants, many Wisconsin towns had a **saloon**, an informal social club for the village men. This presents a sharp contrast to a New England village, where the Puritan ethic (and the local temperance society) would have condemned such a building as a den of iniquity. Stonefield's saloon no longer serves alcoholic drinks, but it still contains a long, highly polished wooden bar.

The **Russell Photographic Gallery** was an important institution in

Stonefield. The photographs now on display capture the many special occasions of small-town life. It is possible to have your photograph taken in the old-fashioned manner at the gallery.

The **Stonefield Gazette Office and Press** illustrate the workings of the weekly newspaper. On display is the leverless press, a lightweight flatbed press introduced in the 1890s. Visitors can see the press, type, and copies of the newspapers, advertisements, and manifestos that were printed on it.

The **Bank of Stonefield** is modeled after the Fox River Bank of DePere, which was established in 1836 as one of the state's first financial institutions. The teller's cages, furniture, and safe were brought to Stonefield from other banks throughout Wisconsin.

The lawyer was one of a small town's important citizens. He was involved in drawing up wills, recording deeds, and conducting litigation regarding land. The **C. & J. Frank Dunn Law Office** is named after the three Dunn brothers who formed the legal firm. Charles Dunn became the first chief justice of the territorial supreme court. Among the office furnishings is a desk once used by Robert La Follette, a Wisconsin governor and senator who became a national progressive leader in the early twentieth century.

The **August Derleth Bookstore** is named after a well-known and prolific Wisconsin regional novelist. One of Derleth's works is *Shadow in the Glass*, a fictionalized biography of Nelson Dewey. The small-town bookstore sold stationery, pens, cigars, tobacco, and magazine subscriptions, as well as books.

The **Cornelius Jewelry Store**, named for a store in Prairie du Chien, is stocked with furniture and equipment from the E. A. Wendt Jewelry Store in Horicon. The store sold jewelry, watches, clocks, silverware, china, porcelain, mirrors, and other decorative items. Jewelry stores of the 1890s also fitted customers with eyeglasses.

The **Confectionery Shop** was as popular with the youngsters of the 1890s as it is with today's children. It was a place of refreshment and relaxation during a shopping trip to town on a hot, humid summer day. Ice-cream cones, sodas, and sundaes made with rich, locally made ice cream were the chief delights; but confectioneries also sold candies such as mint sticks, taffy, rock candy, lemon drops, and red and black licorice sticks. The shop is outfitted with a large marble soda fountain, brass fixtures and decorations, and mahogany booths; it serves lunches, sandwiches, soft drinks, ice cream, and candy to visitors.

The **Telephone Exchange** highlights the technological advances that would transform America. The telephone, invented by Alexander Graham Bell in 1876, was of great importance in speeding communication throughout the country and reducing the isolation of rural life. In small towns, the party line and the local telephone operator became community fixtures. Stonefield's magneto system is still operative and is an excellent example of a typical turn-of-the-century network.

The reconstruction of the **Doctor's Office** was sponsored by the Wisconsin State Medical Society. The office is patterned after that of a physician in Kewaunee. It contains medical charts, diagrams, books, and the examining apparatus used by physicians of the period.

Although tobacco is usually regarded as a crop native to southern states such as Virginia and the Carolinas, it was and still is raised in some areas of Wisconsin. Wisconsin-grown tobacco was particularly esteemed for cigar making, and Stonefield's **Cigar Factory** is furnished with equipment from local tobacco enterprises.

Wisconsin is famous as the nation's dairy state, and both its small towns and its larger cities contained creameries where butter and other milk products were made. The **Creamery** at Stonefield illustrates the technological shift from dairy production on the farm itself to the more efficient production of butter in creameries.

In small-town America, the church was often the center of social as well as religious life. Stonefield's **Church** is patterned after the United Presbyterian Church of Dover; its pulpit and pews are of 1890s vintage.

The **Cheese Factory**, a common sight in many Wisconsin towns, represents an important industry that has retained its national and international reputation. The cheese factory is built of rough-sawed cedar board and roofed with hand-split cedar shakes.

Of vital importance to any town at the turn of the century was the railroad. To be located on a railroad line meant that the town's products could be sent to market in the larger cities. The **Railroad Depot** of Stonefield, like those of other crossroads villages, was the scene of the arrival and departure of goods and people. Stonefield's depot and railroad yard enable visitors to return to the time when railroads formed the country's vital transportation arteries.

Stonefield was located along a main line of the Chicago, Burlington, and Northern Railroad, which was built in 1885. The line, which followed the Mississippi River, connected the Burlington's Illinois system with that of LaCrosse, Wisconsin, and St. Paul, Minnesota. Stonefield's depot contains locomotives, passenger and freight cars, and a caboose, which allows visitors to see the way the railroad crews and track gangs of *gandy dancers* lived and worked.

SIDE TRIPS

The **Nelson Dewey Park** at Cassville is operated by the Wisconsin Department of Natural Resources. Its 800 acres provide facilities for picnicking, hiking, and camping. **Dewey's Farm** is the restored home of Nelson Dewey (1813–1889), Wisconsin's first governor. It is adjacent to Stonefield Village; (806)725-5374.

**Recreated nineteenth-century
ethnic farmsteads**

Address: Route 2, Box 18, Eagle, WI 53119
Telephone: (414)594-2116
Location: Near Eagle, Wisconsin, off State Highway 67. Eagle is 35 miles from downtown Milwaukee and 75 miles from Chicago.
Open: Daily, April 15 to November 15; 9:00 A.M. to 4:00 P.M., April, May, June, September, October, and November; 10:00 A.M. to 5:00 P.M., July, August, and all weekends
Admission: Adults, $5.50; children 5 to 17, $2.50; senior citizens, $4.40
Restaurants: Clausing Barn Restaurant
Shops: Gift shop in Visitors' Center, nineteenth-century reproductions of metal, fabric, and wood household items, toys, games, and books
Facilities: Visitors' Center, picnic areas, provisions available for handicapped

WHERE TO STAY
Camping, Eagle: Ottawa Lake State Forest, 53119, (414)594-2135
Resorts, Elkhorn: Lauderdale Lake Resort, Route 1, 53121, (414)742-2200, $$–$$$

Resorts, Oconomowoc: Olympia Resort and Spa, 1350 Royale Mile Road, 53066, (414)567-0311, $$$$

Motels/Hotels, Waukesha: Algiers, 19035 West Blue Mound Road, 53186, (414)786-3600, $$; Best Western, 2111 East Moreland Boulevard, 53186, (414)547-7770, $$; Holiday Inn, 2417 Blue Mound Road, 53186, (414)786-0460, $$; Quality Inn, 2510 Plaza Court, 53186, (414)786-6015, $$

Camping, Waukesha: Muskego Park, 500 Riverview Road, 53186, (414)548-7790

HISTORY

Old World Wisconsin is a restored recreation administered by the State Historical Society of Wisconsin. It is an outdoor ethnographic museum illustrating the cultural and architectural contributions of ethnic immigrants to rural Wisconsin in the nineteenth and early twentieth centuries. At the present time, four of ten planned ethnic units have been completed: the German, Norwegian, Danish, and Finnish farmsteads. Each clearly conveys the lives of these ethnic pioneers.

Because the basic housing patterns were all created by northern European immigrants, interesting comparisons and contrasts can be made. It is also worthwhile to note how Wisconsin's climate and environment produced variations in the architectural styles that were transported by the settlers from Europe.

Old World Wisconsin's 576 acres, located in the town of Eagle in the southwestern corner of Waukesha County, are within the boundaries of the southern part of the Kettle Moraine State Forest and the Ice Age National Scientific Area. This area was formed at the juncture of the Lake Michigan and Green Bay glacial fields, two massive ice sheets, coming from opposite directions, that deposited glacial materials to create the Kettle Moraine. When the ice melted, channels were cut in the gravel by streams, and the melting buried ice produced depressions known as *kettles*. The region is known for its low, flat, marsh areas running in a north-south direction. The Kettle Moraine area contains native prairie grasses, flowers, shrubs, and trees, such as oaks, junipers, and firs.

The designers of Old World Wisconsin have recreated ethnic life in its natural setting by careful use of space. The farmsteads are scattered throughout the area, which may mean walking some distance. The effect achieved, however, is a harmonious blending of space, time, and nature.

TOUR

The **Visitors' Center** was designed to prepare the visitor for the experience of returning to nineteenth-century rural Wisconsin. It includes **Lueskow House**, built in 1850 and moved from Dodge

County as an example of the German *Fachwerk,* or half-timbered, house. This is where you find administrative and information services.

The center's **Ramsey Barn**, built in 1841, was moved from Fort Atkinson, Jefferson County. It houses the gift shop, restrooms, security office, and orientation theater. The fifteen-minute slide and sound orientation program uses the diaries and photographs of the immigrant settlers to tell of their journeys and experiences. The **gift shop** sells reproduction household items, toys, and games, as well as books on ethnic cooking and nineteenth-century life, crafts, arts, and Wisconsin history.

To complete the Visitors' Center complex, **Clausing Barn**, built in 1897, was moved from its original site in Mequon, Ozaukee County. It is one of the few remaining eight-sided barns built by German immigrants. It has exhibits on the first floor and a cafeteria-style restaurant on the lower level.

Old World Wisconsin can be seen with a self-guided walking tour; guided group tours should be arranged in advance.

Village

The path from the Visitors' Center leads to what will be a **Wisconsin village of the 1870s**. It currently contains Saint Peter's Church and Harmony Town Hall.

St. Peter's Church, built in 1839 to serve German Catholics in Milwaukee, has been restored to its 1889 Greek Revival and Gothic architectural styles. The altar, altar railing, and stations of the cross are wooden. The recessed aisle was meant to keep Wisconsin's cold winter air from creating a draft.

Harmony Town Hall, built in 1876 in Harmony, Rock County, exemplifies the frame clapboard town meetinghouse that settlers from New England brought to Wisconsin.

German Area

Leaving the village, visitors follow the half-mile path leading to the **German Area**, which contains houses, barns, and other farm buildings built by settlers from Germany.

Koepsell House, built by master carpenter Friedrich Koepsell in 1858 in Washington County, has been restored to its 1880 appearance. The house is typical of Pomeranian *Fachwerk* style. This half-timber one-and-a-half-story house has a gabled roof, central brick chimney, and a central hall.

The **Turck-Schottler House**, which is on the National Register, was built in 1847 in Germantown, Washington County, and is restored to its 1875 appearance. An example of German *Blockbau* style, the two-and-a-half-story house is constructed of logs with loam and rye straw chinking.

Schultz House, built in 1856 in German, Dodge County, is in the traditional half-timbered style. It features mud-straw insulation and the central "black kitchen" that was used for baking, cooking, and smoking meat. Although black kitchens were common in southern Germany, the Wisconsin wind and rains made them impractical, and this transplant was eventually abandoned.

Among the farm buildings located in this area are the **Hilgendorf Machine Shed** (1865), the **Hilgendorf Cattle and Horse Barn** (1855), the **Koepke Barn** (1874), the **Witte Outhouse** (1880), the **Held Barn** (1855), the **Jung Barn and Smokehouse** (1875), the **Fassbender Granary** (1865), the **Koepsel Stable** (1855), and the **Gruhe Barn** (1855).

Near the farmsteads are small gardens of onions, cabbage, berries, and flax and pens of livestock such as chickens, ducks, geese, and horses. Guides describe the various skills and crafts that were practiced by the German immigrant farmers.

Norwegian Area

A one-and-one-fifth-mile walk through nature areas will bring you to the **Norwegian Area**.

Fossebrekke House was erected in 1841 in Newark, Rock County. It is constructed of oak logs.

Kualle House, built in 1848 in Dunkirk, Dane County, and restored to its 1865 appearance, features a *svalgong,* or covered porch, which provided additional shelter from harsh weather.

The **Veggli House,** built in 1843 in Plymouth, Rock County, is restored to its 1865 appearance.

Raspberry School, built by three Norwegian families in Russell, Bayfield County, was named after Lake Superior's Raspberry Bay. It has been restored to its 1906 appearance. The school, in operation until 1914, was attended by the children of Norwegian and Swedish families. It is a good example of the one-room, rural school, which housed all eight grades and was taught by one teacher. The building contains educational materials of the period, such as books, papers, and maps.

Other structures in the Norwegian area are the **Dahlen Corncrib** (1875), the log **Sorbergshagen Barn** (1872), the **Lisbakken Granary** (1860), and the **Bosboen Barn** (1865).

Danish Area

The **Danish Area,** adjacent to the Norwegian, contains the **Pedersen House,** built in 1872 in Luck, Polk County, and the **Jensen Barn,** 1886.

Finnish Area

The **Finnish Area,** located seven-tenths of a mile from the Danish, completes the tour of Old World Wisconsin.

The **Ketola House**, built in 1894 in Bayfield County, has been restored to its 1915 appearance. It is an example of the log construction used by Finnish farmers.

Rankihen House, built in 1892, in Oulu, Bayfield County, looks just as it did in 1897.

The **Ronkainen Sauna** (1919) was built in Maple County. The sauna was an essential feature of Finnish farm life.

Other structures found in this area are the **Kortesmaa Dairy Barn** (1910), the **Makeld Stable** (1911), the **Kortesmaa Granary** (1910), the **Lanta Barn** (1919), and the **Rankinen Stable** (1898).

Restoration of an 1850s Swedish religious commune; NRHP, State Historical Site

Address: Bishop Hill Heritage Association, Bishop Hill, IL 61419
Telephone: (309)927-3899
Location: 157 miles west of Chicago, 20 miles east of Interstate 74, 2 miles north of State Highway 34 in Henry County
Open: The Bjorklund Hotel and Colony Church are open daily, 9:00 A.M. to 5:00 P.M., year-round. The Henry County Historical Museum is open daily, 10:00 A.M. to 5:00 P.M., April to November.
Admission: Free except for the Henry County Historical Society Museum, which is $1.00 for adults; children free
Restaurants: Pies un Stuff, Red Oak Tea Room, Valkommen Inn
Shops: Colony Blacksmith Shop, handwoven mats, runners, blankets, iron items, brooms, pottery, baskets
Facilities: Gallery, exhibits, museum

WHERE TO STAY

Motels/Hotels, Galesburg: Holiday Inn, Rural Route 2, 61401, (309)344-1111, $$; Howard Johnson's, 29 Public Square, 61401, (309)343-9161, $$; Jumer's Continental Inn, East Main Street,

61401, (309)343-7151, $$; Regal 8 Inn, 1487 North Henderson Street, 61401, (309)344-2401, $

Camping, Galesburg: Allison Lake Storey Campgrounds, Lake Storey Road, 61401, (309)344-1534

HISTORY

The story of Bishop Hill, founded in 1846 as a commune by 800 immigrants, began in Sweden with the charismatic religious leader Erik Jansson. In 1830, at age twenty-two, Jansson, who was a farmer, suffered a severe attack of rheumatism while tilling his fields. He prayed for and received healing and regarded his cure as a miraculous sign from God and became a lay preacher.

In the early 1840s, Jansson joined the Reader, or Lasare, movement established by Olof and Jonas Olsson. Readers were Fundamentalists who dissented from the formalism of Sweden's Lutheran church. Jansson became a leader of a pietistical group that conducted clandestine prayer meetings. His followers regarded him as a second Christ. They believed that the Bible was the only book that had religious authority. Janssonists attempted unsuccessfully to change the Lutheran church's position on religious books but eventually resorted to burning Lutheran literature, for which Jansson was arrested.

While being transported to prison in 1845, Jansson escaped, and he and his family began their journey to America. After a three-month ocean voyage, a trip across the Great Lakes, and a 150-mile trek on foot from Chicago, Jansson and a group of 400 Swedish immigrants arrived at Bishop Hill, a community previously established, at Jansson's direction, by Olof Olsson. It was named after Biskopskulla, Sweden, where Jansson was born.

The Janssonists settled into dugout living quarters. These shelters, half cave and half timber, were built into the side of a ravine that ran through the town. Worship services were conducted in a tent. Ninety-six colonists died that first winter because of exposure and lack of food.

However, crops were planted in the spring, and a brick kiln was built in which adobe bricks were made for construction of a diversity of permanent buildings.

Approximately 1,500 immigrants left Sweden for Bishop Hill between 1846 and 1854. Many died en route or fell victim to epidemics. Others later became dissatisfied and moved to nearby towns. Approximately 1,100 Janssonists lived in Bishop Hill between 1846 and 1861, although the population never exceeded 800 at any one time. The Janssonists represented a cross section of the Swedish population: blacksmiths, tailors, shoemakers, weavers, tanners, carpenters, farmers, and servants.

Fifteen landowners in Sweden sold their large farms and contributed the money, as all the colonists did, to the communal fund to transport Janssonists to America. Although some left husbands and wives behind, great efforts were made to bring as many relatives as possible to America.

Erik Jansson supervised all activities in the colony. But in 1850, he was murdered by John Root, the husband of his cousin Charlotta. Root wanted to leave Bishop Hill with his wife and son, but their marriage contract stated that if he left, his wife would not have to go with him. Root made several attempts to force his wife and child to accompany him, but Jansson sent men to return Charlotta and her son to Bishop Hill. On May 13, 1850, when Jansson was in Cambridge, Illinois, attending to court cases involving the colony, Root shot him through a window of the courthouse.

After Jansson's murder, the religious leadership of the colony fell to Jonas Olsson. Seven governing trustees were selected, and in 1854, the colony was legally incorporated. Rapid economic growth followed. The colony's landholdings were 12,000 to 14,000 fertile, well-watered acres. Business prospered as the Janssonists sold such products as cloth, clothing, wagons, harnesses, saddles, shoes, furniture, and broomcorn to a growing frontier population. Between 1848 and 1861, Bishop Hill was a major center of commerce and the overnight stage stop between Rock Island and Peoria.

Eventually, dissension arose over religious and social issues; and despite economic prosperity, the colony was dissolved by mutual consent in 1861. Property was divided among the members, many of whom continued to live in the area. Most of today's residents of Bishop Hill and its vicinity are descendants of original colonists or later Swedish immigrants.

In 1946, Bishop Hill became an Illinois State Memorial and is now both a National and a State Historic Site. The Illinois Department of Conservation is custodian of the nearly restored colony church and the partially restored Bjorklund Hotel. The Bishop Hill Heritage Association, a nonprofit corporation interested in preservation, restored the Steeple Building and is also restoring the blacksmith shop, the hospital building, and the colony store.

TOUR

Bishop Hill is not an outdoor museum but a living town that has changed little since the 1850s. No appreciable expansion or construction has marred the mid-nineteenth-century atmosphere. Although some colony buildings are no longer standing, seventeen original buildings remain. Six are either museums or shops; the others are privately owned and not open to the public. There are no reconstructions.

The **Colony Church** (1848), Bishop Hill's first permanent building, was a dual-purpose structure. Community members both worshiped and lived there. The church is a three-story white frame gambrel-roofed building. Two sets of outside stairs lead to the second-floor sanctuary, which is beautifully but simply designed. White walls contrast with pews made of native black walnut and turned maple rungs. The pulpit panels were painted to resemble marble. A center divider separates the men's pews on the west side and the women's and children's pews on the east. The wood and wrought-iron chandeliers, whose design was inspired by the brass chandeliers found in Swedish cathedrals, are reproductions. The unheated sanctuary, which could seat 1,000 people, was used twice each weekday and three times on Sunday for services that lasted two hours or more.

On the first floor and in the basement were twenty dwelling rooms, ten on each floor. Each family had one room, which served primarily as a sleeping room; the cooking, laundry, and bathing were done in other buildings.

The colony church was restored to its 1848 appearance by the Illinois Department of Conservation in the 1960s. The sleeping rooms now contain exhibits. **The Sweden They Left** depicts life in Sweden around 1850. Another room focuses on **The Immigration** and the route taken from Sweden to Illinois. Also displayed are items brought from Sweden by the colonists, including shoes, baskets, wooden and metal boxes, pots, Bibles, coins, and photographs of their homes in Sweden.

Another room displays tools used by the colonists and drums, uniforms, and weapons from Company D Fifty-seventh Illinois Infantry, the company Bishop Hill residents served in during the Civil War. Still another exhibit is devoted to the construction process used in building the colony church.

An extensive collection of paintings by Olaf Krans (1838–1916), also housed in the church, is one of the outstanding features of Bishop Hill. Krans emigrated from Sweden in 1850 at the age of 12. This important American primitive painter's subjects were the founders, buildings, landscapes, and pioneer farming practices of Bishop Hill; the scenes were based on his childhood memories. He began the paintings in 1875 and presented the collection of nearly 100 paintings to the village in 1896 at its fiftieth-anniversary observance.

One distinctive though unsettling feature of Krans's portraits, most of which were based on turn-of-the-century photographs, are the subjects' pale blue eyes, which seem to follow the viewer as she or he moves through the room. The bearded, unsmiling men are usually dressed in black suits and white shirts, and the women wear dark dresses. The paintings are appreciated not only for their artistic beauty but also for their rendering of life in the colony during its relatively short existence.

The **Bjorklund Hotel** was built in 1852 as a two-story brick residence but was converted to a hotel when Bishop Hill became the overnight stop on the stage route between Peoria and Rock Island. A series of additions began in 1857. The first were a barroom on the first floor and the hotelkeeper's quarters on the second. Next, a kitchen and second-story quarters were added, making the building U-shaped. A third floor that included a ballroom and a large tower was the last addition.

The hotel was owned by the colony and managed by a noted clockmaker, Sven Bjorklund. In 1861, when the communal period of Bishop Hill ended, Bjorklund became the owner of the hotel, which he operated until his death. The Bjorklund family ran the hotel until the 1920s, when it was converted into a private residence.

The hotel's first floor and a bedroom on the second floor are open to the public. A clock made by Bjorklund still keeps time in the men's sitting room. Other furnishings include an original cherry table, beds, a table, and a bureau. The kitchen has a bake oven with a forty-loaf capacity, a dry sink, a cupboard with white dishes, cooking utensils, and coffee bean roasters. Baskets, pottery, jars, and wooden boxes are on display in the pantry. A knowledgeable guide in period costume conducts the tour.

The **Steeple Building** was built in 1854 as a hotel but came to be used as a school. This three-story Greek Revival brick structure is stuccoed on three sides. A classical portico dominates the facade, and there is a two-story octagonal wooden cupola. The clock, which was built by Sven Bjorklund, Lars Soderquist, and P. O. Blomberg, has four faces, each with one hand that marks the hours only.

The Steeple Building houses the **Henry County Historical Museum**, with memorabilia from the colony and Henry County. A film, *Bishop Hill*, can also be seen in the museum. The **Bishop Hill Historical Research Collections**, a resource center for the study of Swedish immigration, is also in the building.

The **Colony Store** was the center of the colony's commerce with its neighbors. It sold shoes, clothes, cloth, liquor, medicine, lumber, wagons, and harnesses and provided millwork, grain grinding, and blacksmithing. Today, the store sells Swedish and Bishop Hill craft items and books about the colony.

The **Blacksmith Shop** was built in 1857, at a time when trade and industry were becoming increasingly important. Blacksmiths made hardware for wagons, and a ramp at the back of the building led to the area where the wagons were assembled. The wagons were then lowered down the ramp and taken to the carpentry and paint shops.

The blacksmith shop is now a craft center with handmade items for sale, including handwoven shawls, blankets and coverlets, and antique and originally designed jewelry. Hand-thrown pottery, brooms, candles, baskets, and wooden objects are also available. The **carpenter and paint shop**, built in 1852, is now an antique store that features Swedish items.

In the **Bishop Hill Cemetery**, a white marble monument marks Erik Jansson's grave. Below a small depression near the monument are the remains of the ninety-six colonists who died during the first winter. The site of the dugouts is along the upper edge of the ravine that extends northwest at the north end of Park Street.

The Bishop Hill Heritage Association sponsors eight summer workshops in weaving, spinning, dyeing, basket weaving, and blacksmithing taught by local craftspersons. It also sponsors Old Settlers Days and Jordbruksdagarna (Agricultural Days) in September, Sommarmarknad (Summer Market) in mid-August, and Julmarknad (Christmas Market) in late November.

SIDE TRIPS

Knox College, founded in 1837, is located on Cherry and South Streets in Galesburg, 20 miles from Bishop Hill. **Old Main**, the site of a Lincoln-Douglas debate, is an original building still in use. Tours of the college can be arranged by calling (309)343-0112, extension 223.

The **birthplace and boyhood home of Carl Sandburg** (1878–1967), poet, novelist, and Lincoln biographer, is located at 331 East 3rd Street in Galesburg. It is open daily, except Mondays and state holidays, from 9:00 A.M. to noon and from 1:00 to 5:00 P.M. Admission is free.

Nauvoo

Restoration of an 1830–1850 Mormon historical site; National and State Historic Site, NR, NHL, HABS

Address: Nauvoo Restoration, Inc., Visitors' Center, P.O. Box 215, Nauvoo, IL 62354
Telephone: (217)453-2237
Location: On Route 96 along the Mississippi River
Open: Daily, 8:00 A.M. to 8:00 P.M., May to October; 8:00 A.M. to 7:00 P.M., November to April
Admission: Free

Address: Joseph Smith Historic Center, Nauvoo, IL 62354
Telephone: (217)453-2246
Open: Daily, 8:00 A.M. to 8:00 P.M., Memorial Day to Labor Day; 8:30 A.M. to 5:00 P.M., rest of year; closed Thanksgiving, Christmas, and New Year's Day
Admission: Free
Restaurants: In town of Nauvoo but not at historic site
Shops: In town of Nauvoo but not at historic site
Facilities: Visitors' Centers, film, nearby Nauvoo State Park

WHERE TO STAY
Inns, Nauvoo: Hotel Nauvoo, 1290 Mulholland Street, 62354, (217)453-2211, $
Motels/Hotels, Nauvoo: Village Inn, P.O. Box 191, 1350 Parley Street, 62354, (217)453-6634, $; Pioneer Motel, Highway 96, Mulholland Street, 62354, (217)453-2210, $
Camping, Nauvoo: Nauvoo State Park, Highway 96, Durphy Street, Box 337, 62354, (217)453-2512; Breezewood Camp, Highway 96, Rural Route 1, Box 261, 62354, (217)453-6420
Motels/Hotels, Carthage: Carthage Motel, Highway 136, 62321, (217)357-3119, $; Prairie Winds, Highway 136, 62321, (217)357-3101, $
Motels/Hotels, Macomb: Holiday Inn, 1400 North Lafayette Street,

61455, (309)833-5511, $$; Travelodge, 1414 West Jackson Street, 61455, (309)833-4521, $$

Camping, Colchester: Argyle Lake State Park, Rural Route 2, 62326, (309)776-3422

HISTORY

As a historic restoration, Nauvoo is one of the nation's finest; it has been called the Williamsburg of the Midwest. Located on the east bank of the Mississippi River, Nauvoo's wooded bluffs offer a panoramic view to the traveler. Nauvoo's fame comes from its being a holy city, associated with Joseph Smith, founder of the Church of Latter-day Saints, or Mormons. Nauvoo Restoration, Inc., sponsored by the Church of Latter-day Saints, headquartered in Salt Lake City, maintains the large Visitors' Center and the majority of the restored buildings; the Joseph Smith Historic Center and the Smith Homestead and Mansion are maintained by the Reorganized Church of Latter Day Saints of Independence, Missouri.

Although Nauvoo's foremost historical significance is its relationship to Mormonism, it was also the scene of a later experiment in communal living by the Icarians, a group of French immigrants led by Etienne Cabet. In addition to being the scene of a significant restoration, Nauvoo remains an active small town, with shops, schools, and churches.

An understanding of Nauvoo's importance in both American and Mormon church history begins with its relationship to Joseph Smith, the founder and prophet of the Church of Latter-day Saints. Smith, a farmer's son, was born at Sharon, Vermont, on December 23, 1805. In 1819, the Smith family relocated to Manchester, near Palmyra, in New York. There Joseph experienced a series of divine communications that led eventually to the establishment of the Mormon church. It was in this area of New York that Smith, according to Mormon tradition, found the golden plates on the Hill Cumorah that he translated into the *Book of Mormon*. Smith and his followers formally organized as the Church of Jesus Christ of the Latter-day Saints on April 6, 1830, at Fayette, New York.

From 1831 until they purchased Nauvoo in 1839, the Mormons, who faced hostility because of their doctrines, relocated several times. In their quest to establish the New Jerusalem, they first went to Kirtland, Ohio, in 1831. Six years later, in 1837, they migrated to Jackson County, Missouri, where they again faced opposition. In 1839, the Mormons came to the small Mississippi River town of Commerce, Illinois. They purchased land, drained the swamps, and called their new holy city Nauvoo (Hebrew for "the beautiful place").

In 1840, the Illinois legislature passed the Nauvoo charter, which gave the community virtual home rule. Smith, a skilled administrator as well as charismatic religious leader, organized an autonomous theocratic state within a state, with its own government, militia, school system, and university. Under his leadership, the Mormons created a prosperous community of 12,000 inhabitants, making Nauvoo Illinois's largest city at that time. Homes, shops, schools, a newspaper, and a temple were built as the Mormons once again tried to establish their New Jerusalem. Nauvoo's growing political power and economic prosperity, as well as opposition to the Mormon practice of polygamy, ultimately provoked tension between the Mormons and the residents of the surrounding communities.

As tensions grew in western Illinois, Governor Thomas Ford ordered the Illinois militia to place Smith and his brother Hyrum in protective custody in the jail in nearby Carthage. On June 27, 1844, a mob stormed the jail and killed the brothers.

With the death of Smith, the majority of the Mormons, now led by Brigham Young, left Nauvoo to begin their arduous westward trek to Utah, where they founded Salt Lake City in 1847. An estimated 10,000 Mormons were part of this mass migration, one of the largest and most carefully planned in American history, into the territories west of the Mississippi.

When we visited Nauvoo, we met many Mormons, who had come to Nauvoo from Utah and Idaho to visit the city left by their ancestors. Many tour guides are Mormons, often retired couples who are spending some time in residence in Nauvoo as part of their service to the church.

A smaller group of Mormons, the Reorganized Church of Jesus Christ of Latter Day Saints, rejected Brigham Young's election as leader. The Reorganized church, which has its headquarters in Independence, Missouri, recognizes only direct descendants of Joseph Smith as presidents of the church. Thus, the first successor was Smith's son, Joseph Smith III. The Reorganized church maintains several sites at Nauvoo, distinct from those maintained by the larger church.

Although the physical remnants of the Icarians are few, their effort to found a communal society at Nauvoo is also a fascinating episode in American history. Led by the French political philosopher and utopian theorist Etienne Cabet, 260 persons from France and several other European countries came to Nauvoo in 1849 to establish a communal and egalitarian society. Their name, Icarians, came from the utopia that Cabet had described in his novel *Voyage to Icaria*. Although the Icarian experiment ended in 1860, descendants of the Icarians still live in Nauvoo. An Icarian Weekend is held the third weekend in July each year. The Center for Icarian Studies is located at Western Illinois University at Macomb.

Nauvoo's restoration began in the late 1950s with the efforts of Dr.

LeRoy Kimball, who restored the home of Heber C. Kimball, his grandfather. Dr. Kimball then got the Utah-based Mormon church involved in the project.

Most of the work has been done by Nauvoo Restoration, Inc., sponsored by the Church of Latter-day Saints, with headquarters in Salt Lake City, Utah. The state of Illinois purchased a 148-acre tract, now Nauvoo State Historic Site, to encourage further restoration.

TOUR

The **Nauvoo Visitors' Center**, maintained by Nauvoo Restoration, Inc., is open daily from 8:00 A.M. to 8:00 P.M. This large red brick building should be visited first because its film and exhibits provide an excellent orientation to Nauvoo as a significant location in Mormon and American history. Guide service can be arranged. Admission is free.

The **Nauvoo Temple Site** (1841–1865) marks the location of the Nauvoo Temple and illustrates the role of archaeology in restoration. Paintings of the temple, as well as a model, reveal a design of native gray limestone that incorporated classical, medieval, renaissance, and nineteenth-century styles. Among its unique external features were large "moon stones" that formed the base of the pilasters or buttresses, "sun stones" with a face, and "star stones." The temple was topped by a tower, belfry, observatory, and spire.

Construction began in April 1841, and the temple was dedicated on May 1, 1846. But by that time, many of the Mormons had already departed. On October 9, 1848, a fire caused extensive damage to the temple. It was used by the Icarians from 1849 until 1850, when a storm blew down the north wall. The building was then abandoned.

The **Seventies Hall** was reconstructed by Nauvoo Restoration, Inc., which, through archaeological excavation, uncovered the foundations of the original 1844 building. The hall was designed as an educational center for the *seventies*, laymen in the Mormon church who carry on missionary activities. The first floor was used for classes and lectures; the second, for offices, a museum, and library. The hall was sold in 1846 and used as a school from 1866 to 1895; it was demolished in 1915.

The two-story brick **Noble-Smith House** (1843) restored to its original condition by Nauvoo Restoration, Inc., was the home of Joseph Bates Noble until 1846 and then of Lucy Mack Smith, the mother of Joseph Smith.

The **Brigham Young Site and Residence** was the home of Brigham Young (1801–1877) from 1840 to 1845. Like many of the Mormons, Young was born in the East (Vermont) and, upon joining the church, followed Smith westward in the moves that eventually led to Nauvoo.

Young had worked in the construction trade before his conversion and was a skilled builder and carpenter. Evidence of his craftsmanship can be seen in his house. After living in a log structure, Young completed the two-story brick house in 1843. During the summer of 1844, two wings, each one story high, were added. The east wing, which served as Young's office, was the place where many crucial decisions were made about the future of the Mormon church, especially the decision to move westward. Although the furniture and household items are not those of the Young family, they are authentic to Nauvoo's Mormon period. The outbuildings were reconstructed on their original foundations. The trees and plants are those of a typical 1840s garden.

The **Heber C. Kimball Home** is the restored 1845 residence of Heber Chase Kimball (1801–1868), a Mormon leader, missionary to England, and chief advisor to Brigham Young. Kimball, a migrant from the East, had tastes that were sophisticated for frontier Illinois. His house, in the then-popular Federal style, was constructed of brick in the intricate flemish bond pattern.

The **Jonathan Browning Houses and Workshops** are the residence and factory of one of America's most innovative firearm manufacturers. Jonathan Browning learned his gun-making and repairing skills as a youth in Kentucky, Tennessee, and Illinois. He developed multishot, repeating guns and rifles. His invention of revolving multiround cylinders for handguns and rifles made him well known throughout the American West. His son, John Moses Browning, secured patents for the famous Browning automatic rifle.

In 1843, Browning and his wife, Elizabeth, visited Nauvoo and after meeting Joseph Smith joined the Mormon church. They then sold their property in Quincy, moved with their nine children to Nauvoo, and purchased a lot on Main Street. There Browning built his log house and two-story brick house and workshops. The large two-story brick building has been restored to its original condition, while the log house is a reconstruction.

During the Mormon exodus, Browning was given the special assignment of locating at Kanesville, Iowa, to manufacture weapons for the Mormons who were migrating to Utah's Great Basin in large but separately organized wagon trains. Browning remained in Kanesville from 1847 to 1852. He and his family then joined the Mormon settlement at Ogden, Utah, where he lived until his death in 1879.

The **Wilford Woodruff House** (1843) was the first Mormon building in Nauvoo to be completely restored. Wilford Woodruff (1807–1898) was ordained by Joseph Smith as one of the church's Twelve Apostles. After serving as a missionary in England from 1839 to 1841, he returned to Nauvoo. There, in 1843, he built the Federal-style two-story brick house at the corner of Durphy and Hotchkiss Streets. In

1846, he and his family joined the Mormons in Utah, where he had a distinguished career serving as the fourth president of the church, from 1887 to 1898.

The **Printing Office Complex** consists of three buildings restored by Nauvoo Restoration, Inc. These buildings, erected in 1842, were among Nauvoo's first brick structures. Like other buildings of the Mormon era, they are in the Federal style; the bricks are laid in the flemish bond style.

The complex, the center of Mormon publishing, housed a stereotype foundry, typesetting department, pressroom, bookbindery, and book and stationery store. The Mormon periodical *Times and Seasons* and the weekly newspaper *Nauvoo Neighbor* were published here. After the Mormon exodus in 1846, various local newspapers were printed in the complex. Today, the complex, attended to by a guide, exhibits newspapers, broadsides, and other printed materials. Facsimiles are available for purchase.

The **Webb Wagon and Blacksmith Shop** (1843) was operated by James Webb and his five eldest sons. The shop produced many of the wagons for the westward journey to Utah. The recreated building was erected on original foundations. The bellows, anvils, bench vice, and other tools are originals that were taken to Utah by the Mormons and then returned to Nauvoo to enhance the authenticity of the recreation.

The **Memorial to Women**, sponsored by the Women's Relief Society of the Church of Latter-day Saints (Salt Lake City), is a two-acre memorial featuring a heroic central sculpture of a woman and twelve life-size figures depicting women's roles in society. The Relief Society was founded by Joseph Smith, whose wife, Emma Hale Smith, was its first president. The sculptures were the work of Florence Peterson Hansen and Dennis Smith in the early 1970s.

The **Joseph Smith Historic Center**, established in 1918, is maintained by the Reorganized Church of Latter Day Saints (Independence, Missouri). There you can see a slide presentation on Joseph Smith and the Mormon experience.

The **Old Smith Homestead** consists of the first Smith home in Nauvoo. The log portion was built in 1803 and purchased by Joseph Smith in 1839. Joseph and Emma lived there until 1842, when the **Smith Mansion** was built to accommodate the visitors who came to see the Mormon leader. The new house contained twenty-two rooms and was later expanded into a hotel. Today, the original 1842 structure remains; the hotel wing was torn down in 1890.

Nearby are the **gravesites** of Joseph, Emma, and Hyrum Smith, Joseph's brother.

The **Nauvoo State Historic Site**, housing the **Rheinberger Museum**, is the restored home of Alois Rheinberger, who purchased the house in 1848. In 1851, Rheinberger planted a vineyard, some of which has been preserved behind the house. Rheinberger was a pioneer in the wine-making industry that developed in the Nauvoo area. The house and the wine cellar are open to visitors. A "sun stone," one of two extant from the Nauvoo temple, is preserved at the site.

The City of Joseph, a dramatic and musical pageant based on Joseph Smith's life at Nauvoo, is presented each evening from August 11 through August 15. It is sponsored by Nauvoo Restoration, Inc. **The Wedding of Wine and Cheese** is an annual grape festival held on the Saturday and Sunday of Labor Day weekend.

SIDE TRIPS

The town of Nauvoo has several craft and antique stores. It is noted for its excellent blue cheese, produced at the **Nauvoo Blue Cheese Factory**, and its wines, made by the **Gem City Vineland Company**.

Nauvoo State Park is a 148-acre park with a 13-acre lake, campsites, playground, and museum. Acquired by the state of Illinois in 1948, the park lies along Route 96 on the south edge of Nauvoo. Campsite permits must be obtained from the site manager. For information, call (217)453-2512.

Lincoln's New Salem Village

Reconstruction of an 1830s village; State Historic Site, NRHP

Address: Lincoln's New Salem Park, Rural Route 1, Petersburg, IL 62675
Telephone: (217)632-7953
Location: 20 miles northwest of Springfield on Route 97
Open: Daily, 9:00 A.M. to 5:00 P.M., year-round
Admission: Free
Restaurants: Concession stand
Facilities: Visitors' Center, picnic area, camping, cassette tour, riverboat trip, outdoor drama

WHERE TO STAY
Camping, Petersburg: Lincoln's New Salem State Park, Rural Route 1, Box 244A, 62675, (217)632-7953
Motels/Hotels, Springfield: Best Western State House Inn, 101 East Adams Street, 62701, (217)523-5661, $$; Days Inn, 3000 Stevenson Drive, 62704, (217)529-0171, $; Holiday Inn—East, 3100 Dirksen Parkway, 62703, (217)529-7171, $$; Holiday Inn—South, 625 East St. Joseph Street, 62703, (217)529-7131, $$; Howard Johnson's Southeast, 3190 Dirksen Parkway, 62703, (217)529-9100,

$$; Red Roof Inn, 3200 Singer Avenue, 62703, (217)753-4302, $; Mansion View Lodge, 529 South 4th Street, 62701, (217)544-7411, $$

HISTORY

The village of New Salem, which was Abraham Lincoln's home from 1831 to 1837, was founded on the Sangamon River by James Rutledge and his nephew, John M. Camron, a millwright.

Lincoln's connection with New Salem was strictly an accident. In April 1831, Lincoln, then twenty-two years old, and two other young men planned to pole a flatboat loaded with farm produce down the Sangamon River from Springfield to market in New Orleans. Unfortunately, on April 19, their heavily loaded boat became stranded on Camron's dam at New Salem. Thanks to Lincoln's quick thinking, the boat and its cargo were saved from sinking.

Denton Offutt, the merchant whose goods the flatboat was carrying, came ashore with the crew. He thought New Salem had good growth potential and decided to open a store there when he returned from New Orleans. He asked Abe Lincoln to be his clerk. Lincoln agreed and reached New Salem in late July 1831.

Offutt's store did not last long, but Lincoln decided to remain in town. In March 1832, just seven months after his arrival, Lincoln announced his candidacy for the state legislature. During the campaign, he and some friends joined the Fourth Regiment of Mounted Volunteers to assist in the Black Hawk War. Lincoln was elected captain of his company and served until July 10, 1832; that was his entire military career.

After he lost the election on August 6, 1832, Lincoln purchased Rowan Herndon's share in a store owned by Herndon and William Berry. The firm then became known as Berry and Lincoln. In January, Berry and Lincoln moved to a better location at the Warburton Building, now known as the Second Berry-Lincoln Store. On May 7, Lincoln became New Salem's postmaster and held that position for three years until the office was moved to Petersburg. He was also a deputy surveyor for three years.

He was elected to the Illinois legislature on August 4, 1834, and reelected on August 1, 1836. On September 9, 1836, he was licensed to practice law; and on March 1, 1837, he was admitted to the bar. In April, Lincoln joined the exodus from New Salem to Springfield, where he began his law career.

Because the Sangamon River could not bear riverboat traffic, New Salem declined while other towns in the area grew. In May 1836, when the post office moved to nearby Petersburg, many citizens left the town. On February 15, 1839, the state legislature subdivided Sangamon County, creating Menard County, with Petersburg as the county seat.

This was the final blow to New Salem, and most of those residents who had remained deserted the village.

Interest in the New Salem village site was kept alive by the Old Salem Chautauqua Association. In 1906, William Randolph Hearst, the newspaper publisher, purchased the site and conveyed it in trust to the association. In 1919, the association passed the site to the state of Illinois. The state legislature appropriated $50,000 for "permanent improvements" at the site in 1931, and restoration began in 1932. During the Great Depression, the Civilian Conservation Corps restored the Rutledge-Camron Saw and Grist Mill, the Hill Carding Mill, Miller's Blacksmith Shop, and the church and schoolhouse.

TOUR

New Salem Village, in New Salem Park, contains twelve timber houses, the Rutledge Tavern, ten shops, industries, and a school. With one exception, all the structures are faithful reproductions of New Salem buildings and are on their original foundations as determined by documents and maps. The **Onstot Cooper Shop**, the only original building, was found in Petersburg and brought back to its original foundation. Furnishings include items actually used by New Salem residents of Lincoln's time and other period pieces. Authenticated flower and vegetable gardens and trees help to recreate the original village scene.

All New Salem's houses except Samuel Hill's residence had one story; some had lofts. Usually, they had only one or two rooms. Houses built before the establishment of Camron's Saw Mill had puncheon floors made from split logs. With the mill, planks for floors, ceilings, and siding for houses became available. Fireplaces were made of stone or brick; chimneys, of stone or *cat and clay* (logs and sticks chinked with mud or plaster). Chimneys built inside between two rooms were usually made of stone because they were more fire-resistant than the cat and clay type.

Roofs were made of clapboards or shingles, called *shakes*, secured either by nails or by logs called *weight poles* laid across them. Walls were of logs, notched and fitted together at the corners and chinked with sticks and plaster made of mud and hair. Doors were of frame construction. Houses with leather or wooden hinges and wooden latches and locks predate the blacksmith's arrival at New Salem. After his arrival, fittings were usually made of iron. Houses with wooden latches had buckskin latchstrings, which were tied to the latch and passed outside through a hole above it. When only friends were about, "the latchstring was always out"; but in time of danger, it could be pulled in through the hole.

Most buildings had glass windows, usually situated near the fireplace, where the cooking was done. Cornmeal was a dietary staple, supplemented by hominy, vegetables, milk, pork, fish, and fowl. There was also honey, maple sugar, and in season, grapes, berries, and other fruit.

Furniture was brought to the village from former homes, was homemade, or was made in New Salem by Lincoln's contemporary Robert Johnson. There were rush-seat chairs, cord and trundle beds, plain chests of drawers, and corner cupboards for glasses and dishes. For lighting, candles in brass or iron holders were used.

The village is arranged along a street with cabins on either side. After stopping at the **Visitors' Center**, the first buildings on your right are the Onstot Cabin and Cooper Shop.

The original **Onstot Cabin**, built in 1830, has stone fireplaces, chimneys, and mantels; brick hearths; a sawn-board floor; and iron locks, latches, and hinges. Inside the cabin, a costumed guide demonstrates spinning using thread colored with natural dyes.

The **Onstot Cooper Shop** (1830), the village's only original structure, contains displays of barrels and cooper's tools.

Behind the cooper shop is the **Trent Brothers' Cabin**. Alexander Trent purchased the lot for $50 on August 27, 1832. He owned a grocery and, at one time, the ferry. The Berry-Lincoln Store was sold to Alexander and Martin S. Trent in 1833. Alexander Trent served as a corporal in Lincoln's company in the Black Hawk War.

The next building is the **Mentor Graham Schoolhouse** (1830), a simple round-log structure. Inside are four half-log benches, a table, and a fireplace. The school was not supported by taxes; it was a subscription school. Tuition ranged from thirty to eighty-five cents a month per pupil, depending on the child's age. Church services were also conducted here. Mentor Graham, who came to Sangamon County in 1828, advised Lincoln to study grammar and assisted him in studying surveying.

The **Isaac Gulihur Cabin** was built in 1832; its owner had served in Lincoln's company in the Black Hawk War. The **Robert Johnson Cabin** was built in 1832. A wheelwright and cabinetmaker, Johnson made spinning wheels, wagon wheels, and furniture. The unpretentious cabin has a puncheon floor and wooden latches, hinges, and other fittings.

The **Isaac Burner Cabin** was built on two lots, valued at $10, south of Main Street, in October 1832. In 1836, Burner left New Salem and moved farther west.

The **First Berry-Lincoln Store**, built in 1832, was situated south of Main Street. Today it is used for demonstrations of broom making.

The **Lukins and Ferguson Cabins** were built in 1831 by Peter Lukins, who maintained a cobbler's shop in one of them. Today, it is used to illustrate that craft.

The Dr. John Allen Cabin (1831) is one of the better-constructed cabins in New Salem. A Dartmouth graduate, physician, and business-man, Allen was accustomed to comfortable living. He was a Presbyterian, and church meetings were often held in his home.

Rutledge Tavern was originally built as a home in 1829 by James Rutledge, cofounder with John Camron of New Salem. A native of South Carolina, he was a serious and well-educated man who had a library of thirty volumes and founded a debating society attended by Lincoln. Ann Rutledge, Lincoln's alleged fiancée, was one of his ten children.

In 1831, as Sangamon County's population grew, Rutledge converted his home into a tavern and built an addition for guests. Abraham Lincoln lodged in the tavern's loft. During our visit, there were demonstrations of cooking and dulcimer playing in the tavern.

The museum, a modern, not a reconstructed, stone building, contains an exhibit of Lincoln's surveying tools. Lincoln surveyed parts of Menard and Mason counties, including the town of Petersburg. The museum also has displays of antique quilts, farm implements, furniture, and smaller household objects.

The Herndon Brothers' Cabin belonged to James and Rowan Herndon, who opened a store in New Salem in 1830. In the summer of 1832, James sold his share in the store to William F. Berry; and in September, Rowan Herndon sold his share to Lincoln. On a visit to James and Rowan, their cousin, William H. Herndon, met Lincoln. They were law partners from 1843 until the president's death, and William Herndon eventually became Lincoln's biographer.

The Rutledge-Camron Saw and Grist Mill was built in 1825. The mill drew trade from miles around, and its prosperity inspired some of its customers to settle in New Salem and open businesses of their own.

Clary's Grocery, a simple log cabin warmed by a fireplace, was opened in 1829 by William Clary. The grocery was a convenient place to visit, have a drink, and stock up on supplies while having grain ground at the mill. By 1832, William Clary sold his store to Alexander Trent and moved to Texas.

Denton Offutt's Store, on the bluff above the river, opened in September 1831, with Abraham Lincoln as Offutt's clerk. This general store sold dry goods, furs, seeds, tallow, lard, bacon, cheese, butter, honey, eggs, hops, vegetables, firearms and ammunition, saddles, tools, and liquor.

The Second Berry-Lincoln Store, built in 1831, is a frame structure, which is unusual for New Salem. Its one large room was the store; the rear lean-to served as a storeroom and, for a time, as Lincoln's bedroom.

The business was not a success. New Salem's fortunes were declining, and William Berry consumed much of the store's liquor. Berry had obtained a tavern license so that he could sell liquor by the drink. Lincoln disapproved of the liquor license and dissolved the partnership, selling his share to Berry. Because Lincoln had borrowed money to buy the business, its failure left him in debt as well as unemployed.

The **Hill-McNamara Store** was opened in 1829 by Samuel Hill and John McNeil McNamara. This store, one of the few New Salem buildings to have a porch, was once the center of village social and business life. It was also used as an election polling place.

The **New Salem Post Office** was located in Hill's store because Hill was the postmaster. After some complaints about his service, he was replaced by Abraham Lincoln on May 7, 1833. Lincoln remained postmaster until May 30, 1836, when the office was relocated in Petersburg. Lincoln developed his lifelong habit of reading daily newspapers when as postmaster he had easy access to them.

Martin Waddle's Cabin, built in 1832, has puncheon floors, wooden hinges and locks, and small windows. Waddle was a hatter, and the original iron kettle used in his trade hangs on the east side of the house.

Samuel Hill's Cabin is New Salem's only two-story house. Other unusual features are its porch, front and rear doors, outside cellar entrance, and a sliding window.

Dr. Francis Regnier's Office was bought for $20 in 1832. The son of a French physician, Dr. Regnier was an eccentric and witty young man who lived and worked in the office's single room for four years.

A large two-story log building, **Hill's Carding Mill and Storehouse** was built by Samuel Hill in 1835. The mill's cogs were made of hickory wood, and a yoke of oxen, hitched to a forty-foot wheel, supplied the power by walking on a treadmill. Carding began in May, with some people paying cash for it while others left a percentage of their wool as payment.

Joshua Miller bought the lots for **Miller's Blacksmith Shop** on November 17, 1832, for $25. At his anvil, he forged ox and horseshoes, implements, and household fittings. Miller was also a wagonmaker.

Joshua Miller and John Kelso, who married sisters, built the **Miller-Kelso Cabin**, the only double house in New Salem. Its iron fittings and an unusual sliding window were made by Miller, the blacksmith. Jack Kelso, known as the village philosopher, preferred fishing and poetry to work. To supplement their income, Mrs. Kelso took in boarders. Abraham Lincoln was one of them, and he became an avid listener as Kelso quoted Shakespeare and the Scottish poet Robert Burns.

SIDE TRIPS

After New Salem, a logical next stop is **Lincoln's home** in Springfield. The young lawyer, his wife, Mary, and their son moved to this charming house in 1844, when Lincoln was serving as a state legislator.

Three more sons were born in Springfield, necessitating an extensive remodeling of the second floor to accommodate the growing family. They lived in the house, the only one Lincoln ever owned, for twelve years. Lincoln left Springfield for Washington in 1861 after being elected President.

The **Lincoln Home National Historic Site**, at 8th and Jackson Streets, is federally owned and staffed with knowledgeable National Park Service Rangers, who describe the history of the house and answer questions. The two-story gold frame house is surrounded by a picket fence. It is furnished with some of Lincoln's own and other period furniture. Open daily, 8:00 A.M. to 5:00 P.M., (217)492-4242. Admission is free.

Another interesting site is **Lincoln's Law Offices** on 6th and Adams Streets in the Lincoln-Herndon Building. Lincoln practiced law on the third floor with his partner, William H. Herndon, from 1843 to 1852. In addition to the restored law offices, there is a **federal courtroom**, used from 1841 to 1855, **judge's chambers**, and a **clerk's office**. This is a privately owned building, apparently privately restored. You can visit two floors filled with dusty books, antique desks and cabinets in poor condition, and tables littered with legal documents and deeds; all can be touched. There is also a museum room with cases displaying Lincoln memorabilia. This unusual restoration gives you the feeling of just happening into Lincoln's offices about ten years after they were vacated—authentic, but needing a good cleaning. Open daily, 9:00 A.M. to 5:00 P.M., (217)523-1010. Admission: adults, $1.00; senior citizens and students, 50 cents.

A distinct contrast is the beautiful **Old State Capitol**, across the street from the law offices, on the square in downtown Springfield between 5th and 6th Streets and Washington and Adams Streets. This restored Greek Revival building is an architectural showpiece, with curving stairways, a high cupola, and magnificent senate and house chambers. Attention to detail is evident throughout; the brass is polished, the clocks are wound, and the guides are knowledgeable. The desks in the legislative chambers are reproductions; the other furniture dates from the period, but only nine pieces are original to the Capitol.

The cornerstone of the Capitol was laid in 1837, and·construction was completed in 1854, although the sessions were held there from 1840. Lincoln, a representative in the General Assembly from 1834 to 1841, was instrumental in moving the capital from Vandalia to Springfield. An original copy of the Gettysburg Address in Lincoln's handwriting is displayed in a safelike enclosure on the first floor. Admission is free.

The outdoor **Sound and Light Program** at the Capitol dramatizes events in Lincoln's life. It is presented Tuesday to Sunday at 9:00 P.M., mid-June through Labor Day, weather permitting. For information, call (217)782-4836. Admission is free.

Lincoln's Tomb is located in Oak Ridge Cemetery on North Walnut Street. This impressive monument consists of a 117-foot granite obelisk reached by a double stairway leading to a circular entrance bay. Statuary groups representing Civil War troops are at each corner of the obelisk. It is the burial place of our sixteenth president, his wife, and three of their four sons. Tours through the tomb are narrated by guides. Open daily, 9:00 A.M. to 5:00 P.M. Admission is free. For information, call (217)782-2747.

The **Illinois State Capitol**, built between 1868 and 1889, offers free guided tours on weekdays from 8:00 A.M. to 4:00 P.M. For information, call (217)782-2099. The **Governor's Mansion** (1855), located at 5th and Jackson Streets, is the third-oldest continuously occupied governor's mansion in the nation. Tours are given Tuesday and Thursday, from 9:30 to 11:00 A.M. and from 2:00 to 3:30 P.M. Admission is free. For information, call (217)782-2525.

Conner Prairie Pioneer Settlement

Recreation of a pioneer settlement to 1836; museum program of Earlham College

Address: 30 Conner Lane, Noblesville, IN 46060
Telephone: (317) 773-3633
Location: 6 miles north of the Allisonville Road Exit of I-465 and 4 miles south of Noblesville
Open: Wednesday to Sunday, 10:00 A.M. to 5:00 P.M., first Wednesday in April to second Sunday in December. Closed Easter Sunday and Thanksgiving weekend; open Tuesday to Sunday, May through October.
Admission: Adults, $4.50; senior citizens, $3.75; children 6 to 18 and students, $2.50. Discounts for groups of 15 or more by reservation.
Restaurant: Fare Thee Well Restaurant
Shops: Museum Shop, stoneware, ironware, textiles, craft items, books
Facilities: Visitors' Center, picnic area, kennel, accessible to handicapped

WHERE TO STAY

Camping, Noblesville: Forest Park, Route 19, 50 South 8th Street, 46060, (317)773-2881; Lagoon Lodge, Rural Route 2, Box 68B, 46060, (317)773-3333

Motels/Hotels, Cicero: Waterfront Inn, 409 West Jackson Street, 46034, (317)773-5115, $$

Motels/Hotels, Indianapolis: American Inn—North, 7202 East 82nd Street, 46256, (317)849-6910, $; Dillon Inn, 9090 Wesleyan Road, 46268, (317)875-7676, $–$$; Holiday Inn—North, 3850 De Pauw Boulevard, 46268, (317)872-9790, $$–$$$; Howard Johnson's—East, 2141 North Post Road, 46219, (317)897-2000, $$; Marriott Inn, 7202 East 21st Street, 46219, (317)352-1231, $$$; Red Roof Inn—North, 7520 Valparaiso Court, 46260, (317)872-3030, $; Sheraton Meridian, 2820 North Meridian Street, 46208, (317)924-1241, $$$

HISTORY

Conner Prairie Pioneer Settlement commemorates the life and times of William Conner, a pioneer who played an influential role in the early history of the state of Indiana. Conner was born December 10, 1777, in Ohio. Moving to Indiana in 1802, he established a trading post at White River, twenty miles north of present-day Indianapolis and four miles south of what would become Noblesville. Because he spoke their language, Conner gained the trust of the Delaware Indians who inhabited this heavily forested region of Indiana. His fur-trading business thrived. Conner married Mekinges, daughter of the Delaware Chief Anderson; they had six children.

When Indiana became a state in 1816, the state owned two-thirds of the land. Conner, who had occasionally served as a scout and an interpreter at Indian councils for William Henry Harrison, then governor of the Northwest Territory, helped negotiate the 1818 Treaty of St. Mary, Ohio. With that treaty, Indiana's native tribes, including Delawares, relinquished their rights to a large piece of central Indiana land referred to as the "New Purchase." In 1820, as part of the agreement, a large group of Delawares, including Mekinges and the six Conner children, moved west across the Mississippi.

Conner stayed on, and as permanent settlement began around his trading post, he quickly adapted his business to supply the settlers' needs. In 1823, he replaced his log house with a brick Federal-style building on a bluff overlooking a 200-acre prairie planted with grain. In addition to being a home for Conner, who had remarried, the house served as the county's first post office. For a while, the Hamilton County Circuit Court held sessions there.

Conner and his second wife, Elizabeth Chapman, had ten children, seven of whom were born at the prairie. The other three children were born in Noblesville, where Conner moved in 1837. Conner went on to become a prominent Indiana citizen and was elected to the state legislature three times.

The property at Conner Prairie eventually passed out of family hands and fell into disrepair. In 1934, Eli Lilly, a grandson of the founder of the pharmaceutical house of that name, purchased the Conner homestead. He and his wife, Ruth Lilly, began renovating the house and furnished it with authentic period pieces.

To recreate William Conner's early life, Lilly purchased several log buildings in Brown County and relocated them at Conner Prairie, which became a private museum depicting the life of an early Indiana settler.

In 1964, the Lillys gave the museum and surrounding grounds to Earlham College to be operated as a living outdoor museum, open to the public. Earlham added a village area to the settlement and plans further expansion.

TOUR

Conner Prairie guides play the parts of people who might have lived in the settlement in 1836. They have names, ages, occupations, families, and pasts. When you walk into a house, you are entering a particular person's home; and that person greets you and tells you about himself or herself in a natural, conversational way.

There are three areas to explore at Conner Prairie: the **1836 Village**, the **Conner Estate**, and the **Pioneer Adventure Center**. Settings are pleasant and pastoral; winding paths keep most buildings hidden from view.

In the **1836 Village** is the **Golden Eagle**, a frame two-story inn run by Mrs. Zimmerman and her children. While the women took tea in the first-floor ladies' parlor, the men discussed politics and business in the barroom. In the kitchen, the innkeeper baked cornbread in the fireplace. The barn and farmyard behind the inn were stocked with geese, chickens, and horses.

The **Fenton Cabin** is home to a weaver, who has his loom set up in the one room of the small log house. A bed and a spinning wheel are the other simple furnishings.

Samuel Hastings fought with General William Henry Harrison at Tippecanoe in 1811. He then became a farmer, but after some lean years, he lost his farm. In 1836, he was a pauper maintained by the county. His cabin is furnished so sparsely that there is not even a bed, only a mattress on the floor. **Hastings' Cabin** is a heartrending but undoubtedly realistic picture of the conditions in which some people in that era lived.

The two-room **McClure House** is more sumptuously furnished, with a rope bed, cradle, trunk, spinning wheel, clock, and chest of drawers. Hannah McClure is a young bride who has just moved from a farm to the village. She is having difficulty adjusting to living in such "crowded conditions." She spins and dyes yarn while she talks about herself and her husband, whose carpentry shop, complete with a foot-pedaled lathe, stands behind the house.

The large gold-colored frame **Campbell House**, built in the early Greek Revival style, reflects the income and position of the doctor and his wife, Harriet. The parlor is attractively decorated with wallpaper, a piano, clock, mirror, and a velvet couch. While Mrs. Campbell serves tea to two other women in the parlor, she complains about leaving the sophistication of Lexington, Kentucky, for the roughness of the Indiana frontier. Nevertheless, Mrs. Campbell's kitchen has an iron stove—in 1836 a real innovation in cooking. Dr. Campbell's office is in back of the house; there he leisurely discusses modern medical treatments such as the use of leeches and bleeding.

In the log cabin **schoolhouse**, students attend school in November, December, and January, six days a week from 7:00 A.M. to 4:00 P.M. They study phonics and Noah Webster's spellers; because of a scarcity of books and writing materials, they recite most of their lessons. The schoolmaster is paid three cents per student per day, room and board, and vegetables for his pigs.

Shelves of dry goods, china, and clothes can be found in the one-story frame **general store**. "Spirits" are kept in the store's back room. The storekeeper uses a daybook for his accounts.

In the **blacksmith shop**, Ben Curtis and his apprentice are busy at a well-equipped forge but are not too preoccupied to talk politics. The **Curtis Home**, which Ben shares with his wife and young children, is a two-story frame. The furnishings, which include a beautiful corner cabinet, a couch in the parlor, a dry sink, and a spinning wheel, indicate that the blacksmith's business is fairly prosperous. The **apprentice's domicile**, on the other hand, is a simple log house.

The **Baker House**, a simple structure, reflects the status of the Baker brothers, the settlement's potters. They make their wares in the potter's shed and fire them in a kiln, which is housed in a separate building.

The **Whittaker House** is the home of the storekeeper and his wife. Mrs. Whittaker has a wild-goose-chase quilt on her bed, and you'll find her at work on another quilt, which is set up on a quilting frame. The Wild-Goose-Chase quilt pattern consists of columns of solid fabric interspersed with columns of triangles, which represent the wild geese.

The first column of geese point upward, while in the next column the geese point downward, and so on.

The **Conner Estate** is the nucleus around which Conner Prairie developed. William Conner's house, built in 1823, is a brick Federal-style mansion on a bluff overlooking the 200-acre prairie. It has been beautifully restored and is furnished with pieces owned by Conner and comparable period pieces. The log outbuildings, moved to the site from Brown County, are typical of this period in Indiana. They include the **springhouse**, used for storing perishable foods; the **still**, where corn is distilled into whiskey; and the **loom house**, where textiles were woven.

The **Pioneer Adventure Center** focuses on the crafts of 1836, and visitors are invited to try weaving, cooking, spinning, quilting, log splitting, candle dipping, soapmaking, or playing games such as quoits. During the summer months, special programs such as an old fiddlers' gathering and a discussion of herbal medicine are presented.

SIDE TRIPS

The Indianapolis area offers many features attractive to visitors. The **Children's Museum**, 3000 North Meridian Street, (317)924-5431, is open Monday to Saturday, 10:00 A.M. to 5:00 P.M., and Sunday from noon to 5:00 P.M. It is closed on New Year's Day, Thanksgiving, and Christmas. Admission is free.

The **Indiana State Museum**, 202 North Alabama Street, (317)232-1637, focuses on the state's heritage, culture, and artists. Open Monday to Saturday, 9:00 A.M. to 4:45 P.M.; Sunday, noon to 4:45 P.M.; closed on holidays. Admission is free.

The **Indianapolis Museum of Art**, 1200 West 38th Street, (317)923-1331, features European, oriental, and American paintings, as well as sculpture, furniture, ceramics, and textiles. Open daily except Mondays, 11:00 A.M. to 5:00 P.M.; closed New Year's Day, Thanksgiving, and Christmas.

Indianapolis is also the location of the **President Benjamin Harrison House**, 1230 North Delaware Street, (317)631-1898. Open Monday to Saturday, 10:00 A.M. to 4:00 P.M.; Sunday, noon to 4:00 P.M. Admission: adults, $1.50; students, 75 cents. The **James Whitcomb Riley House**, 528 Lockerbie Street, (317)631-5885, is open Tuesday to Saturday, 10:00 A.M. to 4:00 P.M.; Sunday, noon to 4:00 P.M. Admission: adults, $1.00; children 12 to 16, 25 cents.

In Noblesville, where Conner Prairie Pioneer Settlement is located, the **Indiana Transportation Museum**, Route 19, displays antique trucks, buggies, engines, wagons, automobiles, and railway equipment. Open Saturday, Sunday, and holidays, 1:00 to 6:00 P.M., May to October. From June to August, it is also open Tuesday to Friday, 1:00 to 5:00 P.M. For information, phone (317)733-6000.

Spring Mill Pioneer Village

**Restored early nineteenth-century mill
village in state park**

Address: Spring Mill State Park, P.O. Box 376, Mitchell, IN 47446
Telephone: (812)849-4129
Location: In Spring Mill State Park, 3 miles east of Mitchell on State
Route 60 and 90 miles east of Indianapolis
Open: Monday to Thursday, 8:00 A.M. to 6:00 P.M.; Friday to
Sunday, 8:00 A.M. to 8:00 P.M.; April to October
Admission: Admission to the village is free; entrance to Spring Mill
State Park is $1.25 per car
Restaurants: Spring Mill Inn Dining Room
Shops: Gift Shop, souvenirs and books
Facilities: Boating, camping, cave trips, fishing, hiking, inn, natural-
ist service, picnic areas, horseback riding, Grissom Memorial, pools

WHERE TO STAY
Inns, Mitchell: Spring Mill Inn, P.O. Box 68, 47446, (812)849-
4081, $
Camping, Mitchell: Spring Mill State Park, P.O. Box 376, 47446,
(812)849-4129
Resort, French Lick: French Lick Springs, Route 56, 47432,
(812)935-9381 or 1-800-457-4042, $$$$ (Modified American Plan)
Motels/Hotels, French Lick: Lane Motel, P.O. Box 224, Route 56,
47432, (812)936-9918, $

HISTORY
Spring Mill Pioneer Village, a small but excellent restoration, recap-
tures the era of the early Hoosier settlers, whose economy and society
were based on water-powered gristmills. The mill, which is the central
attraction and focal point of the village, is powered by swiftly flowing
water from the nearby Hamer Cave.

   In the late eighteenth and early nineteenth centuries, towns with
sawmills and gristmills were important trading centers. Farmers brought
their grain to the mills to be ground into meal and flour. Stores opened,

217

and occasionally an inn or tavern was built to lodge traders and travelers. Often the mill owner was the community's leading and wealthiest citizen.

The small community's economic fortunes were tied directly to the mill; it prospered as long as the mill did business. When other sources of energy replaced waterpower, the mill and its village declined.

The village began in 1814, when Samuel Jackson, Jr., an immigrant from Canada, constructed a mill on the site. In 1817, the Bullitt brothers, who had moved to Indiana from Kentucky, purchased the mill and surrounding land from Jackson. They built the large three-story Indiana limestone mill that stands today. The mill's flume, wheel, and woodwork were made from hardwood trees native to southern Indiana. In 1823, the Bullitt brothers sold the mill, its office, and two large homes to the Montgomery brothers of Philadelphia.

By 1828, the village was prosperous enough to become the location of a post office.

In 1832, the mill again changed ownership, when the Hamer brothers purchased it from the Montgomerys. Hugh Hamer changed the name of the village from Arcole to Spring Mill. A prosperous businessman, Hamer was elected to the Indiana legislature.

By the late nineteenth century, other forms of mechanical energy had replaced waterpower. In 1892, Jonathan Turley, the mill's last owner, shut down the entire operation. The abandoned village slowly deteriorated. In 1927, the area became an Indiana State Park; historical reconstruction began in 1937 under the direction of the Indiana Department of Natural Resources. The village is enhanced by its setting in the 1,300-acre Spring Mill State Park.

TOUR

The **George Sheeks House**, built in 1816 by George Sheeks of Rowen County, North Carolina, is one of the oldest residences in Indiana. The house was brought to the village to enhance the restoration and to preserve a significant structure. It is a log structure with a roof of wooden shakes. Inside, there is a working loom once owned by the Sheek family. Rug weaving is demonstrated, and rugs are available for sale.

The **Granny White House**, built in 1824 and restored in 1951, was moved to its present location from Leasville, Indiana. Once owned by Sally Cummins White, it contains period furniture and artifacts.

The **Leather Shop**, built in the early 1800s, was the residence of the David Todd family.

The **Grist and Saw Mill**, erected in 1817, is the dominant structure in the village. The mill, which still operates, is powered by a wooden waterwheel that is twenty feet in diameter. The water that turns this massive wheel flows from Hamer Cave over an elevated flume supported by large stone pillars. The miller demonstrates the grinding of corn, and visitors may purchase freshly ground cornmeal. The mill contains an exhibit of regional artifacts and late eighteenth- and early nineteenth-century tools, including muzzle-loading flintlock rifles, spinning wheels, furniture, and tools.

Of particular interest is the collection of scaled-down samples of cabinetmakers' furniture that resemble dollhouse furnishings. Cabinetmakers and other woodworkers customarily built replicas of their products and took them to communities such as Spring Mill or to farmsteads to show to prospective customers. Customers ordered furniture on the basis of these miniatures. On his next circuit, the cabinetmaker delivered the custom-made orders and solicited new ones.

The **Distillery**, built in 1823, was an important village enterprise. Farmers distilled their grain into whiskey and shipped it to Louisville and New Orleans. Fresh spring water flowing from nearby caves was used by the distillers. Various presses and mash tubs are on display.

The **Montgomery Tavern**, built in 1824 and restored in 1929, is both a tavern and an inn. It was a coach stop on the route between Bloomington, Indiana, and Louisville, Kentucky.

The **Mill Office**, erected in 1818, served many mill managers, who conducted their commercial transactions here.

The **Children's Nursery and School**, built in 1830, was used by the Hamer families. It was also attended by other children of the village and the surrounding area. Inside, there is a display of children's furniture and a small collection of books and educational items.

The **Hugh Hamer House**, built in the early nineteenth century, is a large two-story log house that was the home of the village's leading citizen. Hamer served as a member of the Indiana Senate and House of Representatives.

The **Thomas Hamer House**, also built in the early nineteenth century, was the residence of Hugh's brother and partner. It is a large frame house furnished in the style of the period. Its summer kitchen, barn, and dependency buildings were shared by both Hamer families.

The **Coach House and Stable** houses such items as a sleigh, carriage, coach, and wagon.

The **Apothecary Shop**, built in 1830, was the office of Dr. Jacob Lemon, the village doctor and husband of Polly Hamer, Hugh and Thomas's sister. It contains displays of early nineteenth-century remedies, drugs, and medical apparatus.

The village also has a **hat shop**, a **post office**, a **chapel**, a **general store**, and a **pioneer garden**. Craft displays and demonstrations include milling, weaving, cordwainery, potting, smithing, and candle making. On Saturday evenings in the summer months, there is often a candlelight tour of the village.

SIDE TRIPS

Spring Mill State Park offers many attractions and recreational opportunities in addition to Pioneer Village. There are boat tours of caves in which rare blindfish can be found. There are facilities for hiking, camping, boating, fishing, horseback riding, nature study, and swimming. A **memorial exhibit** is dedicated to Virgil L. Grissom, America's second man in space, who was raised in nearby Mitchell, the "dogwood capital of the world." Grissom died on January 27, 1967, at Cape Kennedy, along with two fellow astronauts during a flight simulation.

New Harmony

**Restoration of an 1814 to 1860 Rappite
community and Owenite utopian
community; State Historical Site, NRP**

Address: Historic New Harmony, Inc., P.O. Box 248, New Harmony, IN 47631
Telephone: (812)682-4474
Location: 7 miles south of Interstate 64 at the intersection of Indiana Routes 66 and 68
Open: Daily, 9:00 A.M. to 5:00 P.M., year-round, except Christmas and New Year's Day
Admission: Master Tour Ticket: adults, $5.00; students, $3.00. Partial tours available. Accompanying guides for groups at a nominal charge. Tour tickets and arrangements are made at the Visitors' Reception Center.
Restaurants: Red Geranium Restaurant, Shadblow Restaurant
Shops: Red Geranium Bookstore, antiques, books on New Harmony, Americana, and many other subjects
Facilities: Visitors' Center, guided tours, picnic area in nearby park, Atheneum

WHERE TO STAY

Inns, New Harmony: The New Harmony Inn, North and Brewery Streets, 47631, (812)682-4491, $$

Camping, New Harmony: Harmonie State Recreation Area, 47631, (812)682-4841; Murphy Park, Main Street, 47631, (812)682-4846

Motels/Hotels, Mount Vernon: Four Seasons Motel, 47620, (812)838-4821, $

Camping, Mount Vernon: Honey Lake State Fish and Wildlife Area, Rural Route 5, 47620, (812)838-2927

Motels/Hotels, Evansville: Drury Inn, 3901 Route 41, 47711, (812)423-5818, $; Holiday Inn, 2508 Route 41 North Business, 47711, (812)425-1092, $$; Ramada Inn, 4101 Route 41 North, 47711, (812)424-6400, $$; Travelodge Evansville, 701 1st Avenue, 47710, (812)424-3886, $

HISTORY

New Harmony, on the banks of the Wabash River in southern Indiana, is both a restoration and a living community. It is noteworthy as the location of two utopian communities, the Rappites, from 1814 to 1824, and the Owenites, from 1824 to 1828. The first community, religious in origin, was established by German Pietists led by George Rapp (1757–1847), a dissenter from the more formal Lutheran church. In 1803, the patriarchal and charismatic Father Rapp led his flock from their native Württemberg in Germany to western Pennsylvania, where they established the town of Harmony. In 1814, the Rappites left Pennsylvania in search of a more congenial location to cultivate grapes and other crops. Rapp selected southern Indiana for his new community, which he called New Harmony. Its location on the Wabash provided excellent transportation to markets.

The Rappites created a thriving agricultural community of 800 residents who cultivated some 20,000 acres. They remained in New Harmony until 1824, when Father Rapp sold the community to Robert Owen, the British industrialist and utopian socialist. The Rappites then returned to western Pennsylvania, where they founded Economy, their third community. Travelers can retrace the Rappite experience in the United States by exploring the three restored villages: Harmony, Pennsylvania; New Harmony, Indiana; and Old Economy, at Ambridge, Pennsylvania, a suburb of Pittsburgh (see page 88). Under Rapp's paternalistic rule, New Harmony prospered. The Rappites were renowned for their industriousness, frugality, and productivity. The town, consisting of 180 solidly constructed buildings, comprised factories, granaries, mills, private homes, schools, and dormitories. Rapp, an astute businessman, diversified the community's agricultural economy to include manufacturing. Its many products, including beer, whiskey, and wine, found ready markets in the frontier towns and farms of Illinois and Indiana.

Rapp sold New Harmony to Robert Owen for $150,000 in 1824 because he believed the establishment of a new communitarian village would rekindle his followers' enthusiasm. Owen brought a very different type of utopian vision to the town.

At the time of the purchase, Owen (1771–1858) was famous for his reform at the mill town of New Lanark in Scotland, where he improved the working and living conditions of the workers. Owen saw himself as the prophet of a new society based on common property. Feeling constrained by England's traditional class structure and customs, he sold his New Lanark mills and came to the United States, where he purchased New Harmony. At a joint session of the U.S. Congress, attended by the president and the cabinet, Owen announced his plan to create a model community and urged interested individuals to join him at New Harmony.

Owen formed an ill-defined partnership with William Maclure, an amateur geologist and philanthropist. Maclure, who took responsibility for the educational phase of the experiment, brought with him an illustrious group of scientists and educators. He sought to combine basic research in the natural sciences with the educational methods devised by the Swiss reformer Johann Heinrich Pestalozzi (1746–1826), who espoused the power of education as a tool of social regeneration. Maclure hoped to turn New Harmony into a scientific and educational center, a kind of nineteenth-century think tank. Among the scientific notables who joined Owen's New Harmony experiment were Thomas Say, a pioneer natural scientist; Charles-Alexandre Lesueur, a naturalist and artist; and Gerard Troost, a chemist and mineralogist.

Maclure, who wanted to introduce a scientifically based, practical education to the United States, persuaded a group of Pestalozzian teachers to staff New Harmony's schools. The ill-sorted intellectuals, educators, scientists, and farmers who joined Owen and Maclure at New Harmony devoted more time to debates than to working. Internal dissension brought disharmony to New Harmony, and Owen's communal experiment ended with his return to England.

The Owenite legacy became a part of Indiana's history. Owen's sons made significant political and educational contributions to the state. Robert Dale Owen, his eldest son, served in Congress; David Dale Owen headed the U.S. Geological Survey; Richard Dale Owen became Purdue University's first president. For a decade after the experiment's end, Maclure's scientists and educators continued their research, publication, and teaching.

Today, New Harmony has many of the qualities that Owen and Maclure wanted to see during their own lives. Its restored buildings illustrate the Rappite and Owenite heritage. Its exhibits highlight science and education. Indeed, conferences of scientific and educational associations are held there throughout the year. To stroll New Harmony's quiet streets at twilight is to walk with Father Rapp, Robert Owen, William Maclure, and those who sought to create a utopia on America's frontier.

TOUR

You should begin your tour of New Harmony at the **Atheneum**, which serves as the **Visitors' Reception Center**. Here tour tickets can be purchased, and groups are organized.

The Atheneum is a shining white building of contemporary design completed in 1979; its architect was Richard Meier. It contains exhibit areas, conference facilities, and a display of books and publications about New Harmony. Visitors can begin their tour with the thirty-minute documentary film, *New Harmony: An Example and a Beacon*, which provides an excellent orientation.

Macluria Double Log House (1775), the oldest building on the site, illustrates early frontier building techniques.

The **David Lentz House** (1822), a Harmonist frame home, illustrates the sturdy and innovative architecture of the Rappite period. [See Old Economy, Pennsylvania (page 88) for a description of Rappite building methods.] It has been restored and furnished with Harmonist artifacts by the National Society of Colonial Dames of America.

Rappite building frames, fastened with mortise and tenon joints, were locked in place with wooden pegs. Rafters were self-supporting. The energy-conscious Rappites insulated their homes with *Dutch biscuits*, a wooden board wrapped with mud and straw. Note the centrally located chimney, which was used for both cooking and heating, and the small windowpanes, which resisted wind while providing a source of light. Of interest is the Christian door, a symbol of the Rappites' religious faith; the upper panels form the cross, and the lower ones represent an open Bible. Among the furnishings are Harmonist chairs; a pie safe, typical of southern Indiana; a small Shaker table; and a Harmonist bed and chest.

The **Early West Street Log Structure**, a potter's shop, and the **Eigner House** (1814–1819) also illustrate life in the Rappite period.

Robert Fauntleroy House, a Rappite frame home, was built in 1822 and enlarged by Robert Fauntleroy, the husband of Robert Owen's daughter, Jane, in 1840. Maintained by the state of Indiana, its furnishings are from the Owenite period.

The **Workingmen's Institute and Library**, built in 1894, has archives and collections on the Rappites and Owenites that attract scholars and authors. There are also extensive collections on Maclure and his scientific and educational associates. The building also houses the **New Harmony Public Library**, a small **art gallery**, and a local **history museum**.

The institute, established in 1838 by William Maclure, was designed as an educational center for working men and women. From 1830 to 1860, the institute's School Press published pioneering scientific books by a number of Maclure's scientific associates, including Say and Lesueur. Be sure to see the portraits of William Maclure and Joseph Neef, a Pestalozzian teacher.

Murphy Auditorium (1913) was extensively restored and renovated in 1975. Funds for its original construction were provided by Dr. Edward Murphy (1813–1900), a New Harmony physician. Today, it is used for lectures, concerts, and other educational and artistic performances.

Lichtenberger Store (1901) now houses the Maximilian-Bodmer collection of hand-colored lithographs called *Travels in the Interior of North America, 1832–1834*. These drawings and sketches were made by the Swiss artist Karl Bodmer (1809–1893), who accompanied the German nobleman Count Maximilian on an expedition through the American frontier wilderness. Especially noteworthy are Bodmer's drawings of Indians, animals, and frontier scenes.

The **Harmonist Shoemaker's Shop** (1817) is an open archaeological dig exposing the foundations of a Rappite building that once stood on this site. In 1837, this building was used by David Dale Owen, Robert Owen's son, as his second geological laboratory.

George Kepler House (1822), a Rappite residence, contains exhibits on New Harmony as a geological research center. It features the surveys of David Dale Owen (1807–1860).

Owen House (1830), restored in the English architectural style of Robert Owen's time, contains furniture and artifacts of the 1830s and 1840s. **John Beal House** (1829), a restored wattle and daub structure, is the location of a printing exhibit.

Thrall's Opera House and Theater Complex, consisting of three buildings, illustrates New Harmony's theatrical past and present. The **Second Harmonist Cooper Shop** (1819) houses a theater exhibit. The **Theater Barn**, built in 1975, provides scenery and costumes for theatrical performances. **Thrall's Opera House**, restored in 1969 and maintained by the state of Indiana, is used for theatrical performances, conferences, and lectures. Originally a Rappite dormitory built in 1824, it was converted into an opera house in 1856.

Solomon Wolf House (1823), a Rappite brick residence, now houses an electronic scale model of New Harmony in 1824, the year of the Rappite departure and the Owenite arrival. The model's sound and light show provides an excellent overview of New Harmony's rich but complicated history.

Dormitory Number 2 (1822), one of New Harmony's earliest restorations, is a fine example of Harmonist architecture. It was put to significant use by both Rappites and Owenites. The Rappites used it as a dormitory for single persons. In the Owenite period, it was the location of Joseph Neef's Pestalozzian School. Neef, once a noncommissioned officer in Napoleon's army in Italy, was trained by Pestalozzi, the Swiss educational reformer, at Burgdorf in Switzerland. Neef came to the United States under Maclure's patronage to introduce the Pestalozzian educational method, which was based on object lessons. Dormitory Number 2 contains exhibits on education and printing and is maintained by the state of Indiana.

Roofless Church (1959), built and maintained by the Robert Lee Blaffer Trust, commemorates New Harmony's spiritual meaning. Although recently created, the Roofless Church, which was designed by architect Philip Johnson, incorporates many symbols of New Harmony's religious past, especially from the Rappite era. The concept of rooflessness unites earth and sky; the rectangular brick wall recalls the egalitarian spirit of the Rappite cemetery; the bronze gates bear the golden rose, a favorite Rappite symbol for the anticipation of the millennium. Within the domed tabernacle is the sculpture *Descent of the Holy Spirit* by the contemporary artist Jacques Lipschitz.

The Roofless Church, near Tillich Park and the Red Geranium Restaurant, is in a beautifully landscaped setting of trees, plants, and flowers. Near it is **Our Lady Queen of Peace Wayside Shrine**, dedicated in 1973 to the memory of Thomas Merton, the Trappist monk, contemplative, and author.

The graves in the **Harmonist cemetery** are unmarked, exemplifying the Rappite principle of equality. The graves were unmarked so that the members of Rapp's society would remain equal in death as they had been in life. The wall surrounding the cemetery was built with bricks from the Harmonist church, which was taken down in the 1870s.

The hedge **labyrinth**, a fascinating maze located eight blocks south of the town, was designed by the Rappites. **Maple Hill Cemetery**, half a mile south of New Harmony, contains the burial sites and monuments of many New Harmony notables, including David Dale Owen and Joseph Neef.

Lining New Harmony's streets are golden rain trees (*Koelreuteria paniculata*), supposedly introduced by the naturalist Thomas Say. The trees bear bright yellow flowers in June that become long seedpods by the fall.

Several buildings of historical significance are privately owned and not open to the public. However, visitors will want to take note of them.

The **Hilarus Henning House** (1823) was originally a Rappite family dwelling and for a time the residence of Joseph Neef and Charles-Alexandre Lesueur.

Rapp-Maclure-Owen Mansion (1844), the town's dominating structure, located prominently on the corners of Church and Main Streets, was restyled and rebuilt by Alexander Maclure, the brother of William Maclure. The white one-story Greek Revival residence was built on the foundation of the residence of New Harmony's founder, George Rapp. From 1850 to 1860, it was David Dale Owen's residence. On the grounds is the tomb of Thomas Say, called the founding father of American zoology, who died in New Harmony in 1834. **Footprint rock** was found by George Rapp; he claimed it bore an angel's footprint.

The vine-covered **granary** (1819), a large stone and brick building, was erected by the Rappites to store grain and supplies. It also served them as a fort. In 1843, David Dale Owen housed his third geological laboratory here.

The **Owen Geological Laboratory** (1859) is an imposing stone building with a turret. It was designed and built by David Dale Owen.

Joseph Neef House (1822), a Harmonist frame and brick family dwelling, became the home of Joseph Neef.

SIDE TRIPS

New Harmony's **commercial district** provides interesting browsing and shopping. A visit to the **Red Geranium Bookstore**, which has a large collection of books on New Harmony, Americana, history, antiques, and many other related subjects, is highly recommended. There are numerous antique stores, art galleries, and interesting gift shops.

Evansville, Indiana, 30 miles south of New Harmony, is the location of the **Evansville Museum of Arts and Science**, 411 Southeast Riverside Drive, (812)425-2406. It features art, history, and science exhibits. Open Tuesday to Saturday, 10:00 A.M. to 5:00 P.M.; Sunday, noon to 5:00 P.M.; closed New Year's Day, Thanksgiving, and December 24 to 31. Admission is free.

The **Angel Mounds State Memorial**, 7 miles east of Evansville on Route 662, features prehistoric Indian mounds and reconstructed dwellings. Open Wednesday to Saturday, 9:00 A.M. to 5:00 P.M.; Tuesday and Sunday, 1:00 to 5:00 P.M.; closed Mondays, New Year's Day, Good Friday, Thanksgiving, and Christmas. Admission is free. For information, call (812)853-3956.

**Inspirationist communal religious society
from 1854 to 1932; NR**

Address: Amana Colonies Travel Council, Amana, IA 52203
Telephone: (319)622-3051
Location: From I-80, Exit 255, take Route 149 to Route 220; five
colonies are on Route 220; additional colonies are on Route 6
Open: Daily; see descriptions for specific hours of museums and other
attractions
Admission: Nominal admissions to museums; see descriptions
Restaurants: Listed in description of each colony
Shops: Listed in description of each colony

WHERE TO STAY

Motels/Hotels, Amana: Amana Holiday Inn, P.O. Box 187, 52203,
(319)668-1175, $$
Inns, Homestead: Die Heimat Country Inn, 52236, (319)622-3937,
$
Motels/Hotels, Williamsburg: Best Western Colony Haus Motor
Inn, Rural Route 2, 52361, (319)668-2097, $$
Camping, Vinton: Hannen Park, P.O. Box 244, 52349, (319)454-
6382
Camping, Oxford: Kent Park, Rural Route 2, 52322, (319)645-2315

HISTORY

The seven Amana colonies—Amana, West Amana, High Amana, Middle Amana, East Amana, South Amana, and Homestead—were founded in 1855 by members of a predominantly German religious sect, somewhat akin to the Pietists, who called themselves "the true Inspirationists." These colonies, which attract thousands of visitors each year, do not fit precisely the definition of a museum village. They are living communities, but they have also retained a rich heritage that makes them worth visiting for those who wish to experience the cultural, ethnic, and religious diversity that is America's past.

Today, the Amanas are bustling with tourists shopping for the sturdy Amana woolens, handicrafts, and food or eating hearty German family-style dinners in the local restaurants. Of course, shopping and dining are part of a visit to the Amanas, but a traveler should take the time to study and tour the colonies. A walking tour of each colony is a good way to discover their meaning.

The Amana story began in southwestern Germany in 1714, when two *Werkzeuge* ("inspired ones"), Johann Friedrich Rock, son of a Lutheran minister, and Eberhard Ludwig Gruber, a Lutheran clergyman, began to receive what they believed to be divinely inspired messages. Rock, Gruber, and their followers were convinced that as in the days of the Old Testament prophets, God revealed His truths to certain inspired persons. The importance that the group gave to divine inspiration led to the name that they later took as a separate church: the Community of True Inspiration.

The Inspirationists, like the Rappites of New Harmony, Indiana (see page 221), and the Separatists of Zoar, Ohio (see page 242), were seeking a simple and direct religious experience that they found lacking in the more formal Lutheran church. Because they deviated from orthodox doctrine, refused to bear arms, and wanted to educate their children in their own religious beliefs, the Inspirationists were persecuted in Prussia and the other German states. Despite their oppression, they survived and kept their faith alive; and in 1842, they began to emigrate to the United States in search of religious freedom.

They first established communities near Buffalo, New York. After spending a decade in New York, the Inspirationists decided to relocate their communities in the fertile Iowa plains. In 1855, Amana, the first colony, was founded; West Amana, South Amana, High Amana, East Amana, Middle Amana, and later, Homestead, on the railroad line to Iowa City, followed.

The Amana Colonies were established as communal societies, where work was shared and property was held in common. Members lived together and went out to work in the fields, pastures, and mills. The Amanas were governed by a Grand Council of Thirteen Elders; each colony also had a Village Elders Committee as its local government.

The committees made the major decisions for the colonies and also assigned the occupations of the members.

Agriculture was the basis of the Amanas' economy. The Inspirationists' landholdings increased from their original 3,000 acres, purchased in 1855, to an unbroken tract of 25,659 acres by 1932. Land, including the village yards, was intensively cultivated; the chief crops were corn, oats, wheat, hay, and potatoes. A distinctive feature still found in the Amanas is the practice of growing grapes on vine-covered trellises mounted on the facades of buildings; this practice not only provides grapes for the delicious Amana wines but also is a natural form of insulation.

In addition, each village had crafts and industries. Each colony had a blacksmith's shop, cabinetmaker's shop, general store, post office, bakery, dairy, wine cellar, and sawmill. The major industry in Amana and Middle Amana was the manufacture of woolen cloth, and the Amanas today continue to be known for their high-quality wool textiles.

Each colony's building plan emphasized internal order and utility. Most of the Inspirationists lived in communal houses without kitchens. Their homes were made of sandstone, brick, or unpainted wood. The usual plan for these houses was a central hall, with two suites, each with two rooms, on each floor. Cooking was done in communal kitchen houses by crews of ten women, directed by a *Küchenbas* ("kitchen boss"). Meals were served in these large houses to thirty or forty people at a time. The kitchen houses, located on the village's main street, were the heart of the community.

Although the Inspirationists were, and still are, intensely religious people, often attending eleven services each week, many visitors have difficulty in locating the colonies' churches. Unlike other Christian churches, with their steeples and crosses, the stone or brick churches of the Inspirationists are similar to elongated houses, with elders' residences built at the ends.

Each church has two or more meeting rooms, the largest of which was used for the general service. These rather austere rooms are furnished with wooden benches on plain wooden floors; walls are painted a light blue. The general worship service consists of readings from the Bible and the testimonies of *Werkzeuge* and hymn singing.

The Amanas developed an educational system that enhanced the occupations of communal life. Children were sent to the *Kinderschule* ("children's school") from age two to age seven. The *Kinderschule*, which was somewhat like a kindergarten, left mothers free to work while their youngsters were cared for by the women who were assigned to the schools. From ages seven to fourteen, children attended the colonies' schools, which followed a conventional curriculum that stressed reading, writing, and arithmetic.

In 1932, when the United States was being economically ravaged by the Great Depression, the Grand Council, after much debate, proposed the reorganization of the Amanas on the basis of private ownership, with each family receiving shares of common stock. The proposal was voted on in a referendum, and more than 90 percent of the community members approved the change. Several factors appear to have motivated the Amanas, including a belief that private initiative might improve the colonies' economic condition, social and technological changes in American life that reduced the feasibility of separatist communities, and discontent among many young people, particularly women, who felt that the communal system restricted freedom of choice. Although the Amanas have advanced into the twentieth century along with the rest of the nation, the descendants of the earlier settlers continue to adhere to many of the values and practices of their forebears.

TOUR

Each of the seven Amana colonies should be viewed both as an individual community, with its own intrinsic design, and as part of a larger, well-knit network of social life. Each has many sites of historic interest, craft shops, specialty stores, and restaurants featuring German-style food.

Amana

The **Museum of Amana History**, located in the village of Amana, is maintained by the Amana Heritage Society, a not-for-profit organization dedicated to maintaining the Amana tradition. The museum complex, which includes several historic buildings, is devoted to the preservation and exhibition of Amana's documents, tools, and artifacts. We recommend a visit to the museum and a viewing of its slide show on the Amanas' history as the first stop on your tour. The museum is open April 15 to November 15, 10:00 A.M. to 5:00 P.M., Monday to Saturday, and noon to 5:00 P.M., Sundays. Admission: adults, $2.00; children 6 to 14, 75 cents. For further information, write to The Amana Heritage Society, Amana, IA 52203; phone (319)622-3567.

The **Amana Artists Guild Community Arts Center**, located in an 1856 building in High Amana, is maintained by the guild, a nonprofit organization founded in 1978 to preserve the Amana artistic heritage. The art gallery features rotating exhibits of early Amana art, folk art, and crafts. The guild also sponsors classes in basket making, fiber art, tinsmithing, and quilting. Open Friday, Saturday, and Sunday, 11:00 A.M. to 4:00 P.M., June to October. Admission is free. For information, write to Amana Artists Guild, P.O. Box 114, Amana, IA 52203.

Village Tours arranges group tours through all the colonies in visitors' vehicles. For information, call (319)622-3269.

The **Amana Bread and Pastry Shop** sells rolls, coffee cake, bread, and pastries from the Amana Society bakery.

Der WeinKeller sells homemade wines, including grape, rhubarb, cherry, blackberry, apricot, and other fruits.

Antique Tower Haus sells antiques, collectibles, dolls, and miniatures. Open Monday to Saturday from 9:30 A.M. to 5:00 P.M.; Sunday, noon to 5:00 P.M.

Colony Candleworks sells handcrafted candles.

The **Amana General Store** offers gifts, wickery, and woodcarvings. Open Monday to Saturday, 9:00 A.M. to 5:00 P.M.; also open on Sundays from April to November, noon to 4:00 P.M.

The **Amana Meat Shop and Smokehouse** is an old-time butcher shop featuring ham, bacon, sausages, and cheese. Open Monday to Saturday, 8:00 A.M. to 5:00 P.M.

At the **Original Amana Furniture and Clock Shop**, the workshop and display room feature walnut, cherry, and oak furniture handcrafted by a guild of Amana cabinetmakers; there are also grandfather and mantle clocks. The workshop area is open for viewing Monday to Friday, 9:00 A.M. to 3:00 P.M.; display rooms are open Monday to Saturday, 9:00 A.M. to 5:00 P.M. For information, call (319)622-3291.

The **Woolen Mill** features yard goods, mill ends, blankets, robes, pelts, sweaters, jackets, and coats. Open Monday to Saturday, 8:00 A.M. to 5:00 P.M.; Sunday, noon to 5:00 P.M. Guided tours of the manufacturing plant are provided Monday to Friday. For information, call (319)622-3432.

Brooms, baskets, and wooden gift items are featured at the **Broom and Basket Shop**.

The specialties served at the **Ronneburg Restaurant**, (319)622-3641, include sauerbraten and dumplings, Wiener schnitzel, and spaetzles. There is an outdoor garden. Open Monday to Saturday, 11:00 A.M. to 2:00 P.M. and 5:00 to 8:00 P.M.; Sunday, 11:00 A.M. to 8:00 P.M.

The atmosphere at **Zum Burghof**, on Main Street, is European. The food served is German-American. Open 8:30 A.M. to 10:00 P.M., Monday to Saturday; noon to 10:00 P.M. on Sunday. (319)622-3648.

The **Ox Yoke Inn** features German and American food served family style. It also has a gift shop and a small museum exhibiting Amana tools and artifacts. (319)622-3441.

West Amana

The 1863 **West Amana Store**, a restored sandstone structure, features antiques, quilts, folk art, and other items made by local craftspeople. Open Monday to Saturday, 9:00 A.M. to 9:00 P.M.; Sunday, noon to 6:00 P.M.

Middle Amana

The **Kraus Old Style Colony Winery** features naturally fermented wines made from fruit, berries, vegetables, and blossoms. Open daily, 9:00 A.M. to 6:00 P.M.

At **Hahn's Hearth Oven Bakery** they still use the original wood-fired oven. Hearth-baked homemade breads and cakes are the specialties. Open from 7:30 A.M., Tuesday to Saturday in April, Monday to Saturday in May through October, and on Wednesdays and Saturdays only in March, November, and December.

The **Community Kitchen, Cooper Shop,** and **Hearth Oven Museum** are open daily, 10:00 A.M. to 5:00 P.M., spring through fall. There is a nominal admission charge.

Amana Refrigeration, Inc., is a well-known manufacturer of refrigerators, freezers, ranges, and air-conditioners. For information, call (319)622-5511.

Hahn Brothers Furniture and Clock Shop sells custom-made handcrafted furniture and clocks. Open Monday to Saturday, 9:00 A.M. to 3:00 P.M.

South Amana

At the **Barn,** you can see farm equipment and tools of the early Amana period and Henry Moore's *Amana and Americana in Miniature.* Open Monday to Saturday, 9:00 A.M. to 5:00 P.M.; Sunday, 1:00 to 4:00 P.M.; closed during the winter months. There is a nominal admission fee.

The **Ackerman Winery and Cheese Shop** features a wide variety of wines made on the premises from fruit, vegetables, flowers, and berries. Open Monday to Saturday, 9:00 A.M. to 6:00 P.M., May 1 to October 31; 9:00 A.M. to 5:00 P.M. during the rest of the year. Open Sunday, noon to 5:00 P.M. in the summer only.

The **Amana General Store—Pottery, Toy, and Christmas Shop** features pottery produced on the premises, other gifts, and specialty items. Open Monday to Saturday, May to November, 9:00 A.M. to 5:00 P.M.; December to April, 10:00 A.M. to 5:00 P.M.; on Sunday, May to October, from noon to 4:00 P.M.

The **Brumwell Flour Mill,** located ½ mile east of South Amana on Highways 149 and 6, features stone-ground flours such as wheat, corn, oats, rye, and buckwheat; pancake mixes; jellies; and preserves. Open Monday to Friday, 9:00 A.M. to 5:00 P.M.; Saturday, 9:00 A.M. to 4:00 P.M.

At the **Krauss Furniture Shop,** the woodshop and salesroom feature custom-made walnut, cherry, and oak furniture and clocks. Free shop tours available. Located ½ mile east of South Amana on Highways 149 and 6. Open Monday to Saturday, 8:00 A.M. to 5:00 P.M.; Sunday, 1:00 to 4:00 P.M., May to December only; closed holidays.

Homestead

The **Amana Home and Blacksmith Shop Museum** is a century-old home featuring a display of antiques. This eight-room brick house contains furniture and other decorative arts of the early Amana period. The interior is painted in the light blue popular in Amana. One of the rooms has an exhibit of children's toys and furniture. There is also a blacksmith shop with hearth, forge, and tools. Open Monday to Saturday, 10:00 A.M. to 5:00 P.M., year-round; Sunday, noon to 5:00 P.M., April to November. For further information, write to The Amana Home and Blacksmith Shop Museum, Homestead, IA 52236; phone (319)622-3976. Admission: adults, $1.00; children, 25 cents.

The **Ehrle Brothers Winery** is the oldest winery in the Amanas. The wines are naturally fermented in oak barrels. Summer hours, 9:00 A.M. to 6:00 P.M.; winter hours, 10:00 A.M. to 5:30 P.M.

The **Amana Meat Shop and Smoke House** features ham, bacon, sausages, and cheeses. Open Monday to Saturday, 8:00 A.M. to 5:00 P.M..

In 1948, Bill Zuber, a former New York Yankee pitcher, returned to his home and established **Bill Zuber's Restaurant** in the 100-year-old **Homestead Hotel**. The specialties include Amana smoked pork, Wiener schnitzel, country fried chicken, and oven-baked steak served family style. Open Monday to Saturday, 11:00 A.M. to 2:00 P.M. and 4:30 to 8:00 P.M.; Sunday, 11:00 A.M. to 8:00 P.M. Phone (319)622-3911.

The **Amana General Store's Yarn and Needlecraft Department** features Amana products and gifts. Open Monday to Saturday, 9:00 A.M. to 5:00 P.M.

SIDE TRIPS

Travelers may wish to visit the **Herbert Hoover National Historic Site**. The Hoover house, museum, and presidential library are located three-quarters of a mile north of I-80 at Exit 63. The house, restored to its 1871 appearance, was the birthplace and boyhood home of Herbert Hoover from 1874 to 1883. Hoover, the thirtieth president of the United States, served from 1929 to 1932. Open daily, 8:00 A.M. to 5:00 P.M.; closed New Year's Day, Thanksgiving, and Christmas. For further information, write Herbert Hoover National Historic Site, P.O. Box 607, West Branch, IA 52358; phone (319)643-2541.

Schoenbrunn Village State Memorial

**Reconstruction of a 1772 Moravian
mission to Indians; NR**

Address: P.O. Box 129, New Philadelphia, OH 44663
Telephone: (216)339-3636
Location: 4 miles east of I-77 on Route 259
Open: Wednesday to Saturday, 9:30 A.M. to 5:00 P.M.; Sunday and
holidays, noon to 5:00 P.M.; Memorial Day to Labor Day. Saturday,
9:30 A.M. to 5:00 P.M.; Sunday, noon to 5:00 P.M.; after Labor Day to
October 31. Open by appointment for groups from April 1 to May
24.
Admission: Adults, $2.00; children 6 to 12, $1.00; group rates
available
Shops: Gift Shop, souvenirs and books
Facilities: Museum, picnic area, accessible to handicapped

WHERE TO STAY
Resorts, Dellroy: Atwood Lake Lodge Resort and Cottages, P.O.
Box 96, 44663, (216)735-2211, $$
Motels/Hotels, New Philadelphia: Delphian Motor Inn, 1281 West
High Avenue, 44663, (216)339-6644, $; Holiday Inn, 131 Bluebell

Drive, SW, 44663, (216)339-7731, $$; Motel 6, 181 Bluebell Drive, SW, 44663, (216)339-6530, $; Penny Pincher Inn, 1256 West High Avenue, P.O. Box 727, 44663, (216)339-6671, $

Camping, New Philadelphia: Tall Timber Lake, Tall Timber Road, Box 1188A, 44663, (216)364-9930 or (216)364-3474; Mushingum Conservancy Lake, 1319 3rd Street, NW, 44663, (216)343-6647

HISTORY

Schoenbrunn Village is a state memorial maintained by the Ohio Historical Society. It is a reconstruction on the site of a settlement built by Moravian missionaries in the 1770s for Christianized Indians (see Old Salem, North Carolina, page 138, for a description of the Moravian movement). Schoenbrunn, which was founded by David Zeisberger, was Ohio's first town.

The Moravians came to Ohio because, as pacifists, they had been plagued by warfare in Pennsylvania and New York, where they settled after emigrating from Germany. Zeisberger had been offered protection by King Natawatwes, the Delaware chief. Schoenbrunn ("beautiful spring" in German) was the first of six settlements built by the Moravians in Ohio.

Unlike other settlers, the Moravian missionaries were sympathetic to the Indians and tried to understand their language and customs while working to convert them to Christianity. The Moravians taught the Indians to build towns, introduced improved agricultural practices and European craft skills, taught reading and writing, and translated hymn books, the Bible, and spelling books into Indian languages. The community was prosperous and had ample harvests of corn, pumpkins, beans, and other vegetables. Hogs, cattle, and horses were raised by the Indians, whose produce and possessions were held in common.

To govern the village, the missionaries enacted nineteen ordinances entitled *Rules of Government for the Schoenbrunn Mission.* Based on the Ten Commandments and the Moravian moral and ethical code, the rules stressed pacifism.

Pacifism became a problem at Schoenbrunn when its inhabitants were caught between the opposing American and British forces during the Revolutionary War. Several attacks occurred near the Moravian Indian settlements. Because of the conflict, Zeisberger ordered Schoenbrunn to be abandoned; and in April 1777, the band moved to Lichtener, south of Coshocton. Schoenbrunn was destroyed in the course of the conflict.

In 1779, a new village was built on the west bank of the Tuscarawas River; it was called New Schoenbrunn. Gnadenhutten, another Moravian settlement nearby, was also resettled.

Still under suspicion, the Christian Indians were removed by British troops to the Sandusky River in 1781, and Zeisberger and the other missionaries were accused of spying and sent to Detroit.

In February 1782, a group of Christian Indians was permitted to return to the Tuscarawas towns to harvest corn and gather their belongings. When they arrived, they encountered a company of American militia who were retaliating for Indian raids. The Christian Indians, whom the Americans accused of giving aid and information to the British, were rounded up at Gnadenhutten. After taking a vote, the Americans decided to kill the pacifist Indians. Sixty-two adults and thirty-four children were massacred, and Gnadenhutten was burned.

After the Revolution, Moravian missionaries returned to central Ohio. When the Indians were removed from the area, the Moravian efforts to convert them to Christianity ended. However, descendants of the Moravian settlers continue to live in the area.

In 1923, an archaeological investigation of the Schoenbrunn site was begun with the support of the Tuscarawas County Historical Society and the Ohio State Archaeological and Historical Society, which acquired the site. The Moravian missionaries left copious written accounts of their work at Schoenbrunn, and their detailed diaries and maps have provided the basis for accurate reconstruction of the village.

TOUR

Schoenbrunn as it stands now has about nineteen structures on their original sites, as determined by archaeological research. These include a school, church, log cabins, museum, trading post, cemetery, and two and a half acres of planted fields. Many of the inhabitants of this serene village became martyrs in spite of their peace-loving ways. Moravian respect for Indian culture, if imitated by other white settlers, might have avoided some of the tragedies of white-Indian relations in early American history.

Schoenbrunn was laid out in a T-shaped plan, with the school and church located at the center of the town. The reconstructed **church** (1773) was built of hewn logs and roofed with wood shingles; the windows were covered with deerskins. Called a *Gemeinde Saal*, the church could accommodate 300 people on simple wooden benches at daily religious services. A bell brought from the Pennsylvania settlement of Friedenshuetten hung in the church belfry.

Next to the church stood the **cabins of the ministers**. The **Indian cabins**, built of unhewn and sometimes squared logs, lined the village streets. By 1775, the village contained more than sixty structures.

In 1772, the Indians began constructing the village **schoolhouse** of hewn and squared timbers. By 1775, nearly 100 children were attending the *Schule*. Zeisberger and John Heckewelder and their assistants were the schoolteachers. They instructed the children in their native

Indian tongue and introduced them to the English language, as well as the Moravians' native language, German. Because they had no books for the children, the teachers had to write them. This large school is said to have been the first in Ohio. Inside the reconstructed school, there is a schoolmaster's desk, students' benches, and a fireplace.

The first cabin was reconstructed in 1927. It was the home of Schebosch, a white man with an Indian name. Schebosch, a Quaker originally named Joseph Bull, was an assistant to Zeisberger. His wife was a Christian Indian. The **Schebosch Cabin**, built in the early 1770s, as were the other log cabins in the village, is simply furnished with crude tables, chairs, and beds. Construction on several log buildings has been stopped at various stages in order to display building techniques.

During the reconstruction work, the Christian Indian cemetery, known as **Gotesacker** (God's Acre), was also discovered at the far end of the village. The original grave markers, flat and ledge-rock stones, are crudely but legibly inscribed. Even the fence post holes were discernible, making the replacement of the cemetery fence possible. Landscaping with indigenous plants and shrubs completes the authentic setting.

Guides dressed in eighteenth-century costumes answer questions as they go about the business of making candles, cooking over a fireplace, sewing, chinking, weaving mats, and working in the fields.

The **museum** tells the story of the Christian Delawares and the Moravian missionaries at Schoenbrunn through exhibits. *Trumpet in the Land*, an outdoor drama about the Moravians and the Delaware Indians in Ohio's Tuscarawas Valley, is performed in the **Schoenbrunn Amphitheater**, Tuesday to Sunday, 8:15 P.M., July to Labor Day. Admission: adults, $7.00 and $8.00; children under 12, $6.00. (216)339-1132.

SIDE TRIPS

A memorial marks the burial site of the more than ninety Indians massacred at **Gnadenhutten** in 1782. There is also an **Indian museum**. Summer hours only. Gnadenhutten, 44629.

Roscoe Village in Coshocton, page 248, and Zoar Village State Memorial in Zoar, page 242, are within easy driving distance of Schoenbrunn.

Hale Farm and Western Reserve Village

Recreated Western Reserve village and
original farmstead; Western Reserve
Historical Society Site

Address: 2686 Oak Hill Road, P.O. Box 256, Bath, OH 44210
Telephone: In Akron, (216)666-3711; in Cleveland, (216)861-4573
Location: In the Cuyahoga Valley National Recreation Area between
Cleveland and Akron
Open: Tuesday to Saturday, 10:00 A.M. to 5:00 P.M.; Sunday and
holidays, noon to 5:00 P.M.; May to October. Open in December on
a limited schedule.
Admission: Adults, $3.50; children 6 to 16, $2.00; senior citizens 60
and over, $2.00; children under 6 admitted free with family. Group
rates and family rates available.
Restaurants: Snack bar, Country Cottage
Shops: General Store and Museum Shop, period reproductions, sou-
venirs, books
Facilities: Admission and Information Booth, picnic areas

WHERE TO STAY

Motels/Hotels, Akron: Hilton Inn, 3180 West Market Street,
44313, (216)867-5000, $$–$$$; Holiday Inn—West, 3150 West
Market Street, 44313, (216)836-8431, $$; L-K Motel, 4015 Medina
Road, 44313, (216)666-3741, $–$$; Ramada Inn, 4073 Medina
Road, 44313, (216)666-4131, $$; Red Roof Inn, 99 Rothrock Road,
44321, (216)666-0566, $
Camping, Fulton: Clay's Park, P.O. Box 182, Canal Street, 44614,
(216)854-3961
Camping, Rootstown: Hickory Hills, 4527 Hattrick Street, 44272,
(216)325-7425
Camping, Streetsboro: Mar-Lynn Lake Park, 187 Highway 303,
44268, (216)653-8998; Woodside Lake Park, 2256 Frost Road,
44240, (216)562-6500
Camping, Peninsula: Tams in Park, 5008 Akron-Cleveland Road,
44264, (216)653-6316

HISTORY

Hale Farm and Village, a living history museum, depicts village life in Ohio's Western Reserve from 1825 to 1850. The history of the Western Reserve goes back to Ohio's settlement. In 1795, the Indian tribes of the Ohio territory surrendered their land to General Anthony Wayne in the Treaty of Greenville. The term *Western Reserve* referred to the Western territories that Connecticut had once retained to meet the claims of its Revolutionary War veterans. Stretching southward from the shores of Lake Erie, the Western Reserve's fertile soil attracted a steady stream of migrants from the Northeastern states of Connecticut, Massachusetts, Vermont, and New York. These settlers brought with them their township government system and their commitment to education.

Ohio, the first state organized out of the Northwest Territory, adopted its constitution in 1802. One of the most democratic documents of the early nineteenth century, it provided for the election of most officials, eliminated property requirements for voting, and abolished imprisonment for debt.

Although industry developed later in the nineteenth century, agriculture, such as that depicted on the Hale Farm, remained the chief occupation in Ohio's Western Reserve. The family farm was the basic economic unit, and most farmers raised corn, wheat, cattle, and hogs, especially the sturdy razorback hog. The region's economic development was advanced by the construction of the Erie Canal, which linked the Hudson River with the Great Lakes. Built between 1817 and 1825 at a cost of $8 million, the canal made it possible for Western farmers to transport their crops to Eastern markets. By the 1840s, the area's farms were producing surpluses for sale in the growing Eastern cities. (A series of canals would be dug in other regions of Ohio later in the century. See Roscoe Village, page 248, for a description of the Ohio-Erie Canal.)

Jonathan Hale's farm represents the operation and development of a typical family farm. Like many settlers in the Western Reserve, Hale moved his family from Connecticut to Ohio. Arriving in 1810, they lived in a log cabin until 1826. By then, Hale was more prosperous and built a large brick house modeled on the architecture of New England.

The Western Reserve Village, a reconstructed community containing buildings from the area that have been moved from their original sites, is laid out on the New England pattern. Because the majority of settlers in the Western Reserve were transplanted New Englanders, they sought to recreate a New England town in the Midwest.

The Hale Farm and Village is a department of the Western Reserve Historical Society, a private, nonprofit organization. Historic preservation and recreation began in 1956 when Clara Belle Ritchie, Jonathan Hale's great-granddaughter, willed the property to the society.

TOUR

The site's service buildings include the **Admissions Office**; a **refreshment center**, serving beverages and sandwiches; and the **carriage shed**.

The **Hale House**, built in 1826 by Jonathan Hale in the Federal style, contains an 1830s kitchen with a bake oven and fireplace for cooking, and a root cellar, which is now a candle-making room. The comfortable living areas, furnished with fashionable period pieces, reflect the family's later prosperity. Craft demonstrations take place behind the house, and a museum shop and General Store is located at the rear of the house. Nearby, a steam-operated sawmill operates on most weekends.

The household garden's variety of plants is typical of farm gardens of the 1830s. An herb garden contains medicinal and cooking herbs. The **apple orchard** is located near the house, between the **north pasture** and the **garden barn**. The varieties of apples are those grown by the Hales during the mid-1830s.

On the east side of Oak Hill Road lies the **Western Reserve Village**. It is plotted in New England fashion on a village green.

The **Law Office**, built in 1830 in Jefferson in the Federal style, was used by a U.S. senator from Ohio, Benjamin F. Wade.

The **Mary Ann Sears Swetland Memorial Meetinghouse**, built in the Greek Revival style in 1851, was moved from Streetsboro, where it served a Baptist congregation.

The **Log Schoolhouse**, built in 1816 in Summitville, was a home and then a church before it became a school. You may even see a class of children dressed in period clothing reciting their lessons for their teacher.

The **Jagger House**, built in 1845 in the Greek Revival style, was the residence of Clement Jagger, a carriage maker from Bath.

The **Federal Saltbox House** was built in 1830 in Richfield. It houses spinning and weaving demonstrations.

The **Glassworks Exhibit**, housed in a log barn built in 1811 in Wellsville, contains the excavated remnants of an early Kent glassworks, as well as examples of early glassware.

SIDE TRIPS

Akron, which is 10 miles from the Hale Farm and Western Reserve Village, offers several interesting attractions. The **Summit County Historical Society**, 550 Copley Road, (216)535-1120, conducts tours of the **Simon Perkin's Mansion** (1837) and the **John Brown Home**. Open daily except Mondays and holidays, 1:00 to 5:00 P.M. Admission, adults, $2.00; children 5 to 16 and senior citizens, $1.50. **Cuyahoga Valley National Recreation Area**, located north of Akron, (216)650-4636, offers extensive recreational facilities and naturalist programs.

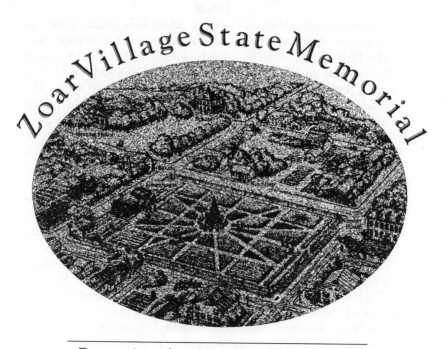

Zoar Village State Memorial

**Restoration of an 1830s communal society
of German Separatists; NR, HABS**

Address: P.O. Box 523, Zoar, OH 44697
Telephone: (216)874-3011
Location: South of Canton, 3 miles southeast of I-77 Exit 93, on Route 212
Open: Wednesday to Saturday, 9:30 A.M. to 5:00 P.M.; Sunday, Monday, and holidays, noon to 5:00 P.M.; closed Tuesday, May 25 to Labor Day. Open weekends, noon to 5:00 P.M. during April, May, September, and October for groups by appointment.
Admission: Adults, $2.00; children 6 to 12, $1.00; special rates for senior citizens and groups
Restaurants: The Inn on the River, in an 1829 canal inn; The Old Homestead Family Restaurant, in an 1831 doctor's office; Zoar Tavern, in an 1831 doctor's residence
Shops: The Store, reproduction pottery, baskets, candles
Facilities: Not accessible to handicapped

WHERE TO STAY
Bed and Breakfast, Zoar: All these accommodations are located in original Zoarite buildings within the twelve-block historic district.

Zoar Weaving Haus, Main and 5th Streets, 52203, (216)874-2237, $; Cider Mill Antiques and Gifts, 2nd Street, 52203, (216)874-3133, $; Cobbler Shop Inn and Antiques, 2nd Street, 52203, (216)874-2600, $; Cowger House No. 9, Park and 4th Streets, 52203, (216)874-3542, $; Lamp and Lanterns, 3rd Street, 52203, (216)874-4736, $

New Philadelphia: See listings for Schoenbrunn Village, page 235

HISTORY

Zoar Village State Memorial is a museum complex of eight restored buildings maintained by the Ohio Historical Society within the town of Zoar. It is the location of a community that was established by a group of German Separatists headed by Joseph Bimeler. Persecuted in their homeland for their religious beliefs, 300 men, women, and children from Württemburg reached Philadelphia in August 1817. There they hoped to practice their religion in peace. The pietistical Separatists, who left the Lutheran church, did not believe in sacraments and refused to enter military service, pay taxes, or send their children to state schools.

In Philadelphia, Joseph Bimeler and his group were warmly received by the Quakers. With their financial assistance, the relatively impoverished Separatists purchased 5,500 acres along the Tuscarawas River in Ohio from Godfrey Haga for $16,500. When Bimeler and a few of his men visited the Tuscarawas Valley, they were delighted to find heavily wooded hills, fertile plains, and several good springs.

The first log cabin in the town the Separatists called Zoar was completed in December 1817. More houses were added during the winter and spring. The first two winters at Zoar were very hard, and the harvests were not adequate to feed the people. Because of the difficult financial situation, Johannes Breymaier, one of the group's early leaders, advocated a communal economy. There would be no private ownership of property, and all resources would be pooled. Although the idea met some resistance at first, eventually communalism was backed enthusiastically.

The Society of Separatists of Zoar was formed April 15, 1819. According to the Articles of 1819, property was owned communally. Members worked where needed in shops or fields in return for being provided the necessities of life: food, clothing, and housing. Officers of the society were elected. Joseph Bimeler held the office of cashier and agent-general from 1819 until his death in 1853.

The economic base of the Zoarites was agricultural. They raised wheat, oats, rye, barley, and vegetables. Beer and wine were produced from their own orchards and vineyards. Among their industrial pursuits were wagon, cooper, and tin shops; a saddlery; flour, woolen, saw, and planing mills; and two blast furnaces. A general store and hotel catered to outside customers.

By 1835, Zoar was practically self-sustaining. The society produced all its own food except tea, coffee, and rice and made its own cloth. The houses were built of Zoar sandstone, roofed with Zoar tile, and heated with Zoar stoves. The shops produced furniture, kitchen utensils, tools, and plows. Revenue from the sale of surplus products paid mortgages and taxes. The society made the last payment on its land in 1830 and reached the height of its prosperity in the 1850s. In 1852, Zoar property was estimated to be worth $1 million. The Ohio Canal crossed the property, opening new markets for Zoar products, and the community owned and operated four canalboats.

Celibacy was adopted at Zoar in 1822 primarily because of economic necessity. Two-thirds of the members of the society were women, which left a small work force of men; women were needed in the workplace, but childbearing interfered with work. By 1830, when the community had achieved a level of prosperity, celibacy was discontinued, and the ban on marriage was lifted.

In a similar effort to free women for the workplace, children aged three to fourteen were placed in nurseries in the care of the older women of the society. After 1840, placing children in nurseries became optional, and in 1860, the nurseries were abolished.

As the community prospered, crude log cabins were replaced with larger frame or brick houses with front and back porches. These houses had large, comfortable rooms but were simple in design. Joseph Bimeler's home, built originally as a home for the aged, was quite elaborate. The Zoarites built a church in 1854 and a school in 1868.

Zoarites were noted for their industry, cleanliness, and love of music and flowers. An entire block in the center of Zoar was occupied by a garden that was designed as a religious symbol. One of the most distinctive features at Zoar was its greenhouse, and the community became known for exotic and varied plants and bulbs.

The communal society that began in 1817 and ended in 1898 was most vigorous and prosperous in the 1830s and 1840s, when its membership increased from 300 to 500. Joseph Bimeler was the driving force behind the development of Zoar. He was a gifted orator, an untrained doctor who was able to effect many cures, a highly successful business agent for the community, and a pastor with an unselfish devotion to his people. Bimeler's death in 1853 was a severe blow to Zoar. Although other good men succeeded him, none had his combination of business sense and religious zeal.

As the first generation of Zoarites, the original immigrants, died off, their children did not have the same appreciation of religious freedom. The Civil War was difficult for the pacifist society, and in spite of their upbringing, fourteen Zoar boys ran off to enlist. Industries at Zoar failed to keep up with the technological changes of the nineteenth century. Their production methods became outdated, and they were unable to compete. Poor investments resulted in heavy financial losses. Discord resulted from hiring nonmember laborers, who not only introduced worldly ways but also received cash payments, which Zoarites never did.

The Zoar Hotel was a disruptive factor in the community. Although hotel business was vigorously pursued because it brought in income, good business meant numbers of people with different beliefs coming to Zoar. Employees of the hotel received cash tips, which they pocketed against society regulations. Many Zoar families started selling produce and craft items to the increasing number of tourists for cash. The best food was served in the hotel and was shared by employees, much to the displeasure of other Zoarites, who felt that they were not receiving equal treatment.

One frequent hotel visitor, Alexander Gunn, a retired businessman from Cleveland, liked Zoar so much that he purchased a log cabin there. He was not a member of the society nor even a German, a prerequisite for membership. Moreover, he used the cabin to entertain the society's leaders, alienating the envious membership from their leaders.

Business declines, outside influences on the membership, internal rivalries, and lessening religious commitment all contributed to the dissolution of the Zoar society. The membership decided to dissolve it on March 10, 1898. Property was distributed among the permanent membership, with families receiving a home, land, personal clothing and furniture, and some cash. Those involved in the society's industries received a share of those businesses.

The Ohio Historical Society acquired several Zoar buildings in the 1940s and 1960s. The buildings have been faithfully restored to their appearance in the 1830s, the period of Zoar's greatest prosperity, and are now open to the public.

TOUR

It is easy to recapture the atmosphere of the nineteenth century in Zoar. Because of its relatively isolated location and peaceful setting, the town has retained much of its simplicity and charm. Each of the restored buildings has a costumed guide who provides a short narration of its history and answers questions. In addition to the state-owned and maintained buildings, a number of Zoarite dwellings are being restored by private owners. A walking tour of Zoar takes approximately three hours.

The **Number One House**, built in 1835, was the home of Joseph

Bimeler and the administrative center of the community. It was originally intended to be a home for the community's aged but was never really used for that purpose. A two-and-a-half-story red brick Georgian colonial mansion, the house contained three separate living quarters for the Bimeler family and two of the trustees and their families.

Some of the furnishings are Zoarite pieces, which are simple and Germanic; some are more elegant Empire-style pieces. Bimeler conducted business from his office in the Number One House, and it contains a desk specially made for him at Zoar.

An exhibit of clothes and coverlets occupies one room. A deep cellar, where the temperature is an even 50 degrees Fahrenheit, was used by the community for storing fruits and vegetables. A slide presentation on Zoar is shown in the house.

A **Greenhouse** and a large **garden** are special features of the community. The formal garden, which occupies an entire block, contains beautiful annuals, perennials, shrubs, and herbs, reflecting the Separatists' love of flowers. The gardens of Zoar became well known and spawned a thriving business in the sale of plants and bulbs.

The garden's design is symbolic of New Jerusalem as described in the Revelation of Saint John the Divine in the Bible. A wide border path symbolizes the earthly road taken by the unredeemed, and twelve narrow walkways lead to a Norway spruce, the tree of everlasting life.

The greenhouse, with its attached **Gardener's Residence**, dates from 1835. The Zoarites raised oranges and lemons, regarded as exotic fruits for Ohio. The greenhouse was heated by a system of pipes under the floor that brought in warm air from an outside charcoal furnace. Seedlings for the garden were raised in the greenhouse, and people from Cleveland sent their best plants to Zoar for the winter.

The simple gardener's residence has been restored and is decorated with Zoar furniture. There is a parlor downstairs and a bedroom upstairs; the kitchen is outside.

The **Bakery**, built in 1835, provided daily bread for the residents of Zoar. Bread was baked in two brick ovens that could hold fifteen loaves each. The baker lived upstairs in the two-story stone and clapboard house.

The **Store** (1833) was the center for the community's commercial dealings with the outside world. It stocked items made in the community and other necessary goods. Society members could take what they needed from the store free. Today, the store has been restored to its original appearance. Visitors may purchase reproduction pottery, baskets, candles, cloth, tinware, and other items.

Several craft shops, which required some reconstruction, are open and operative at Zoar. The **Tin Shop**, which was built in 1825, was torn down in the 1940s. Now rebuilt on its original foundation, the small two-room structure is of brick and timber. This building is a good example of the Zoar method of construction called *nogging*: Soft bricks or sandstone were placed between framing timbers. The inside of the building was then covered with plaster, and the outside was covered with clapboards, brick, or stucco.

The tinsmith produced household products such as basins, cups, buckets, sconces, and milk pails. Similar items are produced in the restored shop; traditional tools and methods are used.

Buggies and farm wagons were built in the restored **wagon shop**, which dates from 1840. The nearby **blacksmith shop** produced any metal tools or parts required by the society. The charcoal-fired forge, with its huge bellows, is going again, demonstrating traditional methods.

The **Bimeler Museum** was the residence of Joseph's grandson, Peter, the community miller. It is furnished as it would have looked in the 1890s, at the end of the communal experience.

The **Zoar Hotel**, scheduled to reopen as a restaurant by the 1986 season, was built in the 1830s. As a popular resort hotel, it was visited by distinguished Ohioans, including President William McKinley.

Many other Zoarite buildings that are privately owned and used as residences or businesses can be seen on a leisurely stroll around the town.

Special events at Zoar include the Spring Home Tour and Luncheon, during which some privately owned homes are open for viewing; the Quilt Show in June; the Schwabenfest in July; the Harvest Festival and the Flower Show in August; six-week antiques seminars in September and October; and a Christmas celebration in December.

Roscoe Village

Restoration of an 1830s Ohio canal town; NR

Address: 381 Hill Street, Coshocton, OH 43812
Telephone: (614)622-9310
Location: In east central Ohio on Routes 16 and 83, near the junction of Route 36
Open: Daily, 11:00 A.M. to 5:00 P.M., September to May; 10:00 A.M. to 6:00 P.M., June to August; closed Thanksgiving, Christmas, and New Year's Day
Admission: Adults, $3.50; children 8 to 18, $1.75
Restaurants: Roscoe Village Inn Dining Room, Old Warehouse Restaurant, Captain Nye's Sweet Shop
Shops: Craft House, pottery, gift items; Village Smithy, ironware; Jackson Township Hall, handcrafted weavings
Facilities: Visitors' Center, slide presentation, gardens, horse-drawn trolley and canalboat rides (additional charge for rides), accessible to handicapped

WHERE TO STAY

Inns, Coshocton: Roscoe Village Inn, 200 North Whitewoman Street, 43812, (614)622-2222, $$
Motels/Hotels, Coshocton: L-K Motel, 275 South Whitewoman Street, 43812, (614)622-9823, $$; Downtown Motel, 723 Main Street, 43812, (614)622-6607, $$; Park Hotel, 325 Main Street, 43812, (614)622-4846, $$
Camping, Coshocton: Lake Park, P.O. Box 644, Route 83, 43812, (614)622-7258; Roscoe Colonial R.V. Park, 43812, (614)622-1695; Shady Grove Campground, People Inc., 405 North 5th Street, 43812, (614)622-2761
Camping, Fresno: Forest Hill Lake, Rural Route 2, Route 425, 43824, (614)545-9642

HISTORY

Roscoe Village is a restored nineteenth-century canal town. In 1816, James Calder, a bankrupt merchant from Coshocton, decided to open a general store and to found a new town on the west side of the Muskingum River. He named the town Caldersburgh.

In the early 1800s, central Ohio was still a frontier region. Although rich in agricultural and natural resources, the farmers of central Ohio lacked a convenient method of shipping goods and produce to Eastern markets. A system of canals, proposed originally by George Washington, was needed to remedy the transportation problem. Construction on the long-delayed Ohio and Erie Canal was finally begun July 4, 1825, at Locking Summit. The Ohio and Erie Canal would connect Ohio's central region with Cleveland on Lake Erie and Portsmouth on the Ohio River, as well as with the older Erie Canal.

On August 21, 1830, the excited residents of Caldersburgh watched as the first canalboat, the *Monticello*, arrived. Caldersburgh's location on the canal near the forks of the Walhonding, Tuscarawas, and Muskingum Rivers made it a potentially important trading port. Realizing that, two speculators, Leander Ransom and Noah Swayne, not only came to Caldersburgh but succeeded in changing its name to Roscoe in December 1830, only four months after the opening of the canal. The newly named town honored William Roscoe, a well-known British banker and abolitionist poet.

On a tract of land north of town, Ransom and Swayne laid out lots between Calder's sixty-seven lots and the Triple Locks. As canal activity increased, the village's business center moved from the old Caldersburgh section to the Ransom and Swayne addition, which was closer to the locks and aqueduct. Eventually, James Calder, again suffering financial problems, left the town that he had founded.

Thanks to the canal, Roscoe became a flourishing wheat and wool depot, providing a much-needed market for area farmers. As the town prospered, industries, including mills, a cooperage, a foundry, and a brickyard, developed. A warehouse was built for the sole purpose of shipping, and local lumberyards built canalboats.

Coshocton County doubled in population in ten years, from 11,000 in 1830 to 22,000 in 1840.

In 1852, the canals carried rails and ties for building the railway. Thus, the canals participated in their own demise as the railroads became the preferred way of shipping goods. The Ohio and Erie Canal continued to do some shipping until the flood of 1913 destroyed most of the system. Towns dependent on the canal, as Roscoe was, slipped into decline.

In 1968, Coshocton businessman Edward Montgomery and his wife, Frances, began restoring Roscoe as an 1830s bustling canal town. The Montgomerys were inspired by an eight-by-twenty-four-foot mural entitled *Canal Days*, which depicts a canal village scene in the mid-1800s. This mural, painted by Dean Cornwell in 1959, is permanently displayed in the lobby of the Coshocton National Bank.

TOUR

Roscoe Village's commercial, industrial, residential, and canal-related buildings, some in Greek Revival style, are of brick construction; many roofs have stepped gable ends, and windows have stone sills and lintels. Some of the restored buildings are used as shops, and there is no charge to enter. Admission is charged only for the exhibit buildings.

The five exhibit buildings are interspersed with old-time shops in canal-era buildings along Whitewoman Street. Brick sidewalks and street lampposts add to the early nineteenth-century atmosphere. Whitewoman Street is named after the Walhonding River, which flows by Roscoe Village; *walhonding* is a Delaware Indian word meaning white woman.

Begin your tour at the **Visitors' Center**, where you'll see a slide presentation, receive a brief orientation, and buy your tickets. A self-guided walking tour of the village takes approximately two hours.

Jackson Township Hall was the seat of community government in the 1880s. Now, spinning and weaving demonstrations are given on nineteenth-century looms. On the lower, or canal, level of the hall, is a model of the railroad that crossed the Triple Locks and Roscoe Basin.

The Georgian **Johnson House** was home to Dr. Maro Johnson, a prominent doctor in Roscoe. It has been restored to its 1840 appearance and is furnished with antiques dating from the 1700s to the 1840s.

The **Tollhouse** (1830) is where canalboats paid the tolls that repaid the cost of building the canal. Jacob Welsh, Roscoe's first toll collector, built his house along the banks of the Ohio and Erie Canal next to the warehouse. The restored one-story brick house, with stepped chimneys at each end, is simply furnished, as befits the life-style of a canal family.

The tollhouse also contains exhibits relating to canal days. There is a working model of a gristmill, and a miniature canalboat travels through a scale model of double locks.

The **Craft House** has working potters and displays crocks made in Roscoe by a man named Rich. His pottery was located at the southern end of the village during canal days. A pewterer demonstrates the art of hand-casting pewter spoons and other utensils.

A blacksmith hand-forges wrought iron at the **Village Smithy** (1830). Demonstrations and explanations of a blacksmith's role in a canal town are given. The authentic tools on display belonged to Tinker Dobson, who was the village blacksmith for many years.

The village has several **flower, herb,** and **vegetable gardens**.

A variety of shops at Roscoe Village sell contemporary merchandise in a nineteenth-century atmosphere complete with appropriate antique artifacts and costumed clerks.

The **Johnson-Humrickhouse Museum**, also located on Whitewoman Street, is owned and maintained by the Coshocton County Public

Library. Exhibits are based on the collections of two brothers, David M. and John H. Johnson. The large galleries house oriental treasures, Indian art and artifacts, decorative arts, and Americana. Admission is free. Open noon to 5:00 P.M., May to October; 1:00 to 4:30 P.M., November to April. (614)622-8710.

Special events at Roscoe Village include Dulcimer Days in May, an art show and sale in June, Americana Festival in July, Coshocton Canal Festival in August, Gay '90s Festival in September, Apple Butter Stirrin' in October, and Christmas holiday activities in December.

Visitors can take a twenty-minute ride on Roscoe Village's **horse-drawn trolley** to the historic **Triple Locks** during spring, summer, and fall. Adults, $1.25; children 8 to 18, 75 cents. A forty-five minute **canalboat ride** on the *Monticello II* is available from Memorial Day to Labor Day. The boat, owned and operated by the city of Coshocton, is docked one mile north of Roscoe Village at the end of the **towpath trail** and travels along a one-mile restored section of the **Ohio and Erie Canal**. It runs 1:00 to 5:00 P.M. daily; adults, $2.50; children 8 to 18, $1.25.

The **Old Warehouse Restaurant**, 400 North Whitewoman Street, (614)622-2222, was the first building restored in Roscoe Village. It serves lunch and dinner and is particularly well known for its peanut butter pie.

SIDE TRIPS

Schoenbrunn Village State Memorial in New Philadelphia, page 235, and Zoar Village State Memorial in Zoar, page 242, are within easy driving distance of Roscoe.

A Brief History of the Shakers

Ann Lee, a blacksmith's daughter born in Manchester, England, in 1736, founded the Shakers. The Shakers, a communal religious sect, established nineteen societies in America during the eighteenth and nineteenth centuries. The total membership reached 17,000.

In 1758, Ann Lee joined a group of Manchester Quakers, led by Jane and James Wardley, called *Shaking Quakers*, or *Shakers*, because of their physical movements during religious services. By 1770, Ann had become the accepted leader of the Shakers and was known as Mother Ann Lee. It was she who introduced celibacy to the Shakers. The need for celibacy was revealed to Mother Ann through a vision, though she herself was married and had given birth four times. None of her children survived infancy.

Mother Ann and her followers were persecuted and imprisoned for their religious beliefs, which emphasized work and worship. Again, acting on knowledge gained in a vision, Ann and eight followers sailed to America in 1774. The United Society of Believers in Christ's Second Appearing, as the Shakers called themselves, established their first communal society at Niskayuna (later called Watervliet), New York, in 1776.

Converts began to be attracted to Shakerism in 1780, and Mother Ann was one of the missionaries who traveled through New England seeking converts. Missionary work continued even after Mother Ann's death in 1784. It is estimated that at the sect's peak in the mid-nineteenth century, there were 6,000 members living in the nineteen communities.

Shaker communities usually began with missionaries holding worship services for local people in the home of a sympathizer or believer. Later, when there were enough believers to form a family, a communal site was agreed upon. Members donated or sold their possessions and gave their money to buy land. Shaker beliefs forbade private ownership of property; all property was held communally.

The meetinghouse was almost always the first structure built in the community, and many were designed by Shaker architect Moses Johnson (1752–1842). Typically, religious services were held on the first floor, with men entering through a left door and women through the right. They then sat on benches facing each other; the space between them was referred to as the *altar*. A section of benches was often reserved for the *world's people*, who were allowed to observe Shaker services.

Religious services, without following a formal ritual, included frenetic dancing and shaking, exhortations, and singing. Blue and white were thought to be heavenly colors, and worshipers dressed in blue and white for the services.

The second floor of a meetinghouse usually contained sleeping quarters for the community leaders, called *elders*.

Shaker communities were divided into families of approximately 100 people, who lived, worked, and took meals together. Each family's dwelling house was the center of domestic life, and all activity was strictly segregated by sex. Many dwelling houses, therefore, have double doors and stairways and wide halls to ensure minimum physical contact between the sexes.

Sleeping rooms were barely furnished; the wooden pegs that line the walls were used for hanging clothes. Because of the size of Shaker families, they often had separate laundry buildings. Brother David Parker of the Canterbury, New Hampshire, community is credited with inventing the first washing machine in 1858. It used water for cleaning and for mechanical power. The washing machine was exhibited by the Shakers at the Philadelphia Centennial Exposition in 1876 and was purchased for use in many large hotels.

Shakers believed in separation from the world, which was every place outside of their villages, because they felt that the world was sinful. They tried to make their communities self-sufficient so that they would have to purchase only a few things from the world. But since productivity often exceeded the community's needs and the quality of their goods was so high, Shaker products were regularly sold to the world.

Shakers strove for perfection through prayer and work to prepare for Christ's Second Coming. Their motto was "Hands to work and hearts to God." Manual labor was required, and adornment of either people or things was forbidden. This led not only to simple dress and functional buildings but also to furniture and artifacts carefully made of the finest materials. Shaker-made became synonymous with the highest quality.

By striving for efficiency and practicality, the Shakers devised many labor-saving inventions in addition to the washing machine: the flat broom, the circular saw, the clothespin, and the threshing machine among them. During the early 1800s, the Shakers monopolized the garden seed and medicinal herb industries because of the high quality of their products.

Shaker villages had schoolhouses even though Shakers did not produce children. Children were brought to the communities when whole families including children joined the sect or when Shakers took in homeless children. Boys and girls had separate buildings in which to live. They were supervised by adults and participated in all aspects of the Shaker way of life. They attended school four months out of the year; girls in summer, boys in winter. In addition to learning crafts and trades, children were taught the 3 Rs.

Within a Shaker society, all people were to be treated equally, including women, which put this sect ahead of the general population. However, the governance of Shaker societies was autocratic. Each family was governed by four people: two elders and two eldresses appointed by the church's central ministry at Mount Lebanon, New York. They were responsible for both the spiritual and the temporal affairs of their family, and their rule was absolute. They, in turn, were subject to the central ministry, composed of two elders and two eldresses, with the head elder or eldress being the official head of the church. Deacons, who were in charge of workshops and food production, and trustees, who conducted business activities with the world, were appointed by the elders.

From the 1830s to the 1850s, the Shakers experienced a period of spiritual renewal known as *Mother's Work*, in which gifts of songs, dance, and drawings were received from Mother Ann and other religious figures by Shaker mediums. Because the Shakers fundamentally banned all ornamentation, decorated Shaker artifacts almost certainly date from this period. *Spirit drawings* are watercolors in the folk art tradition and include pictures of the well-known Shaker tree of life, heavenly populations, and wreaths of flowers. Lyrics and tunes to songs were received and transcribed. The songs were usually about peace, work, and love.

Shaker membership reached its peak around the Civil War and gradually declined thereafter. By 1900, communities began closing; and by 1925, most had folded. By 1950, there were only two remaining communities, Canterbury, New Hampshire, and Sabbathday Lake, Maine, with small numbers of elderly Shakers. Both communities are still active.

INDEX